BUILD TOGETHER

AMERICANS

Adventures in
Intercultural Education
for the Secondary School

BY

RACHEL DAVIS DuBOIS, Ed.D.

With a Foreword by
EDUARD C. LINDEMAN

Publishers
HINDS, HAYDEN & ELDREDGE, INC.
NEW YORK   PHILADELPHIA

To the memory of Malcolm G. Thomas, superintendent of the Woodbury, New Jersey, schools, September, 1914, to June, 1935, for his loyalty and farsightedness.

CONTENTS

FOREWORD

The melting-pot theory, based upon the assumption that a single unified type of American character could be created by the elimination of differences, is now in disrepute. The chief result of the attempt to enforce the melting-pot rule upon Americans has been the precipitation of the minorities issue, that sociological perversion which has bedeviled Europe for more than a century. It has been a hard lesson to learn, but slowly we are beginning to see that all attempts to impose uniformity upon the people leads directly to antidemocratic behavior.

Perhaps the most bitter consequences of the uniformity idea are those experienced by Jews in Germany. In pre-Hitler Germany, the Jews thought of themselves as an assimilated people. They spoke German, taught in German schools and universities, wrote German plays, novels, and poems, composed music with a German accent and in every way participated in German life and considered themselves to be a part of German culture and expressive of German character. The only distinction which they insisted upon maintaining was their religion, and even in this sphere the more sophisticated Jews had long since abandoned religious life, save for a few ritualistic observances. In short, they had become "melted" in the pot of a unified German culture. Their differences, so they thought, had been forgotten and forgiven.

But, alas, it was not so. Their differences had never been understood and hence never appreciated. They were vulnerable precisely because they had become absorbed in a fictitious whole. Whatever there was in Jewish life that possessed intrinsic value had been eliminated or minimized. The Jews at last thought of themselves as being German-Jews and finally as being Germans. The Jewishness of their background and inheritance had been washed out. And it was precisely in Germany, where the so-called assimilated Jews predominated, that there arose the most bestial attack on Jews ever known to history. Why? Because the Jews in Germany had sacrificed their most precious quality—their difference. We have instanced the case of the Jews, but the same reasoning applies to minority groups in nearly all other nations.

The antithesis of the melting-pot theory of human relations is "cultural democracy"—a theory defined and illustrated in this book. As theory, it is a direct derivative of American pragmatic and democratic philosophy. It is based upon the assumption that human differences are relative and not absolute, and hence risks the assumption that persons of widely varied backgrounds and traits are capable of living together in peace. Indeed, this theory goes much further: it even assumes that difference contributes to liveliness and creativeness, while uniformity leads to deadliness.

In spite of the reasonableness and naturalness (natural in the sense that in nature survival depends upon capacity for difference) of the pluralistic theory of cultural democracy, it must be admitted that its adherents are still in the minority. Perhaps the difficulty lies in another direction: this may be one of those examples of a theory accepted on the ground that it bears no relation to practice. Yes, I can already hear the refrain: "Cultural democracy is a beautiful theory but it won't work."

It is at this point that the life and work of Dr. Rachel Davis DuBois becomes important. She not only believes in cultural democracy, but she insists that it works and hence invites others to make the experiment. Her proposition consists of three straightforward articles of faith: she believes that individuals, no matter what their origin, should have pride in their background and

inheritance; she believes that this sense of pride can be awakened
by simple devices and that when properly released these expressed
cultural differences lead quickly and almost automatically to appreciation and understanding; and she believes, finally, that all of
this can be readily taught to children in schools and to adults
wherever they congregate in small groups.

These are not mere items of belief on her part. She has been
trying the experiment valiantly for more than two decades. It
does work. This I know. It works in two directions: it helps new
Americans with a difference to find a spiritual home, and it helps
native Americans toward a deeper sensitiveness and affection for
that American culture which is the unifying product of their
understanding. Rachel DuBois is now reaping the intellectual
fruits of her long and devoted determination to make a good
theory workable. In 1943, she published a book called *Get Together Americans;* its subtitle, perhaps more revealing, is "Friendly Approaches to Racial and Cultural Conflicts through the
Neighborhood-Home Festival." This is an extremely practical
guide for those working with adult groups who really wish to do
something about racial and group tensions—that is, something
more than talk. Her present volume, *Build Together Americans:
Adventures in Intercultural Education for the Secondary School,*
is also a guide and a tool for those who wish to act, but it is much
more. She reaches into the psychological, sociological, and philo-
sophical subsoil upon which her theory and practice rest. The
combination of sound philosophy supported by a wealth of dem-
onstration makes a solid book. It comes at a propitious moment.
We must find ways of healing the wounds of war, and we must
invent methods for bringing the parts of American life together
again. Peace treaties and general international understandings are
essential, but underneath are those face-to-face relations where
prejudice must be conquered. If we cannot live together in the
democratic United States in a way which illustrates the principles

of cultural democracy, then no reasonable hope for peace exists. I share Rachel DuBois' faith. I believe with her that what is now lacking is a practical and simple program of action which can be easily taught. This book helps to supply that lack.

EDUARD C. LINDEMAN
Professor of Social Philosophy
New York School of Social Work
Columbia University

INTRODUCTION

The busy teacher is like the wife of the scientist who had been testing certain theories of the action of vitamins on white rats. One evening he came home elated over a discovery and reported it to his wife. Her immediate reaction was: "That's fine! What does it mean that I should give Johnny for supper?"

And so, teachers everywhere are asking of all those who in books, magazines, press, radio, and innumerable panels are admonishing the schools to do something about the interracial, inter-creedal name-calling, vandalism, and riots, "What does all this mean that I should give Johnny for history and science and assembly programs?"

Most teachers have not been prepared to answer this question either by their professional training or by their school experiences; for the subject has in the past been almost ignored in American schools and teacher-training institutions. To meet their urgent need, a few summer intercultural workshops are now held and some private organizations, concerned about the need for implementing our democratic ideals, are offering teachers a few brochures, newsletters, lists of books, and mimeographed descriptions of what some of the more creative teachers have done about the subject. One school system, that of Springfield, Massachusetts, has been winning much attention on the part of school executives because of having inaugurated "A Community's Total War against Prejudice." One book—*Americans All: Studies in Intercultural Education,* the 1942 Yearbook of the National Education Association—contains twenty reports of pioneer projects, tried and tested by schools in different parts of the country, for promoting goodwill among culture groups. This book shows that a few creative teachers have for years been doing what is now being called *intercultural education*. Another book, *Intercultural Education in American Schools,* by Vickery and Cole, contains "proposed methods and objectives." All this is necessary spadework in a new field. The curricula of most schools, however, have remained uninfluenced by this pressing need for a positive educational approach to the problem of prejudice.

This volume presents a report of intercultural education projects conducted in some hundred schools in different parts of the country over a period of twenty years, under the guidance of the author. During this time, and as a result of this work, a philosophy has evolved, and certain methods in the application of some of the principles of social psychology have proved to be more or less successful in modifying prejudices. The book also presents certain experiences in dealing with the subtleties of inter-group relationships—experiences which may be of aid to the many teachers and school administrators who are puzzling over the kind of intercultural education that shall be given to Johnny.

In this report we do not attempt to meet the emergency situation of race and culture conflict. When riots occur, the executive branch of the city, state, and nation must step in to preserve order. The role of the school is to start the long-term process of planting and nurturing seeds of understanding which take time for growth. Aside from the presentation of the philosophy which guides our work and the analysis of social psychology involved in it, perhaps the unique contribution of this book is the reporting of an effective mobilization of school and community forces in a given area toward a social goal—a mobilization so contrived as to require a minimum of change in the school organization.

Margaret Mead points out that the need today is not for untried blueprints of methods, handed down by armchair social scientists, but rather for a freeing of creative teachers and community leaders to the end that they may invent new ways for breaking down the barriers of prejudice. Too long our society, motivated by materialism, has given recognition to the activity arising from analytical thinking and generally has withheld recognition from the intuitive, integrative activity which characterizes the approach of the creative teacher as well as of the artist to a problem. Both methods of thinking are needed. The role of the social scientist is to recognize the importance of social inventions, to analyze them, and then, through the use of such mass educational techniques as the printing press, the radio, the film, to make them quickly available throughout the country.

The vehicle we used as a means of developing more understanding attitudes was the school assembly. We have no intention, however, of suggesting that the school assembly, used as a core around which to integrate the school activities, is the only approach to intercultural education for high schools. Other schools have found other vehicles. We look upon our approach as merely a natural introduction to an expanding process which should eventually find its way into general education. There must be many ways of working toward the solution of the complex problems of race and culture conflict. Some administrators will readily see how they can use the methods herein described. In a school that may not yet be ready for such a co-ordinated, school-community approach to intercultural education, the wide-awake teacher will be quick to adopt parts of this program for use in her own classroom. We do insist, however, that whatever plans for intercultural education are made during this milling stage be guided by a point of view that is not the result of wishful thinking by members of a dominant group only, but one that is worked out democratically on an equal basis with all those involved: Jew, gentile, old Yankee and recent immigrant, Negro, white, teachers and students, community leaders and school administrators. The means used for attaining any goal are of necessity an integral part of that goal; and unless what we do in intercultural education is as democratic as the goal we hope to attain, we might just as well not do it. Our goal, like the

Kingdom of God, may never be completely reached on earth, and yet it is always being reached. Complete harmony may never come among all our racial and cultural groups; and yet, whenever two or three representatives of these groups gather in a spirit of equality to discuss even an assembly program, as we always did, at that moment our common American culture is richer; for that moment the problem of race and culture conflict is solved.

It was this intangible yet satisfying atmosphere of goodwill which would not let us rest, which has carried us deep into the streams of American culture. The work has been twenty years a-growing and we have grown with it, sharing our heritages with others and finding thereby richer lives. For all this we are deeply indebted to *youth*—those first Woodbury high-school students who brought the courage of the pioneer to an adventure in education (especially Betty Kohler, Loretta Parkinson, and Edward Davis), and those other high-school girls and boys who in later years carried the adventure farther; to *high-school teachers and principals* in schools too numerous to list—in Woodbury (Cora Price, Florence Barber, Margery Baird, and Mary Walton), in San Francisco, in Boston, in Washington, D. C., in the metropolitan areas of Philadelphia and New York; to the *culture group leaders* of sixteen different nationality backgrounds: American Negroes both North and South, Orientals from East and West, Jews, Catholics and Protestants, American Indians whose ancestors "met the boat" and old Yankees whose ancestors were "on the boat"; all have advised us, gone to schools with us; all were patient when we made mistakes, discussed all phases of the problems with us in their homes, and in ours, in school committee rooms, on street corners. Through such co-operation a wealth of experience has been piled up which had somehow to be organized and put on paper.

We are grateful, too, for those who assisted in developing the special project in fifteen schools in the New York City metropolitan area in the school year 1934-1935: Ione Eckerson, who was given a year's leave of absence from the Dwight Morrow

High School in Englewood, New Jersey, and Miriam R. Ephraim
(now Director of Activities with the Y.M.H.A. and Y.W.H.A.
of Pittsburgh, Pennsylvania), our two field secretaries; Emma
Schweppe of the Hunter College High School Faculty, and Rose
Nelson and Ruth Edwards Davis (now doing editorial work in
New York City), in charge of the office and research. We were
grateful also for leadership of some of the faculty at Teachers
College, Columbia University, notably Mabel Carney, Daniel
Kulp II, and Heber Harper; for the research assistance of several WPA workers who supplied some of the factual material;
and for advice given by members of our first advisory committee:

Chairman	*Secretaries*
DR. HEBER HARPER	RACHEL DAVIS DuBOIS
Teachers College	*Executive Secretary*
Columbia	
	EMMA SCHWEPPE
Treasurer	*Research Secretary*
DR. OTIS W. CALDWELL	
Columbia University	IONE ECKERSON
New York City	MIRIAM EPHRIAM
	Field Secretaries
Assistant Treasurer	
DR. F. TREDWELL SMITH	

NATIONAL COMMITTEE

WILL ALEXANDER
  Dillard University
  New Orleans, La.

WILLARD W. BEATTY
  Supt. of Schools
  Bronxville, N. Y.

F. C. BORGESON
  New York University

J. S. BUTTERWICK
  Temple University
  Philadelphia

MABEL CARNEY
  Teachers College
  Columbia

EVERETT R. CLINCHY
  Drew University
  Madison, N. J.

GEORGE S. COUNTS
  Teachers College
  Columbia

LEONARD COVELLO
  Casa Italiana
  Columbia

CRYSTAL BIRD FAUSET
  Swarthmore Institute
  of Race Relations

E. D. GRIZZELL
  University of Pennsylvania

NATHAN ISAACS
  Harvard Law School

JAMES WELDON JOHNSON
  Fisk University
  Nashville, Tenn.

JOHN L. MAHONEY
  Boston University

HEBERT A. MILLER
  Bryn Mawr College
  Bryn Mawr, Pa.

JESSE H. NEWLON
  Lincoln School
  Columbia University

HARRY A. OVERSTREET
  College of the
  City of New York

HARRY W. PFUND
  Haverford College
  Haverford, Pa.

LOUIS S. POSNER
  Board of Education
  New York City

DANIEL A. PRESCOTT
  Rutgers University
  New Brunswick, N. J.

AXEL UVH UPPVALL
  University of Pennsylvania

ROLLO R. REYNOLDS
  Horace Mann School
  New York City

HAROLD E. B. SPEIGHT
  Swarthmore College
  Swarthmore, Pa.

In fifteen schools, during that one school year, we arranged fifty-eight guest assembly programs followed by fifty-eight student-planned programs and the many related activities described herein. The co-operating school systems were Englewood, Fort Lee, Tenafly, Cliffside Park, and Madison, N. J., with two individual senior high schools—Benjamin Franklin High School in New York City and Central High School in Newark, N. J.

We first called our organization the *Service Bureau for Education in Human Relations*. It was that lengthy name which forced us to coin the term *intercultural education*. Having to describe our work, which was wider than race relations and not so wide as international education, though related closely to both, we began to use the term *Service Bureau for Intercultural Education*. It was under this name that the "Americans All—Immigrants All" radio series was produced in co-operation with the United States Office of Education, Columbia Broadcasting System, and W.P.A. It was in 1938-1939, as director of the Service Bureau for Intercultural Education, that the author was responsible for the research for those twenty-six weekly programs which at the end of the year received four national prizes. Ruth Edwards Davis deserves especial credit for that work. Gilbert Seldes of CBS wrote the scripts. In 1940, as so often happens in a democracy, a difference of viewpoint arose within the Service Bureau and the author resigned to continue her free-lance work in what is now being called by everyone *intercultural education*. This work, with Dr. Eduard C. Lindeman as chairman of the advisory committee, is done under the Intercultural Education Workshop. The following are members of the advisory committee:

MABEL CARNEY	E. C. LINDEMAN
GEORGE B. CORWIN	EDWARD LISS
W. E. B. DuBOIS	DANIEL A. PRESCOTT
E. FRANKLIN FRAZIER	RUTH SCOTT
ELIZABETH GILLILAN	H. NORMAN SIBLEY
GEORGE GRAFF	MILTON STEINBERG
LESLIE PINCKNEY HILL	FREDERIC R. THORNE
HOWARD HINTZ	FREDERIC M. THRASHER
LAWRENCE HOSIE	CARL VOSS
DVORA LAPSON	L. HOLLINGSWORTH WOOD

The author wishes also to extend thanks to Malcolm G. Thomas, superintendent of the Woodbury schools, under whom the work was begun; to Eduard C. Lindeman and Hollingsworth Wood for their help and loyalty to the work over a period of years; to George Graff and Lily Edelmann, for their creative co-operation in later phases of the work; and to the individuals and committees who from time to time have contributed financially to keep the work going.

To Frederic Thrasher and Bruno Lasker and Ruth Edwards Davis must go a very large share of appreciation for their patience, advice, and help in developing the manuscript for final publication. Dr. Otto Klineberg of the Psychology Department of Columbia University was kind enough to check the manuscript before publication. None of these people, however, should be held responsible for the points of view contained in the book.

RACHEL DAVIS DuBOIS

1

OUR AMERICAN CULTURE—
ROCK PILE OR CATHEDRAL

> Surely I know that it is not alone
> Your blood in me that suddenly knows its own.
> It is Wyoming that I find
> In Norway now because of old I found
> So much of Norway in Wyoming, where
> You planted all you thought to leave behind.
> And there's no longer virgin ground
> In any land. What cargoes do we bear
> With us unknowing? In what guise
> Travels the pollen by which we fertilize
> New lands with old, and old with new, until
> All lands are kin, in something deeper still
> Than blood, and men may know
> Their own however far they go?[1]

A NUMBER of classroom teachers, on a panel to discuss and share with one another their experiences in attempting to relieve the growing racial and religious tensions in their schools and communities, voiced the following problems:

The problem of the relations between American parents who live "across the tracks" and those who live "on the hill."

The undemocratic tendency in some student bodies which prevents minority-group children from being welcomed at school affairs.

The more overt conflict situations between children of different backgrounds, which often happen on playgrounds or on the streets.

The problem of extreme inferiority feelings on the part of some Negro parents and extreme bitterness on the part of others.

The absence of Negro mothers in the Parent-Teachers' Associations.

The problem of the Negro teacher in the Negro districts who feels that if she understands Negro children that is all that can be expected of her.

---

[1] Ted Olson, *Hawk's Way* (New York: The League to Support Poetry, 1941), p. 42.

The problem of Italian mothers and of other mothers of recent immigrant background. How may they be reached and brought into closer contact with the school and Parent-Teachers' Association?

The lack of information, and sometimes the actual misinformation, in text and reference books, about cultural contributions, especially of minority groups in American life.

The problem of the prejudiced teacher or administrator.

The problem of personality maladjustment of minority-group children, partially due to ethnic-group prejudice; the problem of the lack of sensitivity of dominant-group children.

The acceptance of Nisei—citizens born in this country of Japanese parents—by the communities in which they are resettled.

When one looks over such statements and realizes how common are the problems they present, one concludes that one of the fundamental social problems of our own land, and indeed of the world today, is that of personal relations. If men can first be helped to regard one another as persons, despite differences of race, color, or creed, perhaps even to appreciate and enjoy some of those differences as legitimate in this infinitely varied universe, perhaps they can then live more harmoniously together. This principle obtains on every level, whether men are regarded in families, communities, or nations.

For most people, emotionally satisfying personal relationships out of which grow appreciations rather than prejudices can be built in no other way than by face-to-face contact. And these attitudes of appreciation can be developed, even among adults. But they cannot be developed by magic; nor can their development be left to chance, for time is short and the problems acute.

The recent increase in rioting and acts of vandalism in our cities, the mounting undercurrent of vitriolic criticism of people just because they are members of certain culture groups, are evidences that we are drifting into a situation dangerous to national unity unless something is done quickly and effectively to counteract these tendencies. Nations and civilizations, rotten from the inside, have cracked and fallen apart before, and so may ours. Yet none of us can doubt our ability to pull ourselves together at this eleventh hour. In fact, many of us are as busy as beavers, forming new organizations to do something against intolerance, or attending panels to discuss causes and effects of prejudice; but some of these activities seem to be mainly the result of a blind urge to stem a tide rather than to use it for our own constructive purposes.

We all acknowledge that we should do something to stop the outward expression of hatreds; but few of us realize that we can use our cultural heterogeneity to unite us; nor do we realize that in the process of attempting to build together a richer American culture we may acquire the wisdom to help develop more harmonious relations after the war among all the peoples of the world.

Our more sensitive social observers point to the danger ahead if and when there is, as Henry A. Wallace says, "a purposeful coalition between the international cartelists and those who stand for the K.K.K. type of demagogue at home." A positive approach to the problem in every school and community agency may avert that danger. But to plan school, church, and community programs with only the immediate object of preventing street riots now and economic imperialism later, important as those aims are, is not enough. As in all constructive social movements, the positive, creative, and preventive range of activities is far more important than the curative.

Our personal goals for the most part center around material things: a job that will pay enough for us to live in comfort— and of course a car, or maybe two. Our schools, which to some extent combined us in common purpose, also served as steppingstones of status, and undue emphasis was laid on their use by the Smiths of every generation to have their children reach the place now held by the Joneses. Thus, through the whole educational program, from language study to home economics, there ran the twofold purpose of cultural assimilation and of personal advancement. The obvious inadequacies of an educational system so variously motivated we tried to overcome by more and more stress on scientific method, and eventually by a more thorough examination of the essential question: for what sort of society was the school to prepare the child? One sociological survey followed another; but in the absence of a guiding principle it was difficult to distill from any of them their bearing on educational policy. And so the old conflict of purposes went on. But if we are to build a better world, we must actually find a guiding principle. Fritz Kunkel says: "The power which moves us to love, to strive, to create . . . is the creative power of the ultimate end, the value ahead of us in the infinite future, drawing us like a magnet, training us, transforming us like a breeder who transforms flowers into more beautiful flowers."[2]

But most of us do not want to be transformed—especially by Toni Pasquali in our ninth-grade history class, whose family are "not Americanized yet because they still eat Italian food," or by Sadie Goldberg, who stays out of school because of those holidays in the fall which upset our classes and which we have not taken the trouble to learn anything about, even though they reach back over 5,000 years into our Judeo-Christian culture. Perhaps it is time that we began to respect that hyphenated word, to use it to describe what we are or may become. Yes, we need a guiding principle that will move us to work together—teachers and students, parents and school-board members, social workers: a vision of what American culture—heir to the cultures of all the world—might be. "There *is* a hitherto undreamt-of fullness, freedom, and happiness within reach of our species."[3] What we need is a process of harmonizing those cultural ingredients that have come to us out of so many sets of human experience, until they attain a unity and wholeness of continuing vitality at ever higher levels. But for parents and teachers to take conscious part in that process means, first of all, a quiet maturing of pur-

[2] Fritz Kunkel, *In Search of Maturity* (New York: Charles Scribner's Sons, 1943), p. 42.

[3] H. G. Wells, *Experiment in Autobiography* (New York: Macmillan Co., 1934), p. 11.

pose. There can only be frustration if we continue to run in circles, attend one committee meeting or panel discussion after another, always hoping that out of our unformed ideas there will automatically emerge, for all to see, the bright star of our destiny.

The peace and progress of the world depend not on the physical or cultural amalgamation of its different peoples, though that may happen in some far-distant future. Peace depends on whether individuals of various cultural groups can be taught to acquire such mutual confidence and trust in one another that they will be able to adjust the economic and political problems that concern their living together and thus prevent the subordination of the many to the interests of the few. This end cannot be achieved by any kind of coercion, mental or physical; it can only be arrived at when we have learned to care for one another's welfare. This lesson can be learned in America far more quickly and readily than anywhere else, because here, in the framework of a country rich in natural resources and pledged to democratic policies, we have all of the world's larger culture groups represented. If these groups can increase their mutual respect for one another and implement methods of co-operation, then America can be teacher to the world. But if America slumps back into discrimination and injustice, race hate, lynching, and riots, we will not only fail to teach mankind but we will beckon mankind to relapse toward anarchy, war, and annihilation. We are learning today—the hard way—that:

> Interwoven with the fate of the United States are the fates of countries on the farther side of the world organized on political and social hypotheses and conditions quite different from those prevailing among ourselves. More important still is the process of cultural interchange. If it were as free and full today as our exchange of products, the world, while retaining its picturesque and stimulating cultural differences, might have an agreed code of relationship and behavior with corresponding reduction of the risk of war.[4]

------

[4] Dr. Isaiah Bowman, President of Johns Hopkins University, Annual Report, December, 1943, p. 16.

Our goal then is no less than to begin consciously to build a richer national culture—and hence more harmonious international cultural interchange—by starting in our own homes and schools and communities, remembering that there is time to do it if we begin at once.

More people can be inspired by this goal today than ever before, for it is a rare community that has not had dumped into its lap people of all sorts of cultural backgrounds from all sorts of regional pockets in this varied land and from all sorts of countries. And the war, by mixing people in every country, has greatly increased the number of people who will be conscious of the goal. Our faith in the fundamental equality of all men and in the rightness of *E Pluribus Unum* makes us feel that each of us has a role to play and that we can begin at once. Our first step should be to acquaint ourselves with the "rocks with which we build"—our cultural elements—agreeing with de Saint Exupéry that a "rock pile ceases to be a rock pile the moment a single man contemplates it, bearing within him the image of a cathedral. . . . He who bears in his heart a cathedral is already victorious. . . . Only love can say what face shall emerge from the clay."[5]

We are all familiar with the fact that from the beginning our country has been culturally heterogeneous. Today, people from many countries are still among us—new immigrants fled, as in the old days, from political, economic, and religious persecution; ready, as in the old days, to contribute their best to our developing American culture. It is the old story of "Acres of Diamonds" all over again—acres of unimagined cultural diversity existing in every community for the enrichment of American life, out of which could come a cultural renaissance.

But instead of releasing our creativity, our diversity as yet has been expressed for the most part in intolerance, tensions, and conflict and our various cultural values have tended to cancel one

5 Antoine de Saint Exupéry, *Flight to Arras* (New York: Reynal & Hitchock, 1942), p. 218.

another. Why? Partly because most of us had assumed that our culture was a finished product, built mainly by one people—and that a rather homogeneous and superior people. The later immigrants were made to feel that they did not "belong"; that no matter how quickly in the Americanization process they sloughed off their old-country values and took on American ways (usually the worst ways because of their lack of contact with the best), they were still foreigners.

The feeling of not belonging, growing out of such a narrow conception of Americanization, was carried over to the children of the immigrant in the public schools where they learned from many of their textbooks that the new immigrant was somehow inferior to the old, and where they may have sung:

> Their daddies may be Irish,
> German, Jew, or Dutch,
> But if they're born in Yankee-land
> The rest don't count for much.

In their eagerness to belong, these second-generation young people often came to be ashamed of their parents and to despise reminders of the "old country" in their homes. Some became shy or sullen. A few became aggressive and delinquent. And because such feelings of inferiority tend to kill the sense of personal worth, too many withdrew into themselves and failed to become the participating citizens which they might have become. Louis Adamic estimated in 1934 that about one-fourth of our entire population were of the second generation and expressed the belief that most of them were culturally (and politically) unadjusted individuals.[6] Irvin L. Child[7] has more recently and in more detail described the conflict with its accompanying frustrations in which the second-generation Italian American finds himself. He shows that an individual leaves the parental group en-

---

[6] Louis Adamic, *My America* (New York: Harper & Bros., 1940), p. 210.

[7] Irvin L. Child, *Italian or American?* (New Haven: Yale University Press, 1943), pp. 196 ff.

tirely or stays within the Italian-American group with little contact with outsiders. The attitude of the dominant American group is the important determinant.

While there has been considerable study of the "conflicts of personality" which derive from the "divided loyalty" of the American who is still attached in part to the culture values and habits of a "homeland" which he may never have seen, we hear much less of the conflicts and inner divisions of those Americans of older stock who wish to play their part in the changing life of their country or of their community but are ever pulled back to their roots in a society that is fast vanishing and holds out no promise of creative freedom for the future. In every part of America, there are such ingrowing sets of people anxiously clinging to assumed certainties that are dissolving despite all their affirmations. From these circles quite as much as from the children of immigrants spring many of the disintegrating influences on our national life. A healthy conservatism too often degenerates into the tyranny of unlaid ghosts.

It can be seen, then, why our cultural diversity has constricted rather than released our creativity. Somehow or other we have got into the habit of moving in social worlds made up mainly of people just like ourselves. Old-stock Americans are satisfied that they have "arrived"; that there can be nothing better than what they have or had before the war. Irish Americans in Boston complain that the old Yankee still has the cold "Cape Cod eye." Newcomers want more than anything to feel that they "belong"; and so they try, usually without success, to become what they are not. Not only is the spirit of creativity not to be found in such an atmosphere, but an actual sense of frustration, which we know now is the seedbed of Fascism, spreads. For uniformity wants only its own kind. Ethnocentrism considers inferior all that is alien. Uniformity and ethnocentrism help to breed intolerance, hatred, race riots, and wars.

Not only must there be more social interaction among members of various groups, but that interaction must also be more creative.

When the culture values of all groups are in process of being appreciated and shared or modified and enriched, that process is creative and may be called *cultural democracy.*

M. P. Follett wrote perhaps the most profound treatise on this subject.[8] She used the expression "a creative use of differences" and brilliantly applied it to all levels of social interaction. When individuals from various class and cultural backgrounds work and play and study together—explaining to one another when necessary what lies back of their peculiar cultural values; seeing their differences, yet realizing their common humanity; recognizing their own shortages in some respects, and filling them in through closer contact with individuals from a group which has happened to specialize in those very values—then a creative use of differences is being made. It should be remembered too that a culture trait need not have universal value in order to be granted the right to survive, as long as some social group cherishes it. This right, however, includes the right of any group to try to modify by preachment, example, or in any other peaceful and constructive way, whatever trait in some other group may seem to it to be harmful to the common good. Thus, for example, most Americans, no matter what their antecedents, will have no objection to the cultivation by Italians of their cookery, music, and art. But when American men of Italian birth, for example, continue in the United States those habits of aggressive domination of their wives and children—habits which are or were commonly accepted in Italy but which do not fit into our American pattern—then other Americans may well use whatever means of education are at their disposal to modify those habits, so as to bring them more into keeping with the requirements of American citizenship and democratic civilization. Sociologists, in co-operation with parents of all groups, should focus more attention on this phase of the problem of assimilation.

---

[8] M. P. Follett, *Creative Experience* (New York: Longmans, Green & Co., 1924).

In short, when cultural democracy is practiced in home, school, or community center, nothing of value will be lost. At the same time the possibility for the creating of new values and ways of doing things by all sorts of combinations and inventions is infinite. Such a process of cross-fertilization would insure harmony among our diverse groups. Indeed, a social philosopher warns us that if we fail to learn to behave "in such manner as to create unifying experiences by making use of human differences as though none were absolute, then we can only await the time when among the competing ideological or sectarian groups one becomes sufficiently strong to defeat or assimilate the rest."[9]

Assuming that in our democracy we can escape this danger, then the fact that millions of us have our roots in varying social heritages should promise a rich future for American culture. Rather than worry about the presence of people of Mexican background in the Southwest, of Oriental background on the Pacific Coast, of Polish background in the Connecticut Valley, or of French Canadians in New England, we should welcome the vigor and the colorful diversity which these groups are contributing or may contribute to our common life. As long as we continue to think of our cultural and racial diversity as a *problem*, we will do nothing creative about it. If, however, we begin to see the *promise*, then our creative energy will be released and many prejudices will be forgotten as we begin to build together.

What are some of the values existing in the minds and expressed in the customs of particular culture groups in the United States which might enrich our common life if we could bring about a greater amount of creative interaction among them? American sympathy with Finland during its struggle for independence made the whole country aware of the sterling qualities of the Finns in our midst, not only as individuals, but also as bearers of a great tradition of economic co-operation and

[9] E. C. Lindeman, "Contingency Plus Continuity," *Christendom,* Winter, 1943.

democratic organization. Similarly, the military success of the Russians was reflected in an increased interest in their total cultural life. Speaking of the Chinese, Bertrand Russell referred to their

> Quiet dignity, patience, the pacific temper, dependence on justice rather than force, and love of wisdom for its own sake. . . . These are values which a world bent on mutual destruction through the application of science to man can ill afford to ignore, much less to destroy.[10]

The qualities which the English philosopher found in China, sensitive Americans have found exemplified also among the Chinese in their midst. There is difference of opinion as to the inheritance of such qualities. While a few frontier thinkers, as C. G. Jung[11] and Thomas Mann, are posing the possibility of some ongoing "collective unconscious," most psychologists believe that such qualities are no more biologically inherited than is skill in needlework, musical talent, or ability in animal husbandry. They believe that the social experience of each ethnic group during the course of its history determines what traits are handed on from one generation to another. We as teachers and group leaders should not allow such differences of opinion to prevent our acting. It seems, then, that nothing in human nature should prevent one group from learning what another has learned. The questions that confront us are: What traits are worth learning? How may such learning be advanced?

When considering traits that might be incorporated more widely into American life, let us start with the "mastery through discipline" and certain other specific contributions of one of the oldest of our immigrant groups, the English Puritans who peopled what is still called New England.

> These are the things we should remember: first, that education in New England was not primarily for the clergy but was instead

---

[10] L. V. Cadv, review of *The Problem of China* by Bertrand Russell, *The Nation,* CXVI, 341-2.

[11] Jolan Jacobi, *The Psychology of Jung* (New Haven: Yale University Press, 1943).

instituted for the sake of dignity, of human character, and human imagination; and second, that the glory of Greece, the grandeur of Rome, and the beauty and delicacy of English verse were the heritage of our New England forefathers. . . .

The second thing for which our Puritan forefathers had respect was manual labor. . . .

The third thing . . . was religion. . . . They were men and women who believed that outside themselves were certain objective values, and that life meant nothing else than an approach to these values through daily living and thinking.[12]

This statement, incidentally, shows that we must be careful not to oversimplify the statement of contributions made by particular ethnic groups to American life. The Puritans were not the only English group to leave their stamp on that life. Partly because they had to adjust to a different environment, the Americans of English ancestry in the South developed a different economy and, with it, a very different culture. Then, each of the larger groups of immigrant stock also includes culturally specialized subgroups—in the case of the English, for example, the Catholics of Maryland and the Quakers of Pennsylvania, New Jersey, and New York.

The Quaker group, partly English and partly Welsh, offers an especially interesting example of a cultural particularism that has remained almost unimpaired over many generations and has, after an auspicious but short-lived major influence on the life and thought of Colonial times, only lately commenced again to exert considerable influence on what may be regarded as essentially American traits. One of its traits is especially significant for the present searching inquiry among thoughtful Americans into the nature of democracy. The Friends, among themselves, have always lived democratically; and their tradition-sanctioned procedures include a respect for minority rights which, if widely adopted, would go far to remedy the shortcomings of our political democracy. This respect takes the form of arriving at

---

[12] Mary Ellen Chase, "Head and Hands Working Together," *Common Ground,* I (Autumn, 1940), No. 1.

conclusions by consent rather than by taking a vote through
which those in larger number are empowered to override the
views of the lesser number. To quote Rufus Jones, outstanding
Quaker philosopher:

> By this method the rights of the 'minority' are not overlooked or
> neglected. In fact, there is no majority or minority; there is a group
> striving to arrive at unity. Everybody's judgment counts for what it
> is worth and weighs something if it helps to bring the group to clarity
> and decision.[13]

Less widely known but equally important for democratic procedures is the Quakers' use of silence as a valuable ingredient
in a discussion where high tension might lead to words afterwards regretted, or simply to invite a thought deeper than
that kindled by the rapid give and take of an animated ex-
change of views. Above all, there is in the Quaker tradition
that respect for the individual without which democracy cannot
but be imperfect; there are forms of procedure that prevent "loss
of face" on the part of any individual if he confesses to a change
in his point of view; there is recognition of the value of the
unique experience of each participant.

We hear much of Jewish charity, but little attention is usually
paid to the ethical concern so strongly developed among the
Jewish people from which this purely material manifestation
of one of their cultural peculiarities springs. The Jew's "passion
for social justice" and "sense of a purpose in individual and
national life" is a reaction to an almost unbroken experience of
oppression for two thousands years, a positive, creative reaction
that has its counterpart also in reactions of defense. Now, a
desire for social justice and a desire for family solidarity are
attitudes which for their survival require concrete embodiments
in habits, customs, and traditional forms of behavior. Thus,
Jewish philanthropy may be said to represent a self-imposed insurance that any injustice inflicted on individuals through dis-

---

[13] Rufus Jones, *The Faith and Practice of the Quakers* (New York:
George H. Doran Co., 1917), pp. 66-7.

similarities in fortune shall at least to some extent be remedied. And Jewish family feeling gives meaning to, and in turn is kept alive by, those custom holidays which follow the calendar and outwardly distinguish the Jews from other people.

The courtesy and generosity which we associate with the Italian group, its love of music, of color, of a good time after hard work—are all manifestations of a culture pattern that has made for acceptance of the small joys of life as compensation for much hardship and insecurity.

Here, then, we see that it is no accident that values differ, as diverse culture groups interpret their experience and enjoin their lessons from it upon their children. We also see that most of the values have a significance and acceptance, in varying degrees, far beyond the limits of any single historical folk experience. Nearly always the values which any one group considers highest in the light of its own experience also appear, though differently expressed, in the list of cultural values recognized by other groups. Potentially, then, these groups have more in common than they have apart.

Can Culture Values Be Shared?

Can culture values be consciously shared? No one knows. But we do know that society is dynamic, that all these culture patterns are, as Read Bain says, "either waxing, waning, or in relative equilibrium."[14] Since this state of flux exists, we are justified in asking whether it can be directed toward the common good.

Read Bain says further, "The sane ideal is rationally directed change which will reduce societal friction, tension, and confusion to a minimum and thus prevent the destructive revolutionary upheavals with which history is replete."[15] Sociologists should tell us which values now exist among us that are applied

---

[14] Read Bain, "Cultural Integration and Social Conflict," *American Journal of Sociology,* January, 1939, p. 501.
[15] *Ibid.,* p. 509.

functionally in daily life or come out only in crises and which have perhaps been too quickly sloughed off. Too many genuine values have been sloughed off prematurely because they were considered from the standpoint of an externally applied judgment. Not only this, but anthropologists continually discover culture traits that have been neglected or derided as belonging to more "primitive" culture patterns but whose resurrection may provide important additions to the cultural life of society as a whole. Thus, Aldous Huxley asks, in *Ends and Means,* when comparing the values of the Zuni Indians with those of our Western culture:

> Is it possible for us to acquire their admirable habits of non-attachment to wealth and personal success, and at the same time to preserve our intellectual alertness, our interest in science, our capacity for making rapid technological progress and social change?
>
> These are questions which it is impossible to answer with any degree of confidence. Only experience and deliberate experiment can tell us if our problem can be completely solved.[16]

Besides deliberate, there have always been slow but unconscious, borrowings in American life. The participation of the Negro is an interesting example. Because of his peculiar social experience in slavery in this country, he has been isolated enough to develop his own folk culture influenced only a little by memories of his African background. Yet, because of his close contact in all phases of daily living with white Americans during and since slavery, it was inevitable that he become an integral part of the life of his community, and that his arts, his social customs, even his philosophy of life, should become a part of the social inheritance of those white people. Not only has the Negro thus influenced our American life, but in almost every region of our country instances of mutual cultural borrowings might be observed: for example, the Mexican in our Southwest; the Irish and French Canadian in New England.

---

[16] Aldous Huxley, *Ends and Means* (New York: Harper & Bros., 1937), p. 23.

Some will say that a conscious sharing of cultural values is too artificial a process. The answer might be made that any conscious learning is an artificial process; that leaders of today are turning more and more to rationally directed changes or a planned social economy. The present passion for postwar planning has given great impetus to this movement. Literally hundreds of plans for our economic and political welfare on a national and international basis are being discussed; but little attention is given to planning for an integration of cultural values either within our country or between countries. Such integration would mean the development of the kind of sympathetic attitudes which would insure co-operation in meeting our economic and political problems. Clark Wissler writes of the possibility and the value of such conscious integration. "Imitation," he says, speaking of one form of integration, "plays a big role in human society. Fundamentally it is a natural process, inherent in man, but it also may be rationalized as in deliberate copying, or borrowing."[17] Of ways in which the process of borrowing might take place, he writes:

> We must first of all keep thoroughly informed as to what the other people of the world are doing; that is, we must study their cultures. If we find traits that are truly better than ours, let us make them our own. In doing this we are not sacrificing our individuality, we are merely taking advantage of what the environment offers. We are not throwing away our culture, we are simply building in new and better parts to the same old whole.[18]

This willingness—and ability—objectively to survey what all cultures may have to contribute to a growing world civilization is of the essence of cultural democracy. It does not rest on the assumption that all culture traits are of equal value and have an equal right to survive; and it does not have for its aim a merging of them all in a uniform national or world culture. But, recognizing the advantage of the state of flux in which

---

[17] Clark Wissler, *Man and Culture* (New York: Thomas Y. Crowell Co., 1923), p. 206.
[18] *Ibid.*, p. 210.

practically all cultures find themselves, and further recognizing the need for experimental adaptations, it is predisposed to treat with respect all those values that are cherished anywhere by any group.

No simple graph could do justice to the complexity of the merging process—not least because it is in constant flux. Margaret Mead says that every American has the psychology of the third generation, in that he is "always moving on, always, in his hopes, moving up, leaving behind him all that was his past and greeting with enthusiasm any echo of that past when he meets it in the life of another. . . ."[19] This fluidity adds to the complexity of but favors an experimental approach to the problem. It means that no blueprint can be made out to fit any group or region of the country. It adds to the possibility that all sorts of social interaction as well as cultural borrowings can be, indeed are being, made by all sorts of groups to answer their own needs. We cannot here give adequate attention to the complexity of the merging process, but a backward look at the cultural history of our country gives us hope for the future. Who, for example, could have foreseen fifty years ago that Americans of Italian birth, almost all in very humble stations of life, would give the city of New York its ablest mayor in generations and, what is even more astonishing, would become the financial mainstay of the New York Opera? Or who could have foreseen that the children of illiterate peasants from Poland, Hungary, Slovakia, and other eastern-European countries, with their diversity of language and folkways, would combine to give America its most solid nucleus of trade-union organization? Since our country was built by the released creativity of the common man, why should we fear to destroy imperialism, if, by so doing, the creativity of the common man of Africa, India, or China may be released?

---

[19] Margaret Mead, *And Keep Your Powder Dry* (New York: William Morrow & Co., 1942), p. 37.

Another criticism of cultural democracy is that conscious appreciation for the cultural traditions of his own ethnic group narrows a person's ability to appreciate the values of other groups. On the contrary, if such appreciation is genuine, it sharpens his ability to recognize culture values as such and it tends to release his creativity. A few examples will make this clear. A dance mime was not especially creative until she conceived the idea of interpreting the cultural values of her Jewish background through the medium of dance. To her surprise she found that she could then understand and interpret values in other cultures. A Japanese-American girl resisted her father's attempt to have her learn anything of Japanese culture. Being artistically inclined, she studied Scandinavian art, but she soon realized that Japanese art had influenced what we now term modernistic furniture. She then studied Japanese art and became much more creative in her chosen medium of ceramics.

By citing these examples we do not mean to suggest that individuals should be confined within the limits of their own culture groups. Indeed, many individuals and groups are willing and even eager to lose their cultural identities in American life. Our belief in individual freedom in a democracy convinces us that they should be free to do so.

Real art, however, grows out of experience. The art of a nation should spring from the experience of all the elements that make up that nation. Our poverty of cultural creativity today is caused partly by our long denial of the experiences of individuals who are a part of us. Our social worlds continue to frown upon people for being what they are or for expressing what they feel. A few individuals, of course, rise above this denial. Jim Tully, for instance, was able, by defiance, to make these worlds accept his hobo experience. James Weldon Johnson took Negro sermons which previously had been laughed at and produced his classic *God's Trombones*. Louis Adamic accepted his background and gave the world *A Native's Return*. But for every Jim Tully, James Weldon Johnson, and Louis Adamic, there are millions of Negroes and first- and second-generation individuals who, because of the denial of their heritage, are so ashamed of their backgrounds that they become parts of a dull mass of uncreative citizens. If, through our schools and group work agencies, these young people could be inspired to translate their experiences into art, a veritable renaissance might develop.

It cannot be too often said that we tend to become what our social worlds demand of us, or what we think they demand. It follows then that, by the use of the technique of group approval or disapproval, we have it in our power to determine the cultural future of American life. We need more of this kind of social engineering.

A fifth-grade English teacher proved her ability to be such an engineer by giving social recognition to the children in her class who wrote the following in order that they might share their "differences" with one another:

HANUKKAH LIGHTS

Twinkle, twinkle, little light,
Glowing so small,
But always bright,
Standing in a golden menorah!
One light, two lights, three lights, four,
Growing daily more and more;
Five lights, six lights, seven, eight,
Adventurous stories they relate.

—STANLEY SCLARENCO (age nine)

LACE

Italians are noted especially for lace. They make beautiful collars, cuffs, and petticoats. My mother makes very beautiful lace. Every time I have nothing to do I go watch the women make very beautiful lace. A lady was trying to teach me how to do it, but I get mixed up. But I think its lots of fun making it. I will ask my mother to make me some and send it here.

—JOSEPH DEVIRGILIO (age ten)

These may seem to be insignificant examples of cultural sharing, but they are given to show that no matter what our age level or social position, our creativity can be released. Indeed, a decentralization of the means of self-expression and recreation may well accompany our period of postwar reconstruction. The present interest in the folk arts is a step in this direction. In many communities throughout the country both old and new Americans are enjoying one another in a way that promises well for the future. This movement might well be encouraged by our schools.

2

PREJUDICE AND ITS RELATION TO PERSONALITY MALADJUSTMENT

> Once riding in old Baltimore
> Heart-filled, head-filled with glee,
> I saw a Baltimorean
> Keep looking straight at me.
>
> Now I was eight and very small
> And he was no whit bigger,
> And so I smiled, but he poked out
> His tongue, and called me "Nigger."
>
> I saw the whole of Baltimore
> From May until December;
> Of all the things that happened there
> That's all that I remember.[1]

SOME WAG has said that "prejudice is being down on what we are not up on," and there is as much truth as pun in the phrase. The term means to judge before we know the facts. Prejudice is an attitude which, in the simplest terms, can be described as a tendency to move toward or away from a value. A value (there are both tangible and intangible values) is anything or any idea that we care enough about to avoid or seek. Prejudice can be either negative or positive, though we think of it mostly in its negative sense—as, being prejudiced against Mexicans. Here the value is "Mexican," and there is a tendency to avoid the value, or to do that which expresses hostility toward the "Mexicans." If, on the other hand, the person appreciates "Mexican," then he has a positive attitude.[2]

---

[1] Countee Cullen, "An Incident," in *Color* (New York: Harper & Bros. 1925).
[2] For good analyses of the formation of attitudes, see Otto Klineberg, *Social Psychology* (New York: Henry Holt & Co., 1940). See also Bruno Lasker, *Race Attitudes in Children* (New York: Henry Holt & Co., 1929).

Persons who are maladjusted do not express freely or share their cultural heritages. Among us there are today an alarming number of maladjusted personalities in diverse culture groups, and this applies as well to those of the dominant as to those of the minority groups.[3] Many of those individuals have become maladjusted because of a feeling either of personal inferiority, or of a superiority that imposes upon them a further feeling that they should dominate others.[4] When such prejudices are directed, in varying degrees of intensity, toward millions of Americans, they produce personality maladjustments that tend to impair individual integrity and creativeness, and our common civilization is impoverished.[5]

Although not all figures agree, milder psychological disturbances seem to be greater among Jewish Americans and the foreign-born than among most other Americans. According to a report made in 1936,[6] the number of Jewish patients who seek help in mental hygiene clinics is a disproportionately large part of the total number of individuals who visit these institutions. The explanation, said the report, "lies chiefly in the higher prevalence among Jews of functional mental diseases, particularly those related to environmental stress." The study also found that difficulty in keeping one's emotional equilibrium was more prevalent by half among the foreign-born patients of mental clinics generally and their children than among the native-born. Perhaps every one of these foreign-born patients, in one way or another, had met the kind of paradox of which the authors of this report speak as existing in the particular group studied— that of "not being encouraged . . . to be a Jew or allowed to be

---

[3] See "Thirty Million New Americans," in Louis Adamic, *My America, op. cit.,* p. 210.

[4] In this report, these words are not employed in any technical, psychiatric sense, but according to common usage.

[5] For definition and analysis of prejudice, see Otto Klineberg, *op. cit.,* chap. xiv.

[6] John Slawson and Maude Ross, "Mental Illness among Jews," *Jewish Social Service Quarterly,* XII (June, 1936), 348.

a non-Jew." These findings suggest the weight that change or isolation or uncertainty or all three have placed upon certain groups of Americans.[7] If this is true of one group, it is possibly true of others.

Moreover, through the social conditioning in the intimacy of the home that goes on from earliest childhood, abnormal responses to experience—exceptional shyness, aggressiveness, or simply lack of emotional equilibrium—may continue for generations after the causes of their occurrence have been removed. The compensations sought for lack of freedom in self-expression become habitual; inhibitions that lead to self-frustration are handed on from generation to generation; and an "oppression psychosis"[8] impedes the members of a group in their adjustment to a social environment that is, in the main, free from oppression.

Intercultural education may be said to have a responsibility to point out within minority groups that certain outmoded ways of action should be sloughed off, and outside the group to point out historical causes of certain traits so that no one will think of them as biological inheritances which are bound to persist.

We have said that the heterogeneity of our people presents a task of social adjustment, and that leaders in the field of cultural adjustment realize that the old methods of Americanization, which try to squeeze newcomers as rapidly as possible into a given mold, have not been successful. Such leaders also realize that, as a result of mistaken tactics of Americanization, too often the children of foreign parents tend to become "problem" children.[9] Statistics on delinquency and crime show that, while immigrants do not contribute their proportion to the courts,

[7] See immigrant biographies, such as M. E. Ravage, *An American in the Making* (New York: Harper & Bros., 1917).

[8] Herbert Adolphus Miller, *Races, Nations and Classes* (Philadelphia: J. B. Lippincott Co., 1924), chap. iv.

[9] Louis Adamic, *From Many Lands* (New York: Harper & Bros., 1940).

American-born children of foreigners are much more likely to commit crimes than native-born persons of native parentage. And the reason for this, strange as it may sound to the 100 per cent American, is *not* because they are children of immigrants, but because they are Americans and are no longer controlled by the traditions and customs which keep their parents in the paths of rectitude. In one important sense it may be said that *Americanization* is one of the chief causes of crime in the United States.[10]

Before going further, we need to state as briefly as possible the conception of personality that guides our thinking. Since social psychologists do not yet agree among themselves as to the definition of the personality and just how it develops, we are forced to be pragmatic and glean from the various schools of thought those concepts which seem to work best for our aim. We agree, but not completely, with the behaviorists that personalities can be conditioned toward ends democratically agreed upon. We agree with Gardner Murphy that personality is not just the result of the stimulus and response bonds which the extreme behaviorists once had us believe in, but that we are dealing with a bi-polar situation, and that not only does the situation make the personality, but the personality does much to make the situation.[11] We also agree with Gesell and Ilg that the "infant, to be sure, has great plasticity, great powers of learning, but there are lawful limits to his conditionability."[12]

The classroom teacher holds both of these poles in mind as she arranges educational experiences for her children. On the surface she knows that by giving satisfaction to certain basic wishes, such as recognition and response, and relating these to the desired attitude, she can, if other social worlds do not undo her, make the child "come back for more" until he has ac-

---

[10] Frederic M. Thrasher, "Are Our Criminals Foreigners?" in *Our Racial and National Minorities,* edited by Francis J. Brown and Joseph S. Roucek (New York: Prentice-Hall, 1937).

[11] Gardner Murphy, "Personality and Social Adjustment," *Social Forces.* XV, 473.

[12] Arnold Gesell and Frances Ilg, *Infant and Child in the Culture of Today* (New York: Harper & Bros., 1943), p. 40.

quired the traits of kindliness and goodwill. One of the many statements of college students who were a part of Newcomb's study in the changing of social attitudes is revealing: "It didn't take me long to see that liberal attitudes have prestige value. . . . I became liberal at first because of its prestige value. I remain so because the problems around which my liberalism centers are important. What I want now is to be effective in solving the problem."[13]

On the other hand, the teacher is thankful for "man's capacity to carry the cultures he creates" and that children are the "carriers and sources of life." She is even thankful that the child's personality, which is "an organized and ever-organizing web of behavior patterns closely related to the satisfaction of his wishes," may at times resist her efforts. When he resists, she realizes that she is touching on something sacred and tries all the more to understand his relationship with his parents and his feeling about his cultural background in order to release his creativity.

Since this report has to do mainly with methods of conditioning the child through the arranging of situations in which certain basic wishes[14] are satisfied in terms of appreciative attitudes, we shall now discuss these wishes.

Wish Frustration as a Cause of Personality Maladjustment

Although normal life necessarily carries with it some wish frustration (it has been said that the "adjusted" person is one whose life is more or less balanced between desiring and having his desires fulfilled), yet the experiences which large numbers of persons undergo are often devastating to personality because of the extra amount of wish frustration they produce and the unhealthy compensations that result. If teachers and social workers are to help relieve the situation, they will need not only to

---

[13] Theodore Newcomb, *Personality and Social Change* (New York: Dryden Press, 1943), pp. 39 ff.

[14] Various psychologists call them by various names, as desires, goals, motives, drives, or needs. See Otto Klineberg's discussion, *op. cit.*

know something more about the basic wishes that are frustrated,[15] but also to hold those wishes in mind as they arrange educational experiences for those for whom they are responsible.

Although fundamental wishes, the satisfaction of which with certain limitations is necessary for the adjustment of personalities, are described in various ways by modern psychologists, W. I. Thomas' exposition of four basic wishes[16] has been found most useful for our purposes. He lists the wish for security, the wish for new experience, the wish for response, and the wish for recognition.[17] Faris adds a fifth, the wish to be a part of a cause larger than oneself.[18] A well-adjusted personality, say these authorities, must have all these wishes satisfied to some extent and in some way.[19]

We cannot think of behavior as acting and reacting within such definite and separate categories. Behavior is far more fluid and complex than that. The simplified discussion of the basic needs that follows, however, will aid the classroom teacher and the social worker to understand some of the emotional tensions that arise from prejudice and that may lead to abnormal attitudes and behavior.

The wish for security may be defined as a desire for an assured place in the social world, a desire for ease. It includes physical security, such as freedom from unemployment, sickness, and

---

[15] For a good general analysis of the effect of wish frustration, see D. A. Prescott, *Emotion and the Educative Process* (Washington, D. C.: American Council on Education, 1938), chap. vi.

[16] An example of the application of Thomas' conception of the four wishes in the field of intercultural relations is found in Robert E. Park and Herbert A. Miller, *Old World Transplanted* (New York: Harper & Bros., 1921), pp. 27-9.

[17] W. I. Thomas, *The Unadjusted Girl* (New York: Little, Brown & Co., 1923), pp. 4-40.

[18] Ellsworth Faris, reported by his students from lectures.

[19] For a more thorough analysis, see D. H. Kulp, II, *Educational Sociology* (New York: Longmans, Green & Co., 1932), pp. 158 ff. For a differently stated though similar analysis, see Prescott, *op. cit.*, pp. 110-38; also Robert E. Park and Ernest W. Burgess, *Introduction to the Science of Sociology* (Chicago: University of Chicago Press, 1926), pp. 442-3.

danger. For the child, it might be translated into adequate physical care.

The wish for new experience, or adventure, may be defined as a desire of the individual for freedom to satisfy his curiosity about his environment, to "go places and do things"; in the case of children, it is often the desire to play with other children. People vary in the type of new experience they desire and in the means by which they try to satisfy their desire. For some it may be scientific research; for others, dancing, or travel, or reading, or even seeking illicit pleasures.

The wish for response implies a desire for love or fellowship and the appreciation of beauty. It involves, obviously, relations with people, but includes also response from animals and identification with places, "heroes," and symbols (God, Country, Labor, Profession, Team, Alma Mater, Party, and so forth).

The wish for recognition is basically the desire for *status.* "It expresses itself in devices for securing distinction in the eyes of the public."[20] It is sometimes called the wish for superiority or dominance, and is then explained as the wish to rise as high as possible in one's social worlds; to gain power over people or things; to attain material possessions, intellectual distinction, physical prowess, respectability. It involves adequate participation in group activities. For some people, the fulfillment of this wish is acquired through a feeling of "racial" or group superiority, which results in prejudice and discrimination against members of the "out-groups." We may then call it a wish for dominance.

One might lay at the foot of this wish most of society's ills, for all conflict can be traced to our unlimited striving for superiority and fear of inferiority. And yet the child who starts life with no feeling of being a separate individual must by the struggle to satisfy his basic desires gradually develop his individual personality. However, unless this individuation is balanced

---

[20] Park and Burgess, *op. cit.,* p. 489.

by integration, society comes to be made up of individuals who continually fly at one another's throats. Integration is the process whereby the individual becomes conscious of his membership in the group and of his responsibility to the other members and to the group as a whole.

One's consciousness, then, "should grow until it can include and integrate the qualities, needs, and interests of other groups: it should become universal." "Our consciousness becomes more personal, different from other consciousness, and at the same time more universal: we become alive to our participation in the development of mankind, we become world-conscious. But each individual should find and maintain his own viewpoint, his own individual kind of world-consciousness. There should be no uniformity nor should there be indistinctness nor indulgence in vague generalities."[21]

When we apply this to cultural democracy, we might say that the cultural wealth of our country and of the world depends on the extent to which individuals and the culture groups in which their varied personalities have been developed are permitted and encouraged to express and share what they see, feel, and know.

Some social psychologists include *the wish to be part of a cause larger than oneself* in the wish for response; but we believe that this wish is so important in personality development that special emphasis should be placed upon it. The spread of moral cynicism, decried by Myrdal[22] and others, has been due largely to the fact that extreme behaviorists have been in the policy-making positions of American education and have colored much of our thinking to the effect that a spiritual approach to life is somehow a sign of weakness. Some of us saw the utter inadequacy of this point of view only when the crisis of the war came with its pull on loyalties. Fritz Kunkel[23] shows how re-

---

[21] Kunkel, *op. cit.,* p. 189.

[22] Gunnar Myrdal, *An American Dilemma* (New York: Harper & Bros., 1944).

[23] Kunkel, *op. cit.,* p. 9.

ligion and psychology can be combined in our attempt to help ourselves and others to become emotionally mature. He describes the desire to be part of a cause as the most powerful of all desires. Behind the behavior difficulty, he writes, "is the fear of being excluded from life, and behind the fear, the pain of not being loved, and behind the pain of loneliness the deepest and most powerful and most hidden of all human desires: the desire to love, to give oneself, to be a part of the living stream that we call brotherhood; and the very moment that love is discovered behind hatred, all hatred disappears."

The study and treatment of psychiatric cases of soldiers in World War II highlighted this desire to be a part of a group. It was often found that a flyer's identification with his outfit was so intense that he developed guilt feelings when he had to be brought back from the front. The French pilot de Saint Exupéry expressed this group feeling beautifully in his book *Flight to Arras*. The fact too that so many flyers had to be treated for guilt feelings in reference to bombing may reveal their unconscious identity with humanity as a whole.

What then constitutes personality adjustment? Psychology alone would say that the adjusted person must have some or all of his basic desires satisfied to some extent in ways that are meaningful to him. But the question must then be asked, "How can the individual, becoming more and more conscious of his individual needs, possibilities, and desires, at the same time serve the group and its interest? Is there not a fundamental conflict between social duties and personal enjoyment?" The answer, Kunkel tells us, "involves the acknowledgment of conscious and unconscious psychological functions. . . . Our duties toward ourselves and toward our social environment coincide. Indeed there is only one duty, namely: to grow mature. To find ourselves, our center, our highest value, means to find our group, our spiritual home, and our positive relationship to God. It means unlimited growth, both of individual creativity and of expanding brotherhood. . . . Only our egocentric goals are in conflict with our social duties."[24] One might add that a satisfying religion is one which lessens one's egocentric drives because it gives a greater feeling of security in being a part of the Divine, which implies being a part of the Whole.

Examples of Prejudice and Compensation

Before teachers and group leaders can help to relieve the situation in school and community partly caused by inter-group conflict, they must understand more intimately what members of disadvantaged groups have to face, how the satisfaction of their basic desires is denied, partly because of prejudice against them, and how they tend to compensate for those frustrations.

A Jewish girl, trained to be a stenographer, finds that "only Christians need apply."

A Negro is refused admittance to the theater where a Negro company is playing.

A Nisei, born and raised in this country, who had always felt herself an American, suddenly finds herself in a relocation center behind a barbed-wire fence.

A second-generation Italian boy hears Italians referred to as "dirty wops."

A second-generation Greek boy is slighted at a school party because he is so "foreign-looking."

A Japanese-American boy even before the war is expected to sit at a table set aside for students of his group in the college library.

A German-American boy is bombarded by his school fellows with epithets about Hitlerism.

Members of dominant groups are notoriously callous to the mental anguish of members of the minority groups that results from derision and discrimination. Faris writes:

The effect of race prejudice on individuals who hold it is to limit their power of discrimination. It blinds a man to differences where these would otherwise be easily seen.[25]

---

[24] *Ibid.,* p. 191.

[25] Ellsworth Faris, *The Nature of Human Nature* (New York: McGraw-Hill Book Co., 1937), p. 366.

Few members of dominant groups stop to think that a Negro never knows when he awakes in the morning how soon he will be insulted. The president of a Negro college met for lunch in a downtown New York hotel a friend who is the editor of a well-known Negro magazine. The grumbling white waiter said, "What do you boys want?" It is the unexpectedness of insults like this in the North that is so devastating. In the South, where in general Negroes are "boys," and none is called "Mr." or "Mrs.," there is such a complete separation of the two groups that, for the most part, only the servant group exposes itself— and that only because it is economically profitable to do so— to a situation where the insult can be given. One effect of segregation in the South—where it is possible for the children of each group to go through school, from kindergarten to university, without ever coming in close contact with an educated member of the opposite group—is often to fasten on Negroes a feeling of inferiority so fixed that their inferiority seems even to many of them to be inherent. It is significant that a Negro rural teacher from Georgia, a student in a Northern university, stated in class one day her conviction that Negroes are born inferior to whites.

We need to remind ourselves in passing that members of minority ethnic groups are not unique in being the recipients of prejudice and that they do not react in any peculiar way in their attempts at compensation. For example, L. M., a blue-eyed Nordic, whose father was a foreign correspondent for a New York paper, spent his early years in Paris, then went to school in England in order to become more familiar with his mother tongue. Later he attended school in New York, then in Canada, and finally in a Middle Western community. In every school he was regarded as a member of an "out-group." When in school in England, because of his French accent, he was a "frog"; in New York, with an English accent, he was a "limey"; in the Middle West he was "putting on airs." Because of the persecution from his fellow students, which went all unnoticed by his teachers, he developed a severe case of stammering and an extreme inferiority feeling against which he had to struggle for the rest of his life.

What happens to people who have limitations set upon the fulfillment of their normal wishes? They compensate in some way. Folsom points out that there is no general rule which determines what kind of behavior will be used to compensate for a particular frustration. Each individual compensates in the channel which seems to give him the most relief or satisfaction. If a child's wish for prestige is thwarted because he has been made to feel that he does not "belong," he may attempt to satisfy this wish by behavior that will attract attention, or he may compensate by excessive daydreaming. Similarly, the same kind of behavior may in one person be an indication of a frustrated wish for dominance depending upon what values he is pursuing; in another, of a frustrated wish for personal response.

A few examples will indicate that some of the personality problems which young people exhibit in school and out may have as a basic cause frustrations growing out of group prejudice and discrimination.

SHYNESS

Esther, a Jewish student in a school where there were very few Jews, was noticeably shy. She would not take part in discussions or volunteer to recite. Her grades were consequently low, her oral English mark below passing. The teacher's opinion of her was that she was "dull."[26]

Phillipa was the only Rumanian girl in her school. One of her teachers reported that she was shy and shrinking, afraid to talk in class. She apparently had no friends among the students, for outside of classes she was always alone.

"A young Indian boy of high intelligence was attending a

---

[26] Unless otherwise stated, case stories are taken from the *Field Notebook* of the author.

white school. He did well in his work and seemed a likable chap, but was so plainly shy that he made no social progress. On social occasions he simply said nothing. His white comrades resented his apparent lack of interest in group contacts and left him more and more to himself."[27]

AGGRESSIVENESS

Reports came from schools on the Pacific Coast that some Japanese Americans were trying to gain recognition by excessive attempts to obtain high scholastic marks. In one mixed school ten out of the thirteen receiving honors were of Japanese background. This was out of proportion to their numbers in the school. Many schools in various parts of the country reported a similar compensatory activity on the part of Jewish students.

LACK OF IDENTIFICATION WITH CULTURAL BACKGROUND

A professor in a well-known university in this country said that as a boy he was so ashamed of his Swedish parentage that he hated to study the geography of Sweden. Only when he was in college did he begin to get over feeling ashamed of his heritage.

A Jewish mother says, "I have two sons, sixteen and twenty years old, who have a very bitter antagonism toward their own group. They do not want to be associated with what they think is a despised group. All their friends are Christians, and if ever they meet any Jewish boys or girls, they will have nothing to do with them."[28]

Miss B., of Italian background, never let anyone know that her parents were foreigners. She had changed her name so that it was not recognized as Italian. One day a teacher who had been born in Switzerland was teasing some of her colleagues about "this 100 per cent Americanism." Miss B. entered the

---

27 John Levy, *Conflicts of Cultures and Children's Maladjustments* (New York: National Committee for Mental Hygiene, 1933), pp. 4-5.

28 Bruno Lasker (ed.), *Jewish Experiences in America* (New York: The Inquiry, 1930), p. 111.

room in the middle of the discussion. The Swiss teacher turned
to her and without any introduction said, "Mary, where did your
parents come from?" Miss B. replied, "None of your business,"
and went out, slamming the door.

A nine-year-old Swedish boy was sent to a clinic because
he insisted that he was a Jew. Instead of using his own name,
Carl Swenson, he called himself Isaac Cohen. He carried around
with him a Jewish newspaper which he pretended he could
read. At the clinic it was learned that he was the only Swede
in a community that was largely Jewish, and that the boys he
admired most at school were Jews.

SENSITIVENESS

A Negro girl with a Spanish name, who was evidently partly
Spanish, claimed to be West Indian and not Negro. She was,
however, very sensitive about any slights directed toward the
Negro and often imagined prejudice where none existed. Other
Negro girls brought to her complaints about slights, and she
did the fighting. All the other girls seemed to be afraid of her.

INCORRIGIBILITY

Joseph di Gregorio was seven years old when he moved to
this country. Italian continued to be spoken in the home. At
school Joseph could not understand the work or enter into the
more articulate play life of his companions. The only way he
could make his mark was by cutting up—a solution of his problem which resulted in his being sent to a child-guidance clinic
as incorrigible.[29]

CONFLICT BETWEEN PARENTS AND CHILDREN

A successful teacher, of Armenian birth, went by the
name of Annette Thomas. When asked why she had changed
her name from Zarmig Thomesian, she answered that it was

---

[29] Levy, *op. cit.,* p. 3.

because she could not get a job if she used an Armenian name. When asked whether her parents had not minded, she replied that it had almost killed her mother, but that the latter had eventually seen that it was necessary.

A social worker reports, "I shall never forget the picture of twelve-year-old Tony as he stamped his foot and shouted at his Sicilian father, 'I'll take nothing off a damn Dago like you!' . . . In this instance, as in many others, the break of parental authority had sad results. Three years later a probation officer struggled to pick up the pieces."[30]

How Prejudice in Family Life Acts as a Cause of Personality Maladjustment

It has been said that few individuals can exist happily unless they experience the warm feeling of belonging to an intimate circle within which all the senses of the members are somehow harmonized. The sight of familiar features, the hearing of sister's voice, the smell of father's pipe, the taste of the familiar food, the touch of mother's hand—all these are part of the normal child's sense of security and well-being.

It is the small groups with their face-to-face contacts which, next to the family circle, have most power over our attitudes. These small primary groups are to be found in such institutions as the school, the church, the club, and the summer camp and should be made use of more realistically in an attempt to develop more appreciative attitudes. But in that attempt our first responsibility is to understand the home background and the child's relationship to his parents. Are his parents giving him the kind of response and wise counsel that will enable him finally to feel himself a person independent and yet appreciative of them? Are they able to give him the kind of healthy pride that will enable him to gain the sort of recognition he desires from his peers?

It is the difference of home background, above all, that sets

---

[30] Evelyn Hersey, unpublished manuscript.

up formidable obstacles to emotional habits as soon as the child gets out of the mother's sight to experience contacts with strangers; for even similarities disappear when eyes and ears encounter a new world.

> Among any hundred fathers introduced as a sample of the population at large we should find eighty-eight or eighty-nine "white" men, nine or ten Negroes, and one or two representatives of darker-skinned groups, such as Mexicans, Indians, Chinese, or Japanese.
>
> Of the white men in the representative sampling (eighty-nine in round numbers), fifty-seven are native-born sons of native-born parents; twenty-one are native-born sons of mixed or foreign parentage; and eleven are foreign-born.
>
> Back of census data such as these are the untold life dramas of families which are misfits in the communities in which they live, often lonely and set apart from their neighbors: handicapped by language or color, overwhelmed by sudden changes in their mode of living, and disturbed because of conflicting loyalties which they cannot reconcile.[31]

Added to these disturbances are the conflicting demands of our complex modern social world, intensified by economic pressure and finally by the tensions of war. These demands affect families of all groups and play a large part among the causes of the increase of personality maladjustment. We shall attempt here to isolate only one factor, that of prejudice, and to point out how some situations in home life are responsible for its development.

One's social worlds determine whether or not he will show prejudice toward races other than his own or toward minority groups. If he does show it, it will not be because such prejudice was "born in him"; rather it will be because of his conditioning, because he has seen members of his family or other primary groups so reacting, or because of his own experience with members of other groups. "Wash that lettuce well, dear, you don't know how many dirty Mexicans have handled it," says a mother to her child. For her, this statement may be a reasonable outcome of her own limited experience with Mexicans; but in the

---

[31] Bess V. Cunningham, *Family Behavior* (Philadelphia: W. B. Saunders Co., 1936), p. 88.

child's mind, unless promptly counteracted by other influences, it may develop a generalization that will color his attitude toward all Mexicans.

The person, then, reacts in response to a social situation; and he will so respond until a change has been made, not in *human nature,* which desires only the satisfaction of its own wishes, but in the social situation which plays such a large part in determining how our wishes are to be satisfied or if they are to be satisfied at all.

The Effects of the Feeling of Superiority on the Dominant Group

At first thought it may seem that prejudice causes maladjustment only in children of groups against which prejudice is shown. Children of the dominant group, however, also may tend to become maladjusted, especially if they have developed extreme feelings of group pride and contempt for others.

> In a rather typical Northern suburban community, composed for the most part of wealthy families known as the "best families" (Americans for several generations), there are at least two gangs of boys who, one of their teachers said, would have been in the reformatory if they had come from other homes. On one occasion, these boys came to a school party somewhat inebriated, and turned in a fire alarm, turned on the water in the school, and damaged automobiles. The Board of Education, however, paid for the damages, for the superintendent said, "They come from our best families. Those parents must be spared humiliation." These boys, the teacher said, all have such an exaggerated feeling of superiority about their own background that they will take nothing from the Irish "cop" or the Jewish captain of the police. In the classroom, when immigration or a similar topic is being discussed, they always voice the idea of the "closed door," or say, "send them back where they come from." Even if the teacher and the other members of the class argue against them, they enjoy the isolation that this position gives them. It is then that they feel superior. These children come from homes where the elders say, "you must not play with Dagoes," and where mother blames whatever Johnny does on his association in the public school with Italians, or Irish, or Poles, or other minority-group children.[32]

---

[32] From the *Field Notebook* of the author.

Such double standards, which have been too prevalent in American life, are like boomerangs. The missile used by the "superior" group has returned to weaken our whole democratic civilization. The brilliant writings of Lillian Smith are showing how this applies to the South. "Christianity, democracy, psychiatry, affirm, each in its own idiom, this basic fact: that men cannot cut themselves off from each other and live creative, sane, good lives. Segregation is not a Southern tradition, a regional problem, it is the basic problem of every human being on the face of the earth. It is a problem which every man has to solve in his own life before he can achieve emotional maturity and 'goodness'."[33]

The Effects of Prejudice on Family Life among Minority Groups

The "problem of the second generation" is one of lack of adjustment to American life. It is caused either by misunderstanding between parents and children or by a clash of value judgments, the one derived from an old-world social milieu, the other from contact with American or assumed-to-be American values. Partly because ways of acting here and in the old environment do not have the same meanings, misunderstandings and clashes arise to such an extent that parents are often unable to control their American-born children. This is true of Jewish families recently from Poland, of Italian families from villages in Sicily, of Japanese families from crowded Kinshu, and of Negro families from rural districts in the South. Many of these Negro families have migrated to our Northern cities during and since World War I. Although not from another country, they have come from an isolation that has produced almost a different culture, a culture which is still in the "shadow of the plantation." Southern whites moving to the North also, of course, often enter a cultural setting sufficiently distinct from the one they have left to produce shocks and disturbances to inherited value judgments. But in their case, and indeed in

---

[33] Lillian Smith, in *Common Ground,* Spring, 1944, p. 43.

that of all white Americans moving from one part of the country to another, status is not usually affected by that act: the migrant may find himself at odds with his new neighbors on many matters of taste and judgment; but his children are not drawn away from him, as a rule, by finding his habits and ambitions—or lack of them—a handicap to their own personal success.

In the atmosphere of the immigrant home the conflict between the old and the new cannot fail to show itself. The parents strive to give their children the only values that they know—those of the land from which they have come: the attitude, for instance, of the majority of the people of that land toward work, thrift, and family relations. But the children, attending American schools, playing on American streets, come home with different feelings. The teachers and the other children, they have discovered, do not value the same things that their parents value.

At first, the young child unquestioningly adheres to the standards of his home and even defends them when occasion arises in a war of words with other children. As the children grow older, a gulf begins to develop between them and their parents. Though they seem to have become thoroughly American, the children begin to show in their responses to school situations the emotional disturbances that result from the conflict between the culture of their homes and that of the school and community life. The gulf widens, and the children begin to belittle the customs to which the parents still cling and to ridicule their parents for clinging to them. It widens still further, and the children—young adults now—sometimes even change their names to others that sound more "American." The result is often tragic: pain for the parents and, later on, regret on the part of the children for the pain they have caused. This remorse may reveal itself in a number of ways, among them a sullen renunciation of things American with an exaggerated show of affection for their parents and pride in their home culture. Irvin L. Child in his book *Italian or American?* which should be read by every American teacher, has brilliantly described this conflict.[34]

It must be noted here, however, that this problem of the second generation is a part of the conflict which most young people in western society experience in their growth from dependence upon toward independence of their parents. It must be remembered also that this conflict, universal in western society, has been intensified by rapid social changes in modern times.

The problem of the second generation is exemplified in the following cases:

> Angelina hung back to speak to the club leader after the club meeting. "What can I do?" she asked. "You tell me I shouldn't meet Joe on the street corner, and then lie to my mother about where I was. I know, you will say, try to explain to her! I tell her, American girls bring boys home and entertain them, but she says, 'What would our *paesan* [countrymen] think! They would write to your uncles and grandmother in Sicily and say we are not taking care of you, and that you're not a good girl. No, you cannot do these things. It would bring disgrace. When you or we find a boy you want to marry, then he may come!' " What can Angelina do? The defensive behavior born of these conflicts is familiar to us all. Settlement House directors shake their heads over noisy, painted girls and groan at the hats-over-the-eye "smart alecs" that swarm over their thresholds. Can these be the children of the thrifty, quiet, dignified peasants living in the next block?[35]

> When the Spanish-speaking pupil has spent six or seven years in a school with his own group (in Los Angeles, where he has been segregated in a "Mexican" elementary school), he enters junior high school without personal security and ease in his relations with the Anglo-American group. Moreover, in all too many cases, his academic achievement in language and reading is below the teacher's expectancy for the grade. If and when ability grouping is practiced, he again finds himself segregated and the vicious circle unbroken. Is it any wonder that he acquires a chip on the shoulder, a surliness, an apparent "I don't care" demeanor?

> What is the story when he enters high school?

---

[34] Child, *op. cit.*
[35] Evelyn Hersey, unpublished manuscript.

First, it should be stated emphatically that only those who are strong within themselves are able to "take it" and continue. As a rule, high-school entrance means membership in an even smaller minority. Here he meets the full impact of prejudice.

What chance has a youngster when the head of the commercial department says, "I have no problem with the Mexicans. I take care that the first few days' work is so difficult and involved that they become discouraged and quit," or when a high school principal says, "We just see that none of them get to the tenth grade"? Very casually.[36]

Some second-generation Negro children from our rural South face in our Northern cities the problem of an inferiority feeling on the part of their parents. These parents, not only because of the somewhat different social values in the North, but also because many Negroes have been conditioned to think of themselves as inferior, often have a hopeless and resigned feeling. Sometimes they attempt to cover up their resignation with cheerfulness and laughter, but that does not mean that they are content. Their songs show their sadness. Some Negro parents even believe the fallacy that was utilized in the motion picture *Imitation of Life* that Negroes get "dumb" when they grow up. Such parents fail to instill ambition in their children. This lack produces a condition of mind that prevents the child from making the most of his school opportunities.

At the other extreme, one school, which is 70 per cent Negro, reports that the Negro parents are becoming so aggressive that it is difficult to find any basis of co-operation.

Authorities on juvenile delinquency tell us that an important factor contributing to personality maladjustment today is the broken home, and that the increase in the number of broken homes is caused in part by extreme economic pressure, which affects families of all groups. Because the Negro family is at the bottom of the heap economically and suffers most from dis-

---

[36] C. C. Trillingham and Marie M. Hughes, in *California Journal of Secondary Education,* as quoted in *The Clearing House,* XVIII (March, 1944), 401.

crimination, it is to be expected that this group should produce a large proportion of broken homes and of problem children.

In the survey of the Sub-Committee on Education of the Commission of the Mayor of New York City to Investigate Conditions in Harlem, we find this statement:

> When it actually appears that in one school a survey showed more than 700 broken homes—that is, homes with one parent missing—out of a total representation of some 1,600 families, it is obvious that a social situation exists which constitutes a challenge to the school system and to the life of the city so poignant as to call for most drastic action. . . . No people and children situated as the residents of west Harlem are today could resist the disintegrating influences of extreme poverty, a meagre existence on public or private dole, lack of normal occupation and of almost all adequate social and moral safeguards. It is not a question of race; it is a simple question of humanity which confronts us.[37]

The wise teacher will study the social factors in human behavior and begin to differentiate among their diverse consequences rather than say, "He is delinquent because he is Italian," or make such a generalization as that recently voiced by a white teacher in a school, the population of which was 85 per cent Negro: "All Negroes have loose family morals, so what can you expect?"

The Negro group has had to combat a myth with regard to its loose morals—a myth partly created by former white slaveholders, whose own emotions prevented their seeing the picture as a whole.[38] It was not until W. E. B. DuBois made a thorough historical and sociological study of the problem that we got a more balanced judgment.[39] Though conceding, as he did, the relatively large proportion of illegitimate births, he agrees with the conclusion of the sociologist Reuter that

---

[37] *Report of Mayor's Commission on Conditions in Harlem* (New York: May 22, 1936).

[38] E. Franklin Frazier, *The Negro Family in Chicago* (Chicago: University of Chicago Press, 1932), chap. i.

[39] W. E. B. DuBois, *The Negro Family* (Atlanta, Georgia: Atlanta University, 1908).

the range of Negro home and family standards is as wide as that of any group in the population. The standards are in general those of other Americans of similar economic and educational status; the Negroes conform to the prevailing patterns except as conformity is made impossible by economic, legal, or other insuperable handicaps.[40]

It behooves the teacher to discover what kind of Negro homes the children in her schools are from. No doubt, some of them will be found to come from middle- and upper-class families with traditions dating back to freedom long before the Civil War, or to slave ancestors who happened to have masters who protected and educated them. Others may come from families recently migrated from the rural South, some of whose ancestors may have suffered from the unmoral conditions forced upon the field hands during slavery and the almost subhuman standards of living which many of them have had to face since the Civil War. On the other hand, some may have come from the West Indies; and most of the parents of these children are far better educated than are most of the Negroes from the deep South. The alert teacher will be aware of and make the most of this intercultural situation.

In our study of personality maladjustment we should be careful, however, not to condemn all underprivileged homes. One has only to read Betty Smith's book *A Tree Grows in Brooklyn* to appreciate how one mother in the most squalid surroundings was able to keep intact the personalities of her children; and there are many such mothers among all groups. Crowded homes and poor aesthetic standards are inimical to the development of character and personality; but they are not such important causes of mental suffering in the child as are attitudes of his parents that are in conflict with those prevailing in the community because the parents came from other countries: attitudes, for example, on such matters as the mingling of the sexes, the child's choice of schoolmates, and his discipline. These are exactly the points on which parents brought up in an entirely dif-

---

[40] Edward Byron Reuter, *The American Race Problem—A Study of the Negro* (New York: Thomas Y. Crowell Co., 1938), pp. 221-2.

ferent environment are most often in conflict with their American-born children.[41]

Community Disorganization as a Factor in Personality Maladjustment in Minority Groups

Some students of current life say that only by first setting up a new and co-operative economic system can we be assured of a society in which the individual can satisfy his basic wishes, and that the elimination of inter-group frictions waits upon that change. It is useless, they say, for the school to attempt to develop cultural democracy when the community life in which the pupil lives pulls in the opposite direction. How, they ask, can a San Francisco high-school boy change his attitude toward Japanese Americans as long as a large section of the press depicts all Japanese Americans only as dangerous rivals and spies? How long will a better attitude toward Jews last on the part of a Negro youth in Harlem when he is constantly told that Jewish landlords and Jewish storekeepers in that community exploit his race? How can any white American lad be really appreciative of the Negro people when radio, theater, and movies so largely continue the fictitious notion that all Negroes are lazy, timid, and improvident? How can children of any group have an unprejudiced attitude toward all other groups when they know that their own government in its laws and in many of its departmental "traditions" discriminates against Negroes, Oriental Americans, and Mexican Americans? Where, they ask, can young people get the emotional power to resist pride and prejudice when even their churches often instill in them the feeling that they belong to an elect group?[42]

Economic pressure underlies and gives force to prejudices, and these prejudices are often manipulated in the interests of

---

[41] Cunningham, *op. cit.*, p. 59.

[42] See Bruno Lasker, *Race Attitudes in Children, op. cit.*, pp. 180-2, for an interpretation of the shortcomings of the church, as well as its opportunities.

the system which produces them. But because people are also conditioned by social-psychological relations that are not affected by economic pressure, the school can develop the kind of attitudes which would enable young people of all groups to co-operate in ways that would finally help to break the vicious circle. Thus, we do not need to wait for a new economic system in order to begin to change the social-economic setting in which group relations and attitudes develop. Even in a "new social order" such factors would still have to be reckoned with.

The point we must all come to see is that our attitudes are a result of the total situation, and that education must be undertaken from a community approach. Again to quote Newcomb: "Attitude change was only slightly related to courses of study pursued in college. . . . But the important influences making for attitude changes were clearly of a community-wide rather than of an academic major sort."[43] What first steps schools can take in this direction in their attempt to build appreciative attitudes will be discussed in a later chapter.

Prejudice and Discrimination in the Light of Cultural Anthropology

The lack of appreciative attitudes toward other groups is often based on the false belief that culture groups are primarily distinguished by race, and that races can be measured for inherent superiority and inferiority. Anthropologists, however, point out that there is no standard with reference to which it may be said that one race is inherently superior to any other, and that no culture trait is limited by physical conditions to a single racial group.

The following broad statements uphold this point of view; but since they are taken from their contexts, it is suggested that the interested reader study the sources.

---

[43] Newcomb, *op. cit.*, p. 21.

Ruth Benedict says:

> Since we are forced to believe that the race of man is one species, it follows that man everywhere has an equally long history behind him.[44]

Franz Boas says:

> If we were to select the most intelligent, imaginative, energetic, and emotionally stable third of mankind, all races would be represented.[45]

E. A. Hooton says:

> Each racial type runs the gamut from idiots and criminals to geniuses and statesmen. No type produces a majority of individuals from either end of the scale. There are no racial monopolies of either human virtues or vices.[46]

Even a limited study in the field of anthropology, then, helps us to realize that the ways of our own group are not the only ways to satisfy human desires. Out of thousands of possible lingual sounds, for instance, the French have developed certain combinations and the English others. Out of various ways of eating, the Chinese have selected chopsticks and the Western world, much later, forks. Margaret Mead writes:

> We cannot but be impressed with the many ways in which man has taken a few hints [from] . . . his natural environment, . . . his own physical nature, . . . differences between one animal and another, etc., . . . and made for himself a fabric of culture within which each human life is dignified by form and meaning; . . . [yet] each people makes this fabric differently, selects some clues and ignores others, emphasizes a different sector of the whole arc of human potentialities. . . .[47]

It may be seen, then, that at a given moment not all racial groups are equally well endowed for success in any one set of environmental circumstances; but any modern civilized society has use for all endowments: the superior muscular strength of

[44] Ruth Benedict, *Patterns of Culture* (Boston: Houghton Mifflin Co., 1934), p. 18.

[45] Franz Boas, *Anthropology and Modern Life* (New York: W. W. Norton & Co., 1932), p. 75.

[46] E. A. Hooton, *Apes, Men, and Morons* (New York: G. P. Putnam's Sons, 1937).

[47] Margaret Mead, *From the South Seas* (New York: William Morrow & Co.; copyright 1928, 1930, 1935, 1939 by Margaret Mead).

one, the swiftness of another, even the low metabolism of a third, the acquired resistance to cold of yet another, and so forth. In modern civilized society, however, the relative advantages of one physical endowment or another move entirely into the background compared with those qualities which, experience has shown, members of every racial group can acquire, irrespective of their natural endowment, given the appropriate early conditioning of each generation.

Our reading in cultural anthropology, therefore, brings a realization that although individuals come into the world without any culture and can acquire whatever culture is impressed upon them, yet once the personality is organized around a particular set of habits, it is not easy to change those attitudes which are central to the personality complex and connected by channels of habitual response to the current of its emotions.

> The immigrant comes to the United States with his life direction already established through experiences in the cultural complex of his native habitat; psychologically speaking, his nationalistic character will always be partly European or Asiatic.[48]

We see here, then, a very practical and non-controversial clue to at least one promising form of intercultural education: a more widespread knowledge of some of the truths established by cultural anthropology. If more people could be made aware of the fact that every immigrant faces an inescapable task of personal adjustment—which may take months or years, or may not be accomplished for two generations and even more—we should have a more widely prevalent faith in the immigrant's power of cultural growth, which is so often denied and the denial of which closes so many doors to him and his children. Such knowledge also, as we know from innumerable instances in recorded personal experience, would help the immigrant—or the son of a native minority group who has wandered away from

---

[48] Lawrence G. Brown, *Immigration* (New York: Longmans, Green & Co., 1933), p. 20.

its closely guarded traditions—to understand better the choices before him. He would realize that no culture group ever has successfully in a short time acquired an entirely new set of values, and that it is to his cultural heritage he must look for support of his normal outlook on life and that of his children, until some part of the heritage may become unnecessary and another part, perhaps, may become the common possession of many individuals in many groups. Through such realization of the part which old culture traits might play in a period of adjustment to a new environment, much happiness might result and much energy might be saved; and the cultural luggage which newcomers in former times have been in too great a haste to cast away might henceforth be conserved for whatever heirlooms it may yet be found to contain.

This point of view is especially helpful for teachers who have contact through the children with parents who are refugees. It will aid the teacher to help the child who quickly takes on American ways to see that he has no reason to feel superior to his parents. In addition, by giving social recognition in the class to those who know other languages, home festivals, foods, and ways of doing things, the teacher will aid in releasing the creativity in the foreign-background child.[49] In so far as others share such knowledges, the class is together doing its bit in building together the American "cathedral."

An Intercultural Center

The ultimate goal for each community might be the securing, equipping, and furnishing of an intercultural center (Cleveland has its Intercultural Library and Pittsburgh its Cathedral of Learning) to serve as an educational exhibit of the arts and crafts of our contributing cultures; a workshop in which the

---

[49] For excellent class activities on the elementary level based on this approach see Ethel Duncan, *Democracy's Children—Adventures in Intercultural Education for the Elementary School* (New York: Hinds, Hayden & Eldredge, 1945).

skills, arts, and music of all our people can be shared, dramatized, and taught; a place where common community problems can be analyzed and steps toward their solution undertaken; in short, a place where all elements in the community can find opportunities for self-expression and fellowship.

3

SOME HIGH SCHOOLS BEGIN TO BUILD TOGETHER

It is better to try to write plays than to take courses in drama, better to dance than to go to lectures on the dance, better to do some painting than to study art. . . . It is better to play tennis, even badly, than to watch a championship match. It is better to make a pie or dress than to look into a bakery window or attend a fashion show, better to earn a modest living by your own hard work than to inherit a fortune, better to sing around the piano than to listen to the radio. The joy of creation is always greater than the undoubted pleasure of looking on. . . . Those who have the most fun will continue to be those who do rather than merely look on.[1]

The Role of the School

WE RECOGNIZE that the program for the solution of any social problem is divided into two parts, the long and the short, and that the school should pay more attention to the long than to the short. The short-term program—what to do about preventing riots, vandalism, and the rise of un-American propaganda, immediate treatment of delinquents, adequate housing for minority groups, equality of opportunity in employment—includes problems that should be attended to at once by the executive branches of the city, state, and nation. The schools, of course, should co-ordinate with these immediate programs; but it can be agreed that the main job of the school is to plant and nurture the seeds of understanding. Growth of this sort is necessarily slow.

The task of predisposing the children of different cultural and racial groups for co-operation on a basis of democratic participation is well-nigh impossible when the prejudice of the dominant

---

[1] John Erskine, *The Joy of Creation.*

majority imposes complete separation upon the children and segregates them psychologically as well as physically. Someday we shall understand better the terrific harm this separation does to the personalities of members of both groups. Yet, even in communities where discrimination between classes and groups prevails in its most virulent form, the public school, more than any other institution in our national life, stresses at least some of the elements of national unity. Even where it is surrounded with every kind of barrier against assumptions of social equality, the school still provides, at least in principle, a meeting-ground for diverse cultures, a testing-ground for any effort to overcome social prejudice. The public school, even in the most conservative communities, is usually permitted to offer facilities for the study of America's cultural democracy and, specifically, to spread knowledge about the contributions made to our common life by different culture groups.[2] Although such knowledge cannot be counted upon to revolutionize the community, it can help the community to transform itself by the only method that is really reliable—experimental practice and the development of future leaders.

A School Takes the Lead

It was in the Senior High School at Woodbury, New Jersey, in 1925, that a project was started which became the basis for further study and experimentation and finally the basis for this report.[3] A small group of teachers in that school began to worry

[2] See the excellent pamphlets for school and adult discussion groups on the race question issued by the Commission on Interracial Co-operation, Atlanta, Ga., now the Southern Regional Conference, 710 Standard Building, Atlanta, Ga.

[3] The Woodbury school planned and carried out a three-year cycle of assembly programs. The subject for the first year was that described herein. The second year was given over to the contributions of various subjects to the idea of world interdependence. Thus, language, science and invention, the fine arts, literature, religion, history, mathematics, folk and home arts, and government provided the assembly topics. The third-year subject, based on the premise that "this is a new international world in which we are living, and pioneers are needed to build it as it ought to be," was "Building New Frontiers of Civilization."

about the fact that, because of prejudice, the children of the minority groups in the community seldom took part with those of the dominant white Protestant "old-American" group in extramural school activities. The teachers began to ask the following questions: What is the effect of this situation upon the personalities of the students of both the minority and the dominant groups? What relation does the resulting cast of social attitudes have to American life as a whole? What can we, in the schools, do toward a solution of this problem? They set out to find answers to their questions by integrating some of the activities of their own school around the problem of reducing prejudice and developing more appreciative attitudes among the culture groups in their student body.

Although the questions which those Woodbury teachers asked have not yet been fully answered, the attempt to work out an all-school approach that was made first there, and later in numerous other schools, has been an exhilarating adventure. It has been an adventure in learning to know personally all kinds of interesting people; in bringing them to school and introducing them to the students; in watching the students' faces when their old attitudes toward the Chinese broke down as they listened to Dr. Chih Meng, Director of the China Institute in America, and conversed with him. One boy said, "We never used to go to the Chinese laundry because we were told if you smile or laugh they would stab you with a knife. But now we go to see Lee Poy in the afternoon to talk with him."

The teachers began their pursuit of this adventure by gathering facts about the participation in American life of the peoples who make up our country. They soon found, however, that facts were not enough; *that people generally do not act according to what they know, but according to how they feel about what they know.* Their own students had given them that clue; for, obviously and decidedly, their emotions had been involved in their change of attitude toward the Chinese through personal acquaintance with Dr. Meng. That experience had been pleasant.

Why not, then, plan for such experiences? the teachers asked. Why leave to mere chance the opportunity to meet the director of the China Institute in America, a well-known Negro artist, a member of the British aristocracy prominent in educational movements, a Negro educator from Nigeria now active on an American college faculty, or a Jewish social reformer often mentioned in the newspapers?

The teachers were brave enough to ask such well-known people to give a little of their time as guest speakers on their assembly programs. It was not long before the presence of these and other interesting personalities was making more real to the minds of students the twin ideas that human nature is everywhere basically the same and that many peoples have made valuable contributions to our American life.

Soon after the initiation of the programs a problem arose which had to do with the school's assembly programs. The planning of those programs had always been an extra burden put upon some of the willing teachers. They agreed this time to take their students into their confidence. Together with some of the leaders in the student body, they decided to adopt a unified type of assembly program; and soon students and teachers were working on dramatizations of stories concerning the different ethnic groups in American life. Since almost no plays of this kind were available, they had a good deal of fun writing them as well as acting in them. To find the necessary information became a stimulus for more extended fact-finding by students and teachers alike.

Since there had been little previous experience in work of this kind, the teachers and students who took part in these programs had the special stimulation that comes from conscious experiment in a new and untried field. Each of the schools that in the following years set up such an experiment contributed some new understanding of the task or some new techniques; and each year saw the enterprise stronger in its psychological foundations and more fittingly adapted to a variety of school situations.

In the course of several years these methods acquired greater certainty and precision. They began to be talked about; and from 1931 on, projects of a similar nature were initiated by the author and her associates in other parts of New Jersey, in Philadelphia, the District of Columbia, New York, and California. During one year fifteen junior and senior high schools in the New York metropolitan area were aided in their attempt to integrate their school activities around the study of this major social problem. A teacher and a social worker were released on full time—the teacher working within the schools, helping them plan their assemblies and follow-up activities, the social worker making contacts for the outside talent and guest speakers, and the author giving weekly in-service courses in the principles of intercultural education for teachers and community leaders. The teamwork developed by them and by others drawn into the project was most essential to its success.[4]

METHODS USED TO ACHIEVE THE OBJECTIVES OF INTERCULTURAL EDUCATION

Before discussing in detail the methods and techniques of intercultural education employed in the schools where the projects were conducted, it is desirable to present a brief analysis of the approaches used in the breaking down of old attitudes of intolerance and prejudice and the building up of new responses of mutual understanding and appreciation. Although we recognized that creative teachers have always used these approaches, yet, in the projects, we found it valuable to present them in

---

[4] In 1934 their work was carried further by a WPA research staff of thirty under the direction of the author at Teachers College, Columbia University. Unpublished mimeographed material on the contributions of sixteen groups to American life was developed to help schools throughout the country. From 1934 to 1940 guidance by mail was carried on continuously under the editorial leadership of Rose K. Nelson.

this graphic way along with our application of some of the principles of social psychology.

In general, three approaches were used in the process of changing inter-group attitudes: the *emotional,* or the conscious appeal to the emotions of the students; the *situational,* or the arranging of situations in which the students would have an opportunity to practice new attitudes; and the *intellectual,* or the giving of facts to support the new attitudes.

The means of utilizing these approaches were essentially as follows:

1. *The emotional approach*: guest assembly programs including music, drama, and oratory, in which students had an opportunity to see and hear stimulating representatives of various culture groups. Student-planned follow-up programs.

2. *The situational approach*: smaller face-to-face group meetings and teas, in which representative students had the opportunity to meet and converse with interesting representatives of minority groups.

3. *The intellectual approach*: presentation in the homeroom and the classroom of an array of facts about the cultural heritage of the groups being studied and their contributions to American life.

It is obvious that no hard and fast line can be drawn between these three approaches in so far as the various techniques of intercultural education are concerned. Although the emotional approach, for example, is uppermost in the dramatic assembly program, the situational and intellectual approaches are also present; although the situational approach is predominant in the small-group social situation, the emotional and intellectual approaches are also evident; and although the intellectual approach is used in the classroom, the emotional and situational approaches are by no means absent.

The co-operation of the faculty was obtained before a project was started. In some schools it was found possible to arrange a

series of weekly lecture-discussions for the teachers, to talk over
with them the underlying philosophy and guiding principles of
the work and present to them the pertinent findings of anthropology and social psychology. As the project evolved, opportunities
were provided for the teachers to meet people of the different
ethnic groups to be considered.

The projects were carried on without interfering appreciably
with the regular curricula. Activities of the assembly period,
homeroom period, and extracurricular club periods were co-
ordinated, and supplementary work was carried on in the classrooms. In some schools, depending on local leadership and conditions, the project radiated from the English, in others from the
social studies, department. In still others it was from the outset
woven in an incidental way through the whole curricula.

Although occasionally an administrator was motivated to start
the project by some specific difficulty or conflict experienced in
school or community, the schools were counseled not to take
for the point of departure in this enterprise any group around
which serious negative feelings had developed but rather to
move gradually toward the study of the contributions of such
minority groups. They were encouraged to start with culture
groups represented in the community or groups around which,
for any reason, there had developed sympathetic local or national
interest, as, for example, the Chinese because of the growth of
American appreciation for their effort to preserve their national
life and culture, or the Mexicans or Puerto Ricans in our midst
because of the importance of the good-neighbor policy. Groups
around which serious tensions had developed became the subject
of study later in the year.

The Unified Assembly Program

It was felt that two assembly programs, not more than four
or six weeks apart, were needed in order to produce the cumulative influence necessary for developing attitudes strong enough
to function in everyday life. The first program was followed by

more intensive classroom or homeroom study and at the end of the month by a second, but this time a student-planned, assembly. The last program of the year, given on or near World Brotherhood Day (promoted by the World Federation of Teachers' Associations), May 18,[5] was usually cast in the form of a culminating pageant which gathered together all the groups and focused attention, even more pointedly, on their interrelations in the United States and throughout the world.

The following two patterns of unified assembly programs were used:

1. Dramatizing the cultural contributions to American life of several groups, as those of the Italians in October because of Columbus Day, those of the American Indians and the British in November because of Thanksgiving, those of the Negro in February because of Negro History Week, and those of the Irish in March because of St. Patrick's Day.

2. Dramatizing the contributions of all groups to science, art, and industry.

The "Americans All—Immigrants All" radio series made use of both patterns in its twenty-six programs. If the school represents a virgin field in intercultural education, the probability is that the first method represents the better approach, because, with little or no knowledge of the contributions of our minority groups, the full significance of the second type of program may be missed.

In developing the first type of program, it must be kept in mind that while study is centered for brief periods of time on a given culture group, our purpose is to show the composite nature of the American pattern—to show that nothing is ever done in this country by one group alone. The opening and closing programs of a series should make clear this unification of people

---

[5] This is now generally celebrated as "I Am an American Day." For program suggestions, send for handbook, *Community Recognition of Citizenship* (Washington, D. C.: Immigration and Naturalization Service).

in our democracy. If art or science becomes the focal point of interest, with the intercultural implications secondary, classroom discussions on the culture groups either before or after the assembly programs will add to their value. This second plan of approach to intercultural education, stressing as it does the subject-matter interests of students and teachers, lends itself to the usual school pattern where each department takes its turn in providing an assembly program.

PLANNING TEAS

Because of the policy of making no decision involving culture groups unless some leaders of those groups were present, the key teachers, as a first step in planning a program accorded to Plan I, invited several community representatives of the culture group to be studied to what was called a *planning tea*. In order to make the most effective plans, they discussed outstanding misconceptions held by average Americans, specifically those held in their own community, and considered the best means of counteracting such misconceptions in a positive manner. They then decided on speakers and persons of the chosen group, living in the community or in the nearest city, who were talented in music, the dance, drama, and so on, and who might be asked to take part in an assembly program which was to be used as the motivation for other school activities. A meeting with the committee in charge of assembly programs (it was always urged that students be a part of this committee) was then held, at which available talent was discussed and final decisions were made. Before a person was asked to address a student body, the planning group made sure that he held a view consistent with the aims of the project. These talented leaders, many of whom were nationally known, often gave their services, some of them not once, but several times. Sometimes friends of the school, or culture group leaders, in the community paid the expenses and fees of the guests. Sometimes organizations representing the culture groups to be studied were able to lend to, or purchase for, the school various books, posters, or examples of the folk or fine art representative of the group.

THE GUEST ASSEMBLY PROGRAM

In a few schools the projects started in the classroom and culminated in the assembly.[6] In the majority of schools, however, it was found more workable to start with a guest assembly program. The interest aroused through the guest program permeated the other school activities, some of which culminated in the student-planned follow-up assembly program at the end of the four- or six-week period. At the initial guest assembly, a student chairman presided and introduced the guests. The guests on the platform were of more than one ethnic group, so that the group singled out to be studied would not be isolated in the minds of the students.

Many schools throughout the country have often arranged similar programs presenting a guest speaker along with some folk music and dance, or a short skit. We therefore need present only a brief sampling of our guest assembly programs:

> Mr. Dyson showed slides and talked of the effect of Mexican art on the architecture of the Southwest. This was followed by several folk dances by a group of Mexican dancers from the near-by city.
>
> Mr. Kaloosa, from the Zulu tribe in South Africa, played records showing the development of African music. He sang a Zulu "round," and showed how modern jazz has come directly from African motives and rhythms.
>
> Lady Benn spoke on "England's Contribution to American Life," and then Miss Gadd, director of the English Folk Dance Society, gave a demonstration and quickly taught a group of girls from the audience to dance one of the easier dances.
>
> Dr. Meng spoke on "Chinese Music and Culture," illustrating his talk by recordings. This was followed by a dialogue, "Who Is an American?" by Miss Chin and Miss Lipari.[7]

---

[6] This evolved into a project based on the documentary play method and has been reported on separately. See Spencer Brown, *They See for Themselves* (New York: Harper & Bros., 1944).

[7] See Appendix, pp. 196-8.

A somewhat different but very effective type of guest program was the following:

1. Round-table discussion on the Negro in community life:

Mr. Roland Cheesman (Director of the Settlement House in Madison, New Jersey) is sitting in his office as the curtains part. He is visited by three community leaders to discuss plans for community organization. These are Mrs. Leo Stallings, active in social work in the community, who speaks of the cultural contributions of the Negro and introduces the other two guests: Mr. Arthur Hardy, of the Newark Y.M.C.A., and Mr. Harold Lett, of the New Jersey Urban League.

2. Reading of poetry by outstanding Negro poets, by Miss Gwendolyn Bennett.

3. Piano selections and vocal renditions by Mr. Carl Diton, Negro composer, musician, and vocalist.

THE PLANNED SOCIAL SITUATION

Situations were planned in which the students could meet informally members of the various culture groups and thus have an opportunity to put into practice, or to begin to acquire, new attitudes. In most of the schools it was found possible, after the assembly program, to have a tea at which students met the young Chinese American who had taken part in a play, the Jewish rabbi who had given an introduction to Jewish history, or the Negro artist who had shown his paintings and talked on the history of portraiture. Often, indeed, in such situations, there merged into a momentary feeling of oneness Jew and gentile, French and German, Negro and white, Oriental and Occidental, teachers and students, school and community leaders. These teas were made as informal, colorful, and entertaining as possible, for the aim was to have each student enjoy something more than a mildly interesting afternoon, to have, if possible, what he would call a "swell time."[8] In the larger schools, two delegates usually represented each class or club and afterwards gave

---

[8] These small-group experiences finally developed into the Neighborhood-Home Festival, aimed to meet a similar need for adults. See Rachel Davis DuBois, *Get Together Americans* (New York: Harper & Bros., 1943).

reports of their experiences. The tea also gave an opportunity to invite a few parents and community leaders to join in entertaining the guests.

Sometimes, instead of a tea, the students arranged an informal forum, such as that which took place after a basketball game with Chinese friends from International House in New York City. Once a hundred white students visited the Art Department of Howard University in Washington, D. C., and returned, after having had a pleasant time, exclaiming, "Why, they talk just as we do!" Such expressions showed the tremendous need for such face-to-face contacts, especially in schools made up mainly or wholly of students from one group.

It is important to note the difference between the character of these social affairs and that of the guest assembly programs. While the latter, held in the school auditorium, were necessarily somewhat formal (even though occasionally a guest would break through the formality and talk conversationally or lead the school in song), the social teas had no prepared program. The guests sat while they talked, and there was much conversation between individuals and in small groups. For example, a Chinese folk song just heard would remind a Jewish guest of the similarity in cadence of some traditional Jewish song, and without much persuasion he would give an illustrative example. Or the group would spontaneously hum an accompaniment to some folk song with a vigorous rhythm. Frequently the conversation would take the form of answering specific questions from students about folk customs or some social or economic problem connected with the subject, or the form of a request for recommendation of books to read.

A few comments from the *Field Notebook* in reference to the teas follow:

> Dr. Meng sang a Chinese folk song and taught the group to join in. He also sang a Buddhist Temple hymn. Mr. Huang and Mr. Kao answered innumerable questions.
>
> Miss Haber sang a song in Hebrew and in Yiddish to show the

difference between the two languages. The students asked about the
origin of Yiddish and were interested to know about stories and plays
in that language. The students were fascinated when Dr. Smith, who
had studied for the ministry, wrote a Hebrew phrase on the board
and compared it with the same phrase in other languages. They
learned to say *"Sholom Aleichem"* (peace be with you), the usual
Hebrew salutation. Some of the boys who had learned Palestinian
folk songs and dances at the local Jewish Center taught these to the
other pupils.

It was not always easy to mobilize a school's forces behind
this phase of the project. In one school, for example, the teachers
felt that the planned social situation involved "too much work."
In another school, the assemblies were always in the morning.
Yet, in the schools where an interested teacher or two caught
the value of such gatherings, the school teas were arranged
regularly. The following comment from our *Field Notebook*
reveals the consciousness of their value:

> Would that the M. teachers and pupils could see the flower-decked,
> candle-decorated tables and the dainty sandwiches, cakes, cookies, and
> candies that one teacher of one homeroom of eighth-grade children
> served for all the programs in the E. school. It is not a difficult task.
> It requires only a little time and co-operation.

Often the P.T.A., or an interested church committee, or women
of the culture group involved, volunteered to arrange the tea.
Quite often members of the Board of Education and their wives
attended. In one school, however, Mrs. B., the P.T.A. leader,
could get no mothers to help her because of the feeling among
them in regard to Negroes.

THE HOMEROOM DISCUSSION

In some schools the weekly homeroom period was used to discuss various general phases of the problem which could not be
covered either in the short assembly period or during the classroom activity, with its emphasis on subject matter. In a few
schools the homeroom offered the only opportunity for the presentation of factual material on the culture groups studied. It
was in this homeroom discussion period that the teachers were

more likely to learn whether students were arriving at such generalizations as would tend to function in their everyday lives.

For example, after one program, a non-Jewish girl said during a homeroom discussion, "Too bad that Jews don't have Christmas as we have." To this a Jewish girl smilingly replied, "Most of us do celebrate Christmas in a way. At least we have the holiday. And besides we celebrate Hanukkah, which is very similar." And she went on to describe it. This incident illustrates how new information, even on a relatively minor point, may help to change misconceptions as to the character of another group and the false generalization which so often arises from such misconceptions—that the members of another culture group are, somehow, innately different.

The following chapter contains further analyses of how the homeroom discussion outlines were prepared, and the Appendix contains a verbatim report of a discussion. When it was found that several teachers felt unprepared to lead such discussions, time was arranged in the monthly faculty meetings to discuss the matter. This discussion was led by those who were taking the more intensive weekly course in "Methods of Intercultural Education," for which extension credit was granted by New York University.

Classroom Activities

It was discovered through our survey made (1930) of library reference books and textbooks in ten senior high schools that the school libraries lacked reliable information. Sometimes only the "problems" of a minority group were presented in such books, and not those facts about the group that would arouse curiosity, a desire to know more about it, and a predisposition to meet its members on terms of equality. And so a start was made in collecting data on several different culture groups. These data, in mimeographed form, were given to the teachers with the suggestion that they be used by them as resource material for classroom study in whatever way they saw fit.

For instance, if a class was studying the American Revolution, it was found possible, without using much extra time, for the teacher to call the attention of the students to the fact that the man who did most to finance the war, giving his whole fortune and consequently dying a poor man, was Haym Salomon, a Polish Jew; that, of the important military leaders, von Steuben was German, Pulaski and Kosciusko were Polish, Axel von Fersen was Swedish, and Lafayette was French. In the science, music, and art classes, it was found that the possibilities of calling attention to the contributions that have been made by representatives of the different ethnic groups were almost endless. Care was taken to point out, whenever possible, individuals of various groups who had contributed toward a chain of inventions eventually producing some product or instrument of manifest social utility.[9] The use of the material, of course, depended upon the willingness and alertness of the individual teacher. The biology teacher who, in answer to questions as to his use of such materials, answered, "We only study structure," could hardly be expected to weave into his work the fact that the first successful operation on the human heart was performed by a Negro physician. *Overspecialization in subject matter causes the loss of many good opportunities for educational influences on social attitudes and character.* On the whole, however, it was found that teachers were only too glad to receive factual materials for which they had often felt a need but which they had found neither the time nor the opportunity to collect. Many used the provided classroom materials as sources for developing their classroom units. The subjects of some of those units follow; obviously we cannot list them all. Since our materials, consisting of about a hundred units on sixteen different culture groups, are still in mimeographed form, and therefore not available for wide distribution, we are listing also some available source books.

---

[9] The scripts of the "Americans All—Immigrants All" radio series are full of such facts. These may be secured from the U. S. Office of Education, Washington, D. C.

A. SOCIAL STUDIES

1. The English Inheritance in Our Principles of Freedom.
2. Our Struggle for Religious Freedom.
3. The Negro as a Challenge to Democracy.
4. The Scandinavians Help Extend Democracy through Co-operatives.
5. The Orientals in American Life.
6. All Groups in Industrial Life.

SOURCES

"Americans All—Immigrants All" Radio Scripts, U. S. Office of Education, Nos. 2, 11, 16, 20.

Brown and Roucek, *One American.*

Clinchy, Everett, *All in the Name of God.*

DuBois, W. E. B., *Black Reconstruction.*

B. MUSIC APPRECIATION

1. Irish Music in America.
2. Musicians of Various Backgrounds in American Life.
3. Italian Opera and Folk Music in American Life.
4. The Negro Contribution to Our Folk Music.

SOURCES

Christy, Arthur E. (ed.), *The Asian Legacy and American Life,* chapters on "The Orient and Western Music."

Eaton, Allen, *Immigrant Gifts to American Life.*

Kaufman and Hansl, *Artists in Music Today.*

C. SPORTS

1. Games from the British Isles.
2. The Negro in Athletics.
3. Internationalism and Sports.

SOURCES

> Collins, Frank D., *Popular Sports*.
>
> Johnson, J. W., *Black Manhattan*.
>
> Kieran, John, *The Story of the Olympic Games*.
>
> Krout, John Allen, *Annals of American Sport*.

D. SCIENCE

1. The Negro Scientist.
2. The Italian Influence in Agriculture and Food Customs.
3. Scientific Thinking about Peoples.

SOURCES

> "Americans All—Immigrants All" Radio Scripts, Nos. 17, 21.
>
> Holt, Rackham, *George Washington Carver*.
>
> Kaempffert, Waldemar, *A Popular History of American Invention*.
>
> Powdermaker, Hortense, *Probing Our Prejudices*.

E. HOME ARTS CLASSES

1. The Arts and Crafts of the Pennsylvania Germans.
2. Mexican Influence on American Food Customs.
3. Jewish Home Festivals around the Calendar.
4. Scandinavian Home Customs in American Life.

SOURCES

> Berolsheimer, Ruth, *The United States Regional Cook Book*.
>
> Eberlein and McClure, *The Practical Book of Early American Arts and Crafts*.
>
> Schauss, H., *Jewish Festivals*.
>
> Weygandt, Cornelius, *The Red Hills*.

F. ART CLASSES

1. British Influence on American Painting.

2. Influence of African on Modern Art.

3. Negro Artists in American Life.

SOURCES

"Americans All—Immigrants All" Radio Scripts, No. 22.

LaFollette, Suzanne, *Art in America.*

G. ENGLISH CLASSES

1. The "Natural" Magic of Celtic Literature and Our American Writers of Irish Background.

2. Our Negro Newspapers.

3. A Comparison of Chinese Proverbs and the Sayings of "Poor Richard."

4. Comparison of Immigrant with Second-Generation Biographies and Novels.

5. Regional and National Dialect Poems.

SOURCES

Blankenship, Russell, *American Literature as an Expression of the National Mind.*

Bodmer, F., *The Loom of Language.*

Brown, Sterling, *The Negro Caravan.*

Christy, Arthur E. (ed.), *The Asian Legacy and American Life.*

DuBois, W. E. B., *The Souls of Black Folk.*

Lewisohn, Ludwig, *The Island Within.*

Ottley, Roi, *New World A-Coming.*

Rölvaag, Ole Edvart, *Giants in the Earth.*

Weirick, Bruce, *From Whitman to Sandburg in American Poetry.*

CLASSROOM VISITORS

Often the assembly guest spent all or part of the school day visiting classes, talking with the students and conferring with the teachers. We select the following excerpts from the *Field Notebook:*

Mr. Dipeolu (from Nigeria, West Africa, at the time a student at Teachers College, Columbia University), spoke to five English classes. He spoke on education in Africa, the influence of Christian missionaries, and the evolution of African languages and literature (there are about 160 dialects). He answered many questions on music, art, etc.

Miss Miriam R. Ephraim spoke to five classes on "Nathan the Wise," telling the story of the three rings, the treatment of the Jews in England in the seventeenth century, Scott's sympathy and friendliness to the Jews, his choice of Isaac and Rebecca as characters in *Ivanhoe,* and his supposed use of Rebecca Gratz, Philadelphia girl, as the model for Rebecca.

Aaron Douglas, American Negro artist, spent several periods in the art classes, talking on "The History of Portraiture." His own paintings were on exhibit in the school.

Dr. Chih Meng, Director of the China Institute of America, spent several hours in the school's history classes. The degree of interest was such that a voluntary group of three hundred students remained after school for over an hour.

In a "special" class of mainly Italian-background pupils from low-economic homes, there had been several "problem" children. Arrangements were made to have Aurora Unti, the Italian-born secretary of the Philadelphia International Institute, spend several hours with the pupils, speaking with them in Italian. She talked with them in such a way that they were motivated to start an activity (which their regular teachers then followed) on "A Cultural Treasure Hunt," which led them not only into the richness of their own backgrounds, but also into that of our American cultural diversity and their part in it.

Related Activities

GUESTS PARTICIPATE IN SPORTS

A basketball game was organized between a Chinese team composed of Columbia University undergraduate students and a Tenafly high-school team. Other Chinese friends were also invited. At the suggestion of one of the Tenafly students, the school students were given numbered slips of paper; all even numbers cheered for Tenafly, all odd numbers for the Chinese team. The Chinese rooters were led by cheer leaders dressed in white and using megaphones decorated with a red "20" and a Chinese dragon.

After the game, tea was served. The faculty and wives of members of the local Board of Education were present. The girls sang popular songs, and the boys sang their Alma Mater song. One girl played the piano and another did a tap dance, after which there was general dancing in which the guests joined.

School Exhibits and Trips to Exhibits

Exhibits of Scandinavian art, industries, books, costumes, utensils, etc., were displayed in a showcase in the corridor for the months of November and December.

The entire art department went to the African exhibit at the Museum of Modern Art, New York City. Each student reproduced or sketched at least one object which appealed to him. This formed an exhibit in the art room. A home treasure exhibit and later a hobby exhibit in connection with the Parent-Teachers' Association were held.

Interviews on the Part of Students with Parents and Community Leaders

In one school system the social studies classes of the ninth grade interviewed parents and community leaders of old-stock and immigrant backgrounds and wrote several playlets on "What America Means to Me," based on the real-life histories which they had gathered. In another school an extracurricular group wrote a documentary play on the life of the Negroes of that community.

Community Surveys by Students

In one school the following phases of the community life were reported upon in the light of the participation of each of the community's racial and cultural groups: economic life, health, education, recreation, civil rights, residential facilities, musical, artistic, and literary activities. The discussions which followed the collection of data were organized according to the following topics: (1) defining racial justice; (2) exploring the situation with relation to actual community conditions in each of the above categories; (3) searching for possible procedures which might change the situation; (4) planning what should be done.

EXCURSIONS AND VISITS

Some teachers made arrangements for classes to spend a day and in some cases two days being introduced to culture group leaders in personally conducted tours of fellowship in a neighboring city.

Student Follow-up Assembly Program

After about a month's study of a culture group the students gave their own assembly program, listing their objectives and building accordingly. Indeed, it was felt that a cycle was not complete until the students themselves had an opportunity to act in, or witness, a program or dramatic sketch of their own making which showed some phase of the culture of the particular group being studied. *It was found that these vicarious experiences tended to modify attitudes.* Especially was this true for those who took part in the dramatic presentations. The students who played the roles of Italian immigrants, telling why they came to America, actually lived for a brief while the lives of those immigrants. The gentiles who acted with their Jewish fellow students in a play depicting Jewish experiences would hardly forget their experiences during the time when they were a part of the ways of thinking, feeling, and acting of that culture group. White students who with Negroes planned and performed in a program on the cultural contributions of the Negro were more sensitive to what members of this group face in American life. A few examples of student programs follow:

Specific Programs

ENGLISH

1. Illustrated Lecture: "English Gardens in America."
   Slide lantern operator—Richard Bell.

Short Talks: American Democracy and the English
   Struggle for Freedom—
   Donald Branch,
   Ross Clinchy,
   Garalyn Disbrow,
   Marjorie Allison.
2. Three English Folk Dances:
   a. Gathering Peascods—Freshman Girls.
   b. Selanger's Round—Eighth-Grade Girls.
   c. Sweet Kate—Seventh-Grade Girls.

ITALIAN

1. Original Sketch: "Interview with Leonardo da Vinci," by
   Alvin Childress.
   Leonardo—Thomas de Palma.
   Boy Reporter—Harry Wann.
2. Quartette: "O Sole Mio" and other songs—
   Harry Stilwell,
   Richard Coogan,
   Mary Shean,
   Winifred Ryan.
3. Senior Chorus: "Italia" and "Aida."
4. Dance: "Tarantella"—Freshman Girls.
5. Cornet Trio: "Santa Lucia"—
   Betty Shay,
   Thomas Overman,
   Howard Griswold.
6. Talk on Della Robbia—Nan Parsons.
   Display of Della Robbia Plaques.

NEGRO

1. "Spring Song"—Chorus of Negro and White Children.
2. Original Sketch: "Interview of Frederick Douglass with
   Abraham Lincoln," by Alvin Childress.

Frederick Douglass—Earl Morgan.
Abraham Lincoln—James Hanlon.
Senator—Stanley Muchmore.
Secretary—Fred Dotson.

3. Pageant: "Two Races," by Inez M. Burke.[10]
Sam, a Negro boy—Ralph Ford.
Gilbert, a white boy—William Mowen.
Spirit of Progress—Leona James.
Spirit of Adventure—Janice Eckels.
Spirit of Invention—Harriet Michnor.
Spirit of Music—Delight Fletcher.
Spirit of Poetry—Peggy Smith.
Spirit of Art—Jessie Joyce.
Spirit of Science—Jean Hancock.

4. Spirituals: Bottle Hill Quartet—
Earl Williams,
Theodore Morgan,
Stephen Williamson,
Charles Little.

5. Description of Spirituals, Their History and Meaning—
Agnes Branch.

6. Spirituals: Colored Chorus led by Lester Suitt:
"Steal Away."
"Climbing Jacob's Ladder."

7. Recitation from *God's Trombones*—Agnes Branch.

General Programs

To offset the possibility that a feeling of separateness might develop, general programs were used after a series of programs on specific groups. The pattern usually followed by the students was that of presenting an introductory and a final program for

[10] From Willis Richardson, *Plays and Pageants from the Life of the Negro* (Washington, D. C.: Associated Press Publishers, 1930).

the year's series which would stress the interdependence of mankind and portray the groups working together in American life. These programs were often of the pageant type. Since the scripts of the "Americans All—Immigrants All" radio programs[11] became available, numerous schools have been using them as models for mock radio programs.

Among the general programs reported in the *Field Notebook* was the following student-planned skit, "The Spirit of the Scientific Mind":

> The Spirit of the Scientific Mind looks through a telescope and the Spirit of Intolerance looks into a mirror. Together they discuss what constitutes superiority among races—such qualities as moral courage and perseverance, spiritual vision and high aims, physical adaptation, mental keenness and thirst for knowledge.
>
> The Spirit of the Scientific Mind says he can find those qualities in all races, creeds, and classes.
>
> The Spirit of Intolerance says he can find them only in his own group.
>
> The Spirit of the Scientific Mind finally discovers that the Spirit of Intolerance is looking at a mirror, so he invites him to look through the telescope which brings closer the people of other groups, so that their good qualities become distinctly visible. (Short statements about various groups followed.)

The School and the Community

It has been pointed out that as many sociological data about the school and community as possible were obtained before any programs were arranged; that culture group leaders helped to arrange programs; and that interested people from the communities were always present at assembly programs and other events when outside guests were invited. It was soon found that these planned situations were providing learning experiences for community leaders as well as for high-school students. The following examples are pertinent:

> In one town the members of the Board of Education had asked to be invited to all programs. It was interesting to note the look of surprise on the face of one of the several members who came regularly

---

[11] See Appendix for a sample.

when, at a tea, in answer to a question of his, he learned from Dr. Meng that Orientals could not become American citizens.

After Louis Sharp, Negro actor from a current Broadway play, had visited the school several times to teach spirituals to both white and Negro students, eight white parents told him that they appreciated the opportunity that was being given their children. One white parent, however, objected.

At a number of schools the Parent-Teachers' Associations and the Women's Clubs arranged their programs to gear into what was being done in the schools, so that outside guests might fill both appointments on one trip. Students who had put on a successful program were sometimes asked to repeat it for the evening meeting of the P.T.A. One P.T.A. secured funds for the school programs by arranging a series of nationality suppers. High-school students helped to arrange the entertainment and to wait on the tables.

It was not, however, all smooth sailing. Our *Field Notebook* reveals occasional difficulties:

> When February rolled around and Lincoln's Birthday suggested a program on the Negro, the P.T.A. committee, without consulting those conducting the project, planned a chicken dinner—to be cooked by the Negro mothers and the domestic science classes—in the sewing room, which was to be transformed into a "Cabin in the Cotton," with Negroes, dressed in "mammy" costumes and overalls, singing spirituals on the cabin porch.
>
> Plans were well on their way when the project leaders discovered that the Negro parents were not co-operating; that they had forbidden their children to serve the dinner because they had been asked to wear "bandanas and large white aprons."
>
> Visiting the sewing room with the principal, Mrs. E. pointed out the error to her and suggested that she persuade the P.T.A. committee to paint the cabin white instead of brown, cover it with artificial wisteria, and make a hollyhock garden with a white picket fence.
>
> By chance, the P.T.A. committee arrived at that time. When the mistake was pointed out to the chairman, Mrs. H., she exclaimed, "Why, I love the Negroes! I wouldn't hurt them for anything! I was brought up in the South. We had three colored mammies in the house. Besides, when we asked the Negro mothers to co-operate, they said they would. But they haven't helped at all. The Italian parents were so much better. We just don't seem to be getting anywhere with these darkies!"

"Of course, they hated to say 'No,' " Mrs. E. said. "I'm sure they would have co-operated if instead of making up your own minds first and then asking them you had made all the plans together."

In the discussion that followed, Mrs. E. reminded the women of a few of the accomplishments of American Negroes in the arts and sciences. To save the situation, she promised to visit the homes of two or three leading Negro women, explain the error, describe the proposed changes and ask them to work out a short pageant, "The Spirit of Negro Progress," for the evening's entertainment. Co-operation of the Negro mothers was then assured, and the white and Negro high-school girls who served dinner came in their ordinary dresses protected only by small aprons. The affair was held in the sewing room according to plan, but it was now a cottage covered with wisteria, surrounded by hollyhocks, "with one field of cotton left for Mrs. H."

The experience, frankly faced in a spirit of goodwill, seemed a valuable one for all concerned. When the guest assembly participants came a week later, both white and Negro mothers co-operated in assisting the Home Economics department to arrange the school tea. Later the Superintendent of Schools wrote:

"We were more than pleased with the results from this program which you supervised in our school. The little flurry over the colored question has subsided, and I think the net results have been good."

On the whole, however, the relations between school and community leaders were more harmonious. An important result of the planned social situations was that culture group leaders themselves became more realistic in their understanding of conditions that faced them, as they discussed at the planning teas actual misconceptions of their groups. Sometimes factions within the groups co-operated with one another as they had not done before. Chinese foreign students from the university and second-generation Chinese became better acquainted with one another. Polish or Italian first-generation persons of "good family" found it easier to identify themselves with the "common men" of their group, as both attempted to show the contributions of their nationality to American life. At these planning teas, a beginning was made of the selection, in terms of needs in American life, of those values or culture patterns in each group which, in the students' own appraisals, should be held on to and shared. Thus did students and teachers make a small start toward building a cathedral out of our American rock pile.

4

DISCUSSION PERIODS AS AN AID TO INTERCULTURAL EDUCATION

> There are birds of many colors—red, blue, green, yellow—
> yet all one bird. There are horses of many colors—brown, black,
> yellow, white—yet all one horse. So cattle, so all living things—
> animals, flowers, trees. So men; in this land where once were
> only Indians are now men of every color—white, black,
> yellow, red—yet all one people.[1]

As THE PROJECTS in intercultural education developed, the
question most often asked by teachers was: "Even though
we arrange inter-group experiences for the student and supply
him with information about the participation of various culture
groups in American life, how can we be sure that he will be led,
first to the acquisition of new attitudes, and then to putting the
new attitudes into practice?"

It was acknowledged by those conducting the projects that
only the impossible task of objectively checking all overt actions
in school, playground, and home would assure that students had
acquired not only new attitudes but also new behavior patterns
to conform with the new attitudes. However, many of the teachers reported on incidents which showed that the projects were
having a positive effect on students. The Neumann Attitude In-
dicator was given to 4,000 students and standardized by Kulp
and Davidson from our data. Later we made adaptations of the
Bogardus Social Distance Scale to suit our needs.[2] Since the

---

[1] Natalie Curtis, *The Indians' Book* (New York: Harper & Bros., 1933),
quoting a chief of the Sioux Indians.
[2] For a good discussion of attitude testing, see S. Stansfeld Sargent,
The Basic Teachings of the Great Psychologists (New York: The New
Home Library, 1944); "Education for Racial Understanding," *Journal
of Negro Education,* Summer, 1944.

scores always showed a statistically significant change toward more tolerance, it seemed a waste of effort to test later projects.

Although the teachers, then, could arrive at no conclusive answer to their question, they came to feel, as the work progressed, that in order to be most certain of results it was important to help students to arrive at generalizations that would function in real-life situations wherever they might occur. The teachers decided that this help might be best given through the intelligent and objective guidance that would follow the assembly programs and other planned social situations. After having seen the Mexicans dance, after having met the visitors at tea, students were found to be eager, and now perhaps for the first time able, to take part in a discussion about people of Mexican background and our relationship with them.

The teachers found that Professor Hugh Hartshorne had verified this technique of following experiences with objective analysis when he wrote that the attitude of goodwill should not be discussed until after a sufficient number of experiences have occurred, for only then is it possible to separate this aspect of the total experience from other aspects of it, as, for instance, color is separated from weight. Once it is separated and named, it can be discussed, and the relative value of situations where it is present and where it is absent can be consciously appraised and debated.[3] In the homeroom discussions, then, questions such as these arose: What happens when the attitude of goodwill is present? When it is absent? What arouses the attitude? What kills it? Which consequences are to be preferred?[4]

It was discovered at this point that there was an especial need for guidance which would prevent the student from resuming his old attitude of indifference or even antagonism. Although much of this guidance took place in the homeroom

---

[3] Hugh Hartshorne, *Character in Human Relations* (New York: Charles Scribner's Sons, 1932), p. 306.

[4] See Appendix for a report of a homeroom discussion.

and classroom periods, the teachers were asked to remember that the informal discussions that might arise at any moment and at any place were also very important; that such guidance can take place whenever and wherever a real teacher meets a willing pupil, be it on the proverbial log, in a classroom, or on the athletic field.

If this guidance of the students toward functional generalizations was to take place to any adequate extent in our large public schools, however, it was found that special provision had to be made for it. This provision, it was decided by the teachers, could best be made in the homeroom and classroom discussion periods. Aside from presentation of facts about various culture groups, some schools used materials from the Institute for Propaganda Analysis to show methods used by enemy forces to inculcate race conflicts. It was possible under especially well prepared teachers to discuss prejudices held by members of the class and others: how these prejudices were acquired, and how people can change their own attitudes, if they will.[5] When this openness of mind was coupled with the goal for building together a richer American culture, it was found that the student, through his newly acquired respect for representatives of other ethnic groups, would without manipulation take advantage of opportunities to meet more of them, to learn more from them, to share more with them his own thoughts, his own sense of values.

Teachers' Generalizations

The first step toward providing for the arrival of students at functional generalizations was taken when teachers themselves decided to hold in mind certain generalizations which most of them could agree upon. This step seemed necessary because it tended to clarify the teachers' thinking and to make them more likely to guide the students, in both their formal and informal discussions, to similar conclusions. The teachers were aided by

---

[5] For list of books on this subject see Appendix, pp. 255-6.

those guiding the experiments in intercultural education to form, from various sources, a list of generalizations which were agreed upon and then mimeographed and distributed. The following short list of generalizations is presented as illustrative, but it is suggested that teachers be encouraged to make their own lists from their readings.

> So God created man in his own image, in the image of God created he him; male and female created he them.—Gen. 1:27.
>
> Akin by nature, men are made strangers by their surroundings.— Confucius.
>
> Citizens, peoples and all men, thou, recalling their common origin, shall not only unite among themselves, but shall make them brothers. —Pope Benedict XV, "Encyclical Letter," May 23, 1920.
>
> America is a land of but one people gathered from many countries. All have come bearing gifts.—Allen Eaton, *Immigrant Gifts to American Life*, p. 28.
>
> The only sound basis for society lies in getting each individual to recognize the worth of other persons and their philosophies of life. —Harold Rugg, *Culture and Education in America*, p. 235.
>
> Race prejudice is not instinctive but the result of social experience. —Bruno Lasker, *Race Attitudes in Children*, p. 37.
>
> No man has ever proved that a human being through descent from a certain group of people must of necessity have certain mental characteristics.—Franz Boas, *Aryans and Non-Aryans*, p. 11.

Students' Generalizations

The teachers were asked to try to discover when and how the students arrived at such generalizations of their own, by listening in on informal discussions organized as part of the homeroom and classroom procedure in connection with the project, and on conversations between two or more students. In this way it was possible for the teachers to record, as evidences of development, new and interesting ways in which the students expressed their new-found conclusions. A few of the generalizations[6] arrived at by some of the students follow:

> I thought the program about the Italian contribution was the most important because up to that time I had no idea Italians and other

---

[6] See Appendix for a longer list of student generalizations.

peoples had helped America. I had thought it was Americans who helped and protected the dumb foreigners, as I called them.

I have learned that Scotch people are not always stingy; Italians are not all dirty; Polish are not all sullen; Jews are not all bankers; Germans are not all goose-steppers; Mexicans are not bandits and do not play guitars all day; Latin Americans are not half-naked in a very hot country; Chinese are very prosperous sometimes and are not all laundrymen or bandits; and Negroes—well, I've always felt as though they were like me, being around them all my life.

I was obliged to go to Hebrew school but did not want to learn Hebrew. When I heard that girl singing in Hebrew, I was more interested in learning the language.

I believe I have learned to realize that you can't judge a country by one person in it.

More Harmonious Living Together

Reports made by the heads of departments in the schools proved that a more harmonious living together and sharing of experiences among students of different culture groups actually had resulted from the arranged inter-group situations when they were followed by discussions of this kind. After the talks given by outstanding Negroes, for example, a marked increase of respect on the part of other students toward their Negro classmates was observed. The increased confidence of the latter in themselves led to their greater participation in discussion, and this, again, aided the process of identification and shared experience. Similar positive results, it was found, revealed themselves among other groups. Shy as well as aggressive children of Italian background, who previously had denied that their parents were born abroad, also acquired more confidence when they saw the culture values of those parents given public recognition by their teachers and fellow students. One boy who had vigorously denied that he could speak Italian surprised his fellow students by conversing in that language with Italian guests at a tea. A Polish student who had changed his name asked for further factual material and titles of books about Poles in American life. Minority-group students, who before had been ignored, were chosen for class officers, or their classwork became of higher caliber because they were more relaxed about themselves. In two high schools the senior students formed cosmopolitan clubs.

After a number of such instances had occurred, the alert but tactful teachers were able to help even those students who had been least eager to take part in classroom discussion to analyze why shared experiences based on goodwill are of more value than experiences gained in the isolation of prejudice or of silent resentment. Such a teacher could also help the group to understand how to deal with prejudice situations, and even perhaps assist students of the minority group to work out their own techniques when confronted with such situations. The following example presents one student's experience and shows how he discussed it with his teacher and his fellow students in a homeroom period:

> A Negro boy who trusted his teacher told his fellow students in the homeroom how, on a previous Sunday, he had been almost evicted from a museum by a guard who took it upon himself to discriminate. He had previously worked out a technique of his own for use in meeting such situations, which was to talk so loudly, though calmly and intelligently, to anyone blocking his entrance that near-by white people would come to his assistance. He used the technique on this occasion, and through its use gained entrance to the museum. His method of solving his problem was discussed by him and his schoolmates in a way which, according to the teacher, was decidedly helpful.

Special Discussion Outlines

Special discussion outlines were prepared to lead students to objective analyses of their social situations involving intergroup relations. The purpose of these outlines was, more especially, to relate particular situations or experiences to a larger view of the social and psychological factors at work. In most schools, a small committee of teachers, appointed for the purpose, combined into one outline enough suggestions to fit various expected needs of the students and to allow each teacher to choose from it those questions and references to information that would best fit the requirements of her class.

Some outlines started with subjects in which the students

were known to be interested. Adventure stories, such as that of Mat Henson, the Negro who accompanied Peary to the North Pole; accounts of the achievements of athletic stars representative of various groups; short biographies, such as that of Lu Gim Gong, the Chinese-American "Luther Burbank"—were used to advantage. Other outlines started with a few real-life situations gathered from or at least checked with the culture group advisors. These real-life stories reflected what members of the particular group were at that time facing in social or economic discrimination because of color or creed.

The discussions were planned as far as possible according to the demands of creative discussion,[7] because this embodies the principles and methods of sharing individual experiences. It was found helpful for the teacher to make clear the difference between discussion and argument: that the former is an honest attempt to marshal the facts from all angles, but that argument is usually based on an attempt to put over only one's own point of view. While each teacher was urged to build her own discussion outlines, it was found that the average teacher, because of her lack of familiarity with the different ethnic groups, needed more help in this than in most other phases of the work.

For those pupils who were unable to think abstractly, who could not readily see the issues involved, more concrete activities were suggested in the outlines. Examples of interdependence, not only within our country but among all countries, were examined, to show the many ways in which almost all the peoples of the world depend on one another for some of their resources in everyday life. The discussions were used also to offset stereotypes of race and nationality diffused by popular entertainment films, or to augment the influence of films of the better sort.[8]

Teachers were asked to be alert to the calling of names.

---

[7] See Bibliography for list of books on this method.
[8] See "Educational Programs for the Improvement of Race Relations: Motion Pictures, Radio, the Press, and Libraries," *Journal of Negro Education*, Summer, 1944.

They took advantage of situations, all too common in school, in which students indulged in the use of such terms as "wop," "greaser," "kike," "Jap," "squarehead," and the like. It was made clear to students that whether or not the use of such a name is wrong depends upon whether it is intended to hurt the feelings of the person against whom it is used. On the other hand, there was agreement with the idea of Pearl Buck that "we must teach the foreign-born to laugh when silly children cry, 'You wops— you heinies—you sheenies; we're Americans!' " and with her conclusion, "The truth is, Americans are all something else, too, and are going to be for a long, long time, and the truest American knows it."[9] A unit on regional and ethnic-group dialect poems made it possible to take an objective view of this subject. It was made clear to the teachers, therefore, that only by knowing something about the various groups can one know what names are anathema to them.

Thus, when the subject was brought into the open for discussion, it was relatively easy for the informed teacher to help the students to come to the conclusion that the use of opprobrious names, aside from being unkind and impolite, is a recourse of the ignorant and thoughtless or of the cowardly and the stupid.

Students Influence One Another

Since students are especially open to suggestion from those of their own age level, another method of assisting them to arrive at functional generalizations was that of encouraging them to teach one another. In one of the white high schools of Washington, D. C., a few student leaders were chosen each month to give four-minute talks, in each of the forty homerooms, on phases of the contributions of the various culture groups to American life. It gave one a pleasant shock to hear a fourteen-year-old white boy say, in his Southern drawl, "Believe it or not, but

---

[9] Pearl Buck, "On Discovering America," *Survey Graphic,* June, 1937, pp. 313-5, 353, 355.

the first successful operation on the human heart was performed by a Negro physician, Dr. Daniel Williams of Chicago," and to hear him end his speech with a plea for fair play and justice for the Negro.

When asked what he felt after having met the Negro guests at school assemblies devoted to the intercultural program and the fine representatives of the Negro group who had taken him and his schoolmates through the Howard University Art Department, and after having learned some facts about the contribution of the Negro to American life, this boy answered: "At one time I thought that Negroes were all low-down and no-count and mean. Now I know that some of them are fine and good." The sincerity of this answer made one feel that he, like a good many others, would at least try to carry the new learning outside the school and act upon it.

The Need for Reconstructing School Practices

It cannot be too strongly emphasized that generalizations cannot function except in real-life situations. There are some schoolroom situations, however, which prevent that functioning. Kurt Lewin's comparison of what happened in democratically and in autocratically set up classroom situations is of special importance here. He reports about thirty times as much hostility expressed among pupils in the autocratic groups as among those in the democratic groups. The democratic groups showed 47 per cent more feeling of "we-ness" and the autocratic groups 27 per cent more feeling of "I-ness." This aggressiveness was not directed openly against the autocrat—the teacher—toward whom the children generally were rather submissive, but tended to find an outlet in the easy and less dangerous way of attacking a scapegoat—one of their own members.[10]

---

[10] Kurt Lewin, "Field Theory and Experiment in Social Psychology: Concepts and Methods," *American Journal of Sociology*, May, 1939; and (with others) "Patterns of Aggressive Behavior in Experimentally Created Social Climates," *Journal of Social Psychology*, May, 1939. See also *Social Frontier*, July, 1939.

It can easily be seen that intercultural education can be really effective only in the classroom which has a democratic atmosphere and that to pay attention merely to curriculum revision is to put the cart before the horse. Then too, there must be a rethinking of what the dual system of education in several states, with its consequent lack of shared experience, means. Private schools, for the most part, show this same lack, as also do schools in the North in homogeneous neighborhoods.

In such schools special attempts should be made to arrange for interschool visitations in large and small groups. Even in the deep South, no revolutionary principle is involved if for certain purposes of learning—say, for example, that of learning about concrete problems in community planning—members of the two races come together to share what they know at first hand.[11] But there need be no uniformity. The important point is that certain educational practices—such as exchanges of visits between schools, joint discussions, joint participation in symbolical exercises—have sufficiently proved themselves to justify their more general adoption; and that here and there new advances are possible on the experimental level.

Some educators contend that learning brought about by such contacts cannot, any more than book learning, insure permanent results, until economic discrimination based on false theories of race is wiped out. There can be no denial of the importance of economic justice; but before people can hope so to work together as to solve their common problems of an economic nature, there must be developed a state of mutual understanding and trust. The point to be remembered here is that this mutual confidence must extend to peoples of all cultures, races, religions, and classes, and this aim has never seriously been a part of the curriculum of American schools.

---

[11] For further suggestions of what can be done in Southern communities, see Lillian Smith, *Humans in Bondage* (New York: Council for Social Action of the Congregational Christian Churches, 1944).

The aim of intercultural education is to draw our attention to what should always have been done in general education in a democracy: to lead each generation to understand that all cultural groups in this country have made valuable contributions to its growth; to show that we can create a democratic atmosphere in our social groups in school and out; and finally, to make it clear that the "quality of a future civilization in our country will be superior or inferior in just the proportion that all peoples and races foregathered as its citizens give to each other the best of their traditions, customs, and folkways."[12]

The educational procedures which have been outlined in this and the preceding chapter were designed to aid in making democracy in American life more real. They do not assume that we already have full democracy and need only to implement it, nor do they assume that the concern for democracy has yet to be created from the start. They function, rather, in a situation not uncommon in dynamic societies: the concern for a given objective is widespread; the ideals have been variously yet clearly enunciated; but the realization of the ideals is lagging far behind. If we do not quickly bridge this gap, even calm sociologists predict that "anything can happen." The responsibility rests heavily upon our classroom teachers but even more heavily upon the administrators and community leaders who determine the economic security and hence the professional proficiency of the classroom teacher.

---

[12] Malcolm Dana (ed.), "A New Americanism," *The Country Life Bulletin,* Congregational Church, V (December, 1933), 5.

5

USING SOME PRINCIPLES OF SOCIAL PSYCHOLOGY TO CHANGE ATTITUDES

> Where all men's reasoning is weak
> To take the answer that is sent,
> What man shall have the right to speak
> Who has not dared experiment?[1]

Now that the peoples of the world have been brought even closer together, it is imperative that concerned leaders experiment with methods of producing more friendly attitudes. Whether or not a school follows the particular plan of the projects described herein, an analysis of the principles of social psychology used in our experiments should be of value.

The initial step toward any objective is taken when that objective is clearly stated. But clarity is not enough; the problem must be stated dramatically. Once stated in such a way as to stir the imagination, energy is released that makes it possible for action to be taken, which in itself tends to clarify the objective.

When our projects were started in 1925, although school and community situations even then were producing hurt personalities, the need for intercultural education was not generally recognized; in fact, the term had not yet been coined. Hence our first step was to try to stir the imagination of the teachers by a vivid presentation of the problem and of the goal and, through the teachers, the imagination of the students.

In each school, preliminary conferences were held with the principals and teachers. Here we attempted to show that, although intercultural education is needed in all schools, the make-

---

[1] Richard Lattimore, *Symbol's Dyad.*

87

up of the school's population would determine what approach should be made. In the culturally homogeneous schools, the first reaction often was, "We have no problem,"—evidence that the teachers were conscious of a problem only when they saw overt conflicts due to racial or religious prejudices. In a homogeneous school population, however, there is all the more need to create in the students a sense of interdependence between the various social classes and culture groups in the United States. And apart from the more general lessons to be drawn from American history and from the literature of American idealism, the most effective first step toward that recognition is to acquaint students with the actual character of the various ethnic and culture groups and with their contributions to American life. Without guidance, they will often be unable to draw the correct conclusions from social facts—in their own community, for example —with which they might be supposed to be familiar; but vast numbers of young Americans have never become even distantly acquainted with the most elementary facts about important population groups untouched by their own personal lives.

In most of the schools, the following educational objectives were stated:

1. More appreciative *attitudes* toward the specific groups to be taken up.
2. The *skill* of getting along more harmoniously with members of those specific groups.
3. More *facts* about the cultural contributions of those groups.
4. An increased *sensitivity* to the problems of everyday relations which members of minority groups have to face and a consciousness of what all this means in terms of democracy.
5. An increased *ability* to interpret data found in newspapers, magazines, cinema, etc., in relation to the problem.
6. A richer American culture.

Such statements, though good for lesson plans and reports, are still not alive enough to stir the imagination either of the teacher or, through her, of the pupil. We attempted, therefore, to show the teachers that intercultural contacts and the variety of experiences and friendships which may develop are so enriching for one's own life that one does not count the cost of extra time and strength in making them. Only the leader's own enthusiasm and sincerity can determine what facts should be presented and what experiences should be drawn upon to paint a convincing picture for his audience.

Today most teachers and administrators are conscious enough of the problem of prejudices; but aside from realizing that we must do something to stop the outward expression of hatreds, very few have done much thinking about the cultural richness which could evolve from our heterogeneity. They are not "gripped by a goal"; only the immediate object of preventing street riots seems to arouse their interest. Most panel discussions and educational conferences on the subject are confined to a discussion of methods, as "The Relation of Frustration to Racial Prejudices"; "How to Overcome Racial and Religious Prejudices in our Schools and Communities." The participants hear first one method and then another, and are warned not to imitate what is being done in other schools or communities. They often go away paralyzed into inaction, their own frustrations added to their burden. They talk about freedom of religion and equal opportunity for members of all races. But these concepts are conditions, not goals. Freedom and equal opportunity for what end? We talk about better *economic democracy*. Yes, in the "new world a-coming" there must be a more equitable distribution of goods. We talk about better *civil* and *political democracy*. Yes, since our problem is national and not sectional, a way must be found, for example, to help the white South get over the fear it expresses in sending to Congress men who block every bill aimed at better political democracy. We must continue to be aware of the shortages of political democracy for all disadvantaged groups, as Negroes and Orientals. But better *cultural democracy?* Few educators have even heard the term. If such a goal really gripped us, it would be easier to gain economic and political democracy; for the feelings which move us to grant such equality lie in the realm of how much we care about people. Do we know as friends persons in various minority groups? Do we have confidence and trust in Negroes, Chinese, and Mexicans? in Catholics, Jews, and Protestants? in owners and workers? Do we see that the problem of race is also a moral problem? If so, we can work together more easily to adjust the economic and political problems that concern our living together and can prevent the subordination of the many to the interests of the few. Such questions sincerely faced today should arouse the interest of America's classroom teachers.

When we had aroused the interest of the faculties of the schools in which our projects were inaugurated, *our next step was to point to the importance of the scientific approach.* In their discussions, the teachers were led to see that only by recognizing their efforts to be an application of the science as well as of the art of human relations, only by thinking of themselves as social engineers, could they avoid sentimentality. They were reminded at this point that astronomy was once only astrology, and chemistry only alchemy; that some four hundred years ago, Copernicus, sitting in a cathedral tower night after night and watching the movement of the stars, proved that our earth is not the center of the universe; that later Galileo, for embracing the Copernican theory, was repudiated by fellow scientists; but that, because of the sacrificial pioneering of these and other scientists, we now have a physical world which to a large extent is predictable.

From this discussion the question arose: "Can there be a science of human relations?" The teachers were reminded that science is a method, not a body of facts; a method which Dewey defines as "patient, co-operative inquiry, operating by means of observation, experiment, record, and controlled reflection."[2] They

---

[2] John Dewey, *A Common Faith* (New Haven: Yale University Press, 1934), p. 30.

were reminded that this method can be applied to the problem of prejudice by putting emphasis on honesty in recognizing facts as an essential part of the scientific—as well as of the democratic —approach to life. For example, when a person says that he dislikes Jews and that this dislike is based on his experience, it would be unrealistic immediately to ascribe his dislike to prejudice. He has mentioned his experience; and the social scientist should know what that experience is and how it has affected the person before concluding as to the nature of his attitude. The worst lack of realism in the classroom, more especially, would be that of the teacher who denounces all expressions of dislike for some other culture or racial group as "prejudiced" instead of helping the student to analyze his experience and to separate actual and justifiable causes of dislike from those generalized applications which alone embody prejudice.

Hunches Are the Beginnings of Hypotheses and Educational Practices

All creative scientists have something of the mystic in their make-up. From the source of all creativity came Newton's hunch which led to his formulation of the law of gravitation; from that same source came Pasteur's hunch which led to the purification of milk and the saving of millions of lives. The inquiry which leads to the hunch is continued in further reflection and, if the scientist is still creative, into another hunch. Thus it might be said that hunches are the beginning and end of scientific knowledge. Educational theories are built on the hunches of social psychologists, but nothing is ever done in the field of education until the classroom teacher starts doing it.

Educational theories must be experimented with by the teacher; but because social psychology is a growing body of knowledge, there is not complete agreement among the various schools of thought. Can our experimentation be called a science? Our favorite answer is that the way to be scientific is to be as scientific as one can. To do otherwise is to rely on chance or magic or on just muddling through, and there has been too much of that in our classrooms. The teacher who takes her calling seriously will, while making a lifelong study of human behavior as it is interpreted to us by various schools of psychology, check these theories as best she can in actual situations and take from each what she finds to be useful.

Principles of Social Psychology That Guided the Work

Gradually, over a period of years, guided by certain principles of the social psychologists, a body of educational practices was formulated out of our own observation and experimentation. We offer this now to America's teachers, but we do not feel that it is final. Many of these practices may already have been outmoded by other schools and teachers pioneering in the same field or by more scientific studies of the social psychologists. We trust that every teacher and school administrator will be critical as well as pragmatic—taking only what he thinks is wise and adapting it to fit his own unique situation. Our only warning is that to do the best we can in sincerity of purpose and with an open mind is better than to do nothing about the problem.

The list of principles will be found in exact quotations from authorities at the beginning of each subsequent subdivision of this chapter. The reader will be able to see the relation of these principles to the planned activities. The list should not be considered to contain all the principles involved in the complex phenomenon of social behavior, but simply some of those that were used consciously or unconsciously by the teachers who were carrying out the projects.

Satisfying Basic Needs as a Part of the Reconditioning Process

Individuals learn to satisfy basic needs by means of certain activities, and these activities then become themselves the objects of striving. Continued relevance to these basic needs is essential to the maintenance of derived motives. . . . The effect of attaining the goal, then, is to establish the tendency to approach again in the future, by repetition of similar acts, the situations in which the goal has been attained.[3]

All uniformities with which social psychology has to deal are the product of social conditions.[4]

The act must come before the thought, and a habit before an ability to evoke the thought at will.[5]

Our conduct in any new situation is a transferred response, a response determined by its similarity to some situation in which we have been previously conditioned.[6]

Attitudes, like habits, represent the stable and organized aspects of a personality, and these tend to persist so long as they work well and allow our conduct to proceed in a satisfactory way. The key to our problem lies, it seems to me, in the concept of crises. . . . A crisis is to be found just in those situations where existing attitudes fail to satisfy our expectations.[7]

Values show their presence through manifestations of loyalty to such ideas as "the golden rule," "rugged individualism," etc. . . . These values furnish the integrating fabric which holds life together and gives it unity and significance.[8]

Personality is the organization of wishes and habits around a dominant wish which creates for the person a status or role in his group or social world.[9]

In approaching problems of behavior it is possible to emphasize— to have in the focus of attention for working purposes—either the attitude, the value, or the situation. The attitude is the tendency to act, representing the drive, the effective states, the wishes; the value represents the object or goal desired, and the situation represents the configuration of the factors conditioning the behavior reaction.[10]

---

[3] Child, *op. cit.*, p. 52.

[4] W. I. Thomas and Florian Znaniecki, *The Polish Peasant in Europe and America* (Boston: The Gorham Press, 1918), p. 40.

[5] John Dewey, *Human Nature and Conduct* (New York: Henry Holt & Co., 1922), p. 30.

[6] Gardner Murphy and Frederick Jensen, *Approaches to Personality* (New York: Coward-McCann, 1935), p. 64.

[7] Faris, *The Nature of Human Nature, op. cit.*, p. 139.

[8] Prescott, *op. cit.*, p. 105.

[9] Kulp, *op. cit.*, p. 126.

[10] Ernest W. Burgess (ed.), *Personality and the Social Group* (Chicago: University of Chicago Press, 1929), chap. i, p. 1.

On the secondary-school level many habits of wrong thinking and acting in reference to intercultural relations have already been formed and must be broken before new habits can be developed by reconditioning. A new experience, such as the guest assembly program followed by a tea or some other small face-to-face gathering, was relied upon most frequently to start the reconditioning process. Many similar experiences with different groups of guests during the year challenged old attitudes and helped to develop new habits, while the classroom and home-room discussions gave the necessary facts and meanings to enable the students to "evoke the thought at will."

Faris has said that the key to the problem of behavior lies in the concept of crises.[11] It is during such shock experiences that existing attitudes of prejudice may fail to meet the needs of the personality. Then it is that the individual will try to find his way out of the situation by means outside his habitual modes of response. Often he acts blindly, and afterwards gives himself reasons for so acting. At this time he may follow suggestions made by others, or even imitate their actions; for, when a person is confronted with a crisis, he is especially open to influence. Waller reminds us that "when a situation is defined we know what our attitude toward it is."[12] It is the responsibility of a leader or a teacher so to define or help the individual to define the situation that he will be able to move from the old attitude to the new. This process should not be left to chance.

This role of the teacher to define situations is clearly seen in the following example from Newcomb's study: "I've always

---

[11] Recently the term "crisis" is being used in connection with depth psychiatry. Kunkel, for example, describes how, when the self-sufficient philosophy fails in individual or group life, an inner crisis begins. It might be better if the social psychologists were to use the term "shock experience" to describe a social situation in which old attitudes cease to work but in which the depths of the individual are not necessarily touched. We shall therefore use "shock experience."

[12] Willard Waller, *Sociology of Teaching* (New York: John Wiley & Sons, 1932), p. 318.

had a strong underdog complex. I needed the security of personal recognition. Then I found that intellectual self-respect meant more to me. I guess I got my notions of what intellectual self-respect meant from two or three faculty members. By that time my attitudes were really a part of me and so I wanted to work for the causes I believed in."[13]

At this point a few typical illustrations will show the shock experiences which developed in the situations planned by the teachers in the schools and communities where our experiments were conducted:

> A senior high-school girl was afraid of Chinese people because she had been conditioned to think that all Chinese were bandits and "dope fiends." She was given an opportunity at the school tea to meet and shake hands with a Chinese student from International House. To her surprise, she not only felt no fear but, she reported, had "a thrilling time."
>
> A junior high-school girl of French descent who had been taught by her grandmother to hate all Germans was present at an especially enjoyable assembly program on the German contribution to American life. The very attractive personality of the refugee professor, who not only gave information but soon had the whole group singing German folk songs and some of them doing folk dances, so affected the girl that she wrote afterwards: "After I had danced and sung their songs, I found I no longer hated all Germans."
>
> A second-generation German girl whose father "cussed out all Jews" had an enjoyable time in a small mixed group where everyone sang, along with other songs, some Palestinian folk songs led by their Jewish friends. During the evening activities, in a spontaneous way the girl was given special recognition by a Jewish person, which met in part her need for status. After that she attended regularly a series of forum discussions in which she acquired some facts to which she had before been blinded.

Of course, there are all sorts of ways other than integrated assembly programs for youth to develop appreciative attitudes. Yet the importance of planned situations which tend to open closed minds cannot be overstressed. These situations became, in the experiments carried on in the high schools and later in Parent-Teacher groups, the media that called forth the very

---

[13] Newcomb, *op. cit.*

behavior which, it had been hoped, would result; and when similar reactions to like situations happened again and again, it was evident that, as initial steps toward the desired change in attitudes, these functions served their purpose with success.

As the work progressed, we saw ever more clearly the need for the school-community approach. At first a few community leaders were brought into the planning and the conducting of school experiences; later a group of teachers started experimentation with the Neighborhood-Home Festival, which made it possible to arrange for the parents experiences similar to those that their own children had been having. This will be discussed in a later chapter.

Introducing Suggestion and Imitation Among Students

Man has one capacity which is of the greatest possible service for collective aims—the power of imitation. . . . Without it mass organizations, the state and the ordering of society are simply impossible. Imitation embraces suggestibility. . . . Imitation and not laws and statutes is responsible for the ordering of society.[14]

The process of suggestion . . . is to release under the appropriate social stimuli mechanisms already organized, whether instincts, habits, or sentiments.[15]

Imitation . . . is a process of copying or learning. . . . Through imitation we appreciate the other person.[16]

Art is an experience, a sort of vicarious experience; and yet, however vicarious it may be, it is an emotional experience and always modifies our emotional attitudes.[17]

When, in rehearsing the past, emotional situations are reenacted, taking the role of another sometimes gives rise to a new attitude which is so like the attitude of the other person that it is often called imitation.[18]

We have said that when a crisis or shock experience is reached, an individual is likely to follow suggestions made by others or

---

[14] C. G. Jung, *Integration of the Personality* (New York: Farrar & Rinehart, 1939), p. 161.

[15] Park and Burgess, *op. cit.*, p. 346.

[16] *Ibid.*, p. 344.

[17] Faris, *The Nature of Human Nature, op. cit.*, p. 364.

[18] *Ibid.*, p. 80.

even to imitate their actions; that when an individual has reached such a situation, he is especially open to influence.

It is not within the scope of this report to discuss the social processes of suggestion and imitation; they may be summed up in the word "rapport." It was our aim to invite to the schools the kind of people from any group who would more quickly develop rapport with the students, and we were careful to plan situations other than the assembly in which the processes of suggestion and imitation could more easily function. But we always held in mind the desired new attitude. The "planned situation" does not in itself determine what this attitude is to be. It does two things: first, it brings the student into rapport with personalities whose unexpected existence (that of a gifted and educated Negro, for example, where previously only underprivileged Negroes have been known) challenges previously held opinions about the particular group and makes the habitual attitude and behavior toward members of that group untenable; second, it carries within itself, by the presence and leadership of people who have prestige for the pupils, suggestions for more suitable attitudes and forms of behavior which, in various ways, students begin to imitate. The student is led to identify himself with persons of the group being studied, to see the mutual relation from their point of view, to recognize new standards of value by which to judge both the group and his personal relation with it, to become curious about that group and predisposed to appreciate its contribution to his own life and toward the common good. The following thoughts were voiced: "It never occurred to me how much we depend on the Negroes for our comfort and enjoyment of life." "I see now that I can add to the depth of my own life by experiencing some of these Jewish festivals. The Old Testament becomes more alive to me." "I guess the Orientals have what we don't have—we can supplement each other."

At other times the feeling of rapport comes by sensing the

similarities: "We all care for good music and humor." "We are all Americans." Sometimes it is brought about through a common interest in nature or in science, through common love of the beautiful, or simply through sharing in the æsthetic experience of rhythmic movement in dance, through common admiration for heroic deeds, through common appreciation of refinement in manners, diction, or personal appearance. In short, there is no end to the variety of pleasant thrills of recognition for common values by which one individual may feel himself drawn to another, especially in the small face-to-face groups following the assembly; and it is through these thrills that a rapport is established which naturally extends to other situations. And out of that rapport, experience has shown, spring suggestions for changed attitudes and conduct that fertilize the whole subsequent learning process. Then the classroom teacher has the opportunity to follow such opening-up experiences with the kind of reading and discussion that will lead to intellectual self-respect.

When assembly speakers were chosen, the effect that they might have not only upon students of the dominant group but also upon members of their own minority groups was also considered. When Jessie Fauset, the Negro novelist, and Frank Wilson, the well-known Negro actor, were on a program together the Negro students actually sat up straighter while they listened. The English teachers reported that after the program those colored students took a more normal part in classroom discussion. Sophisticated white senior students said: "We want Frank Wilson back again; we want to ask him some more questions." Schools often fail to recognize the value of prestige and hero worship in the development of attitudes. Jesse Owens, for example, was idolized by an all-white group of students because of his position in the world of sports.

The student follow-up programs which ended the assembly cycle consisted mainly of dramatic sketches, planned and written, for the most part, by the students themselves. Music, song, and dance were also freely used. The positive effect of these experiences through art demonstrated the truth of Faris' statement that such experiences always modify emotional attitudes.

Resemblance of Guest Speakers to Students

The sympathy between two groups is directly proportionate to their consciousness of resemblance.[19]

When there is consciousness of kind or awareness of resemblance, then two or more minds respond in like ways to the same stimulus.[20]

The greater the difference between one organism and another, the more difficult is any imitation of one by the other.[21]

The above generalizations may explain why people who are prejudiced toward others often rationalize in their attempt to keep themselves from feeling any resemblance to those others. The rationalizations which such people indulge in to bolster their own feelings of superiority when members of other ethnic groups excel them would be amusing if they were not sometimes tragic in their consequences. Among such rationalizations we have found are: "Mexican Indians are born with a peculiarly shaped hand and hence are good artists." "Negro runners won so many honors in the Olympics because of a certain elongated heel bone, and Japanese swimmers because of a 'secret stroke.' " Another example of such rationalization occurred when a well-known writer went to a Harlem night club and heard a Negro play Chopin. The writer exclaimed in his column, read by thousands: "Imagine a Negro playing Chopin divinely!" Where such rationalizations are indulged in, there is no real consciousness of resemblance; hence, little understanding can develop.

The idea of difference is built up in many ways. It is built up by many of our civics books, which draw a sharp line be-

---

[19] *Ibid.*, p. 364.

[20] Franklin N. Giddings, *Introduction to Sociology* (New York: Mac-Millan Co., 1901), p. 64.

[21] *Ibid.*, p. 92.

tween the "old" and the "new" immigrant, and by our history texts, many of which contain historical rationalizations.[22] It is built up by our naturalization laws which, through such expressions as "aliens ineligible for citizenship," have fixed even more deeply a sense of difference between ourselves and the Oriental. Because this "ineligibility" is based not on difference in individual capacity but on membership in a racial group, the logic of the child mind easily concludes that the exclusion from citizenship is based upon an insurmountable "racial" difference.

Since prejudiced pupils are likely to use any outward difference as a rationalization for their attitudes, care was taken to choose for guest speakers persons who, though from different groups, yet resembled in many ways those teachers or other adults whom the students most admired. The first visiting rabbi in the Woodbury school was a young man who looked and acted like a Y.M.C.A. secretary whom the students greatly admired. Mr. Dipeolu, who was from Nigeria and was dark-skinned, spoke beautiful English. Louise Chin, a third generation Chinese-American girl, was a typical American college girl. The mere act of taking to the schools with these guests one or two of their old-stock American friends was enough to suggest to students that they too could identify themselves with people of foreign appearance or background. When possible, leaders from traditionally antagonistic groups were invited to come together. The German guests were introduced by a Jewish, or the English by an Irish, leader. In the student-planned programs, if any "boasting" was to be done about one group, members of another group were chosen to do it.

Since all the programs stressed the interdependence of peoples, it was found that students could easily move from feelings of difference based on outward dissimilarity to feelings of loyalty

---

[22] The reader is urged to read chap. xvii, "The Propaganda of History," in W. E. B. DuBois, *Black Reconstruction* (New York: Harcourt, Brace & Co., 1935).

based on belongingness. In fact the generalizations of Faris and Giddings should be counteracted here by a generalization from Kurt Lewin: "A group does not need to consist of members which show great similarity. As a matter of fact, it holds for social groups, as for wholes in any field, that a whole of any high degree of unity may contain very dissimilar parts." (See p. 84, note.) Witness the family unit of man, wife, and baby.

Prestige of Guest Speakers

Prestige is the leadership aspect of collective behavior. If a group is suggestible to a leader, then he has prestige.[23]

Now number, age, prowess, sanctity, inspiration, place, money, ideas, and learning, are genuine features; there is power in them; those who possess them can exert pressure because of them.[24]

The factor of prestige was considered in choosing culture group leaders to speak at assembly programs. Whenever possible, speakers of wide reputation who held respected positions were chosen: an internationally known economist, a member of Congress, an English lecturer. Since students are always interested in accomplishment, attention was called, in introducing speakers, to what they had done. Well-known musicians, poets, novelists, artists, actors, scientists, and champion athletes were among the guests. Today, returned soldiers who approve of the need for developing appreciative attitudes and who have ability may be chosen.

Because there is a positive relationship between the prestige of a person and the extent of identification with and hence of imitation of him, great care was taken that a guest representing a different culture and speaking in assembly about his own group was not one who would disparage another culture group. This point was stressed in a tactful preliminary interview with the guests. It was found that a speaker's attitudes, no matter what his profession, could not be taken for granted.

---

23 Kulp, *op. cit.*, p. 280.
24 Frederick L. Lumley, *Means of Social Control* (New York: The Century Co., 1925), p. 332.

Participation of Students

> To the extent that children share in the purposing and achieving
> of adults as well as other children do they acquire character.[25]

It was urged that the teachers, instead of doing all the planning themselves, should form student committees which would
have the responsibility for arranging the student-produced assembly programs for a semester. This procedure not only resulted
in the students' identifying themselves with characters in the
programs which they had themselves helped to plan, but it also
brought about a more democratic sharing of experience. In a
school that was preparing a program on the Negro, the committee of students consisted of four white and two Negro boys.
A white boy quickly started the planning by saying, "Let's have
a plantation scene and wear gingham aprons and overalls." The
Negro boys offered, "Say, Jim, we want to get away from all
that." The resulting program was not of the gingham-apron
type but a dramatization of an annual meeting of the National
Association for the Advancement of Colored People. These and
similar experiences made those responsible for the projects realize
that democratic participation not only provides sympathetic understanding among those who plan and work together but also
gives students status in the administration of the school program
and tends to develop attitudes of personal responsibility and
initiative. The importance of the democratic atmosphere in
school cannot be overestimated.

The process of participation was also intentionally used in
the assemblies when speakers called for members of the audience
to come to the platform to take part in folk dancing or singing.
This procedure never failed to arouse the interest and enthusiasm
of the students and thus developed rapport between them and
the guests. The process of participation was used again in the
tea situations when it was planned to get the group to do together one or more of the following: singing, performing rhyth-

---

[25] Hartshorne, *op. cit.*, p. 23.

mic movements such as clapping of hands, laughing and talking, and eating together. In other words, an effort was made to
mobilize as many senses as possible—sight, sound, taste, and
touch—toward the objective, in this case identification with
members of a particular culture group.

Use of Humor

Laughing with people attracts; laughing at people repels.[26]

Laughter is a powerful aid in developing and retaining social co-
operation.[27]

Sielly thinks the practice of laughing together is a great promotor
of social sympathy.[28]

The fear of ridicule is the most dominant of our feelings, and that
which controls us in most things and with the most strength.[29]

Another stimulus which develops rapport is that of humor.
Humor entertains and gives students pleasure. It can be used
to ease tense situations. No one likes to be laughed at, but all
enjoy having others laugh with them. The first kind of laughter
separates people and leads to antagonism; the second brings
them closer together. Laughing together helps them to feel that
they have something in common. The fear of ridicule, of being
laughed at, has driven many a second-generation boy to despise
his cultural background and even his parents.

The difference between laughing at and with a group is shown
when we compare the following story with all those about
Negroes stealing chickens, eating watermelon, and the like:

The candidate for admission to the colored church was giving his
religious experience—his soul had visited hell, and had seen Satan
and all his hosts, but finally got away. "Find any white folks down
there?" "Yes, sir, lots of white folks down there." "Any cullud folks
there?" "Yep—some cullud folks there too." "Well—how do the
white folks an' the cullud folks get 'long down there together?"

[26] Lumley, *op. cit.*, p. 271.

[27] *Ibid.*, p. 280.

[28] *Ibid.*, p. 281.

[29] M. A. Michaels, *World of Humor and of Laughter*, as quoted by
Park and Burgess, *op. cit.*, p. 375.

"Jes' about ez heah—cause soon ez I got there, fust thing I noticed wuz evah white man had him a Negro holdin' him between him an' the fire!"[30]

Stories of Jews burning down stores for insurance, of penny-pinching Scots, of "dumb" Swedes, producing the kind of laughter that leads to false generalizations, are used consciously or unconsciously to degrade those groups. They presuppose and further stimulate feelings of superiority on the part of those who use them and inferiority on the part of many members of the groups about whom they are told. Much of the dangerous divisive anti-Semitism, anti-Negroism, anti-foreignism, is carried on a wave of "Have you heard the story about—?"

Repetition of Attitude-Changing Situations— a Battery of Experiences

One planned social experience where students met members of a culture group was not relied upon alone to alter old attitudes or to build new ones; a whole battery of varied and pleasant experiences was provided. In one school, for example, Louis Sharp, who was then singing in a popular Negro show on Broadway, went five times to train a group of white and Negro students to sing together some of the spirituals used in that play. In all schools, from ten to sixteen assembly programs, both guest and student follow-up, were given during the year. It was found necessary, in order to build resistance to those influences in school, home, and community which were pulling away from the desired attitudes, to see that the students had acquired enough facts and experiences and wish satisfactions to counter-act the pull. A number of teachers reported on the value of the cumulative effect on student behavior of a series of programs, all of which pointed toward fundamental human likenesses and

---

[30] William Pickens, *American Aesop—Negro and Other Humor* (New York: The author, 260 West 139th St., N. Y., 1926). This book contains anecdotes, catalogued according to culture groups, which have been used by Dr. Pickens in his lectures throughout the country.

interdependence and yet stressed the importance of recognizing and sharing differences in cultural expression. Care was taken to provide enough programs to hold the interest of the students, but not enough to kill interest. This latter point has become especially important, now that so many schools and teachers have become suddenly aware of the need for intercultural education. In some schools, it has been reported to us, so many references have been made to "democracy" and "prejudice" in class after class that pupils have begun to rebel.

Criticism of the Work

Having recounted some of the basic principles underlying our programs of intercultural education, we must now consider a criticism which has often been made of the "culture group" approach used in many of the unified assembly programs. This criticism was usually put in the form of the question: "Are you not, by singling out first one group and then another for special attention in assembly programs, developing rather than reducing a sense of separateness among groups?"

The first answer to that question was that many members of ethnic groups are already set off in the pupils' minds in a negative way. Many Jewish students, for example, are absent from public schools during holidays which others do not share. Other children are set off by obvious physical differences, and still others by rather extreme cultural differences in home life. An answering question was formulated: "If members of ethnic groups are already set off in a negative way—in a way, that is, which makes for dislike or antagonism—do we not need to set them off in a positive way in order to make difference appear interesting and attractive?" It is by first having his negative values changed into positive ones that the individual can be enabled finally to rise above feelings of separation and to acquire a sense of interdependence and belongingness.

Another criticism of the culture group approach was that Jews were included among the culture groups. Some critics believe that since all Jews have come from some nation, as England, Poland, Germany, or Russia, they should be considered as of English, Polish, German, or Russian background. We realize, of course, that Jews have taken on characteristics of whatever countries they have lived in; but if we are attempting to change the attitudes of gentiles toward Jews, we accomplish nothing when attention is focused only on the concepts *Poles, Germans,* or *Russians.* These critics remind us too that Judaism should be considered as a religion on a par with Catholicism or Protestantism and not as a nationality or a race. They are right, of course, but in our public-school programs we were not focusing attention on religion but on cultures; and, from one angle, Judaism may be considered as a subculture within American life.

Some critics have said that, rather than point to cultural differences, even differences that are socially valuable, it is best to arrange experiences together around some common interest. The value of this latter approach must be granted; but is not mutual understanding and confidence basic to any effective coming together around a common interest? Is it not the role of the school to help people to take this first step? In schools there are two interrelated ways of bringing about that readiness: one, the study of specific culture groups; the other, the integration of those groups around a common activity, as the pursuit of scientific knowledge or of the arts.

It still should be admitted that in the application of either the subject matter or the culture group approach, when not guided in every detail by someone experienced in bringing out the desired learning values, mistakes sometime occur. Such a mistake, for example, is made when the teacher in charge of a dramatic production by students permits students of one ethnic group to impersonate members of another group in such a way as unduly to accentuate peculiarities of speech or gesture that reflect unfavorably on that group's reputation; or when the present cultural status of a group which has as yet made few important contributions to the arts and sciences of this country (whatever may have been its cultural history) is presented with such exaggeration of emphasis as to make the whole effort appear insincere; or when actual characteristics of a group are denied instead of being explained; or when an emphasis on minor achievements of individuals is permitted to becloud the very large contributions which a group, not as yet far advanced in economic status, is making to one of the more humble fields of common national effort. All these faults may occur. But nobody has as yet successfully challenged the teaching of history or home economics on the ground that it is sometimes of doubtful quality. In a new field of teaching, more especially, errors of judgment must be expected to occur until those who pioneer in it have had far greater opportunities than now exist to acquire the requisite knowledge and to train themselves in effective practice. How some teachers aided in their own further education will be discussed in a later chapter.

6

FIRST AID TO WOUNDED PERSONALITIES

> We do not share the skepticism against education as a means
> of mitigating racial intolerance which recently has spread
> among American sociologists as a reaction against an impor-
> tant doctrine in the American creed. The simple fact is that an
> educational offensive against racial intolerance, going deeper
> than the reiteration of the "glittering generalities" in the
> nation's political creed, has never seriously been attempted in
> America.[1]

IT WAS STATED in a former chapter that the experiences
through which large numbers of people go in facing personally
unmerited discriminations and antagonisms are often devastating
to personality because of wish frustrations and undesirable compensations which often result. These psychological by-products
of unfortunate situations in the community cannot be entirely
removed by the schools; but schools can do much to provide
opportunities for the satisfaction of the basic wishes within the
framework of their own social worlds. In the experiments on
which the present study is founded, many such opportunities were
found to help students of disliked minorities to overcome specific
personality maladjustments partly due to failure of the basic
wishes to find satisfaction.

Because any social situation may provide for satisfaction of
one or more wishes, it was difficult to distinguish and to plan
situations that might help to satisfy one particular wish rather
than another. We shall attempt, however, for purposes of clarity,
to list under each of the four wishes, in so far as possible,
those situations and outcomes which seemed to the leaders of

---

[1] Myrdal, *op. cit.*, pp. 48-9.

the experiment to minister to a given kind of wish and thus to assist in overcoming personality maladjustments caused by the frustration of that particular wish.

Finding Ways for Satisfying the Wish for Recognition

The desire for recognition expresses itself in devices for securing distinction in the eyes of the public. A list of the different modes of seeking recognition . . . would include courageous behavior, showing off through ornament and dress, the pomp of kings, the display of opinions and knowledge, the possession of special attainments—in the arts, for example. It is expressed alike in arrogance and in humility, even in martyrdom. Certain modes of seeking recognition we define as "vanity," others as "ambition." The "will to power" belongs here. . . . It would be difficult to estimate the role the desire for recognition has played in the creation of social values.[2]

Certainly, the role which the desire for recognition plays in the school is an important one. Schools depend upon it for motivation, not only of formal tasks but also of extracurricular activities. "Recognition is the one string of the human instrument which it is permissible for the schools to play upon at will."[3] In our intercultural education projects several ways of satisfying the wish for recognition were found workable.

Since, in brief, this wish finds satisfaction when opportunities are provided in which the individual student gets recognition for what he himself is, for what his family is, and finally for what his culture group is, it seems best to divide our discussion into those three parts. It should be pointed out again, however, that we are concerned here only with the satisfaction of the four wishes as it applies to the elimination of frustration caused by intercultural conflict and the social attitudes connected with it.

Providing Recognition for "What the Individual Is"

The importance of the satisfaction of the desire for recognition in personality adjustment made the teachers feel that, if enough different kinds of social distinction to go around might

---

[2] Park and Burgess, *op. cit.,* pp. 489-90.
[3] Waller, *op. cit.,* p. 290.

be created, no one would have to be neglected. And such distinction might be conferred in such a way as to emphasize how all groups in America work together. In some schools, students who had shown the best co-operation in preparing for the Italian program, for example, were given free tickets to the Italian opera, and those who worked on the British program were invited to a tea given by the English Speaking Union. A similar basis for selection was used for choosing those who should go on museum trips and visit art exhibits. Students who showed tact were given the privilege of being hostesses at teas or were placed on reception committees for meeting guests at the station. Opportunities for exhibiting their handiwork were given those who produced the best scrapbooks, compositions, paintings, and so on. In one school a Jewish girl made a portrait of her grandfather which won for her a fellowship to study art. Several schools had hobby exhibits. The interest of local newspapers was aroused; indeed, newspapers were often glad to take photographs and to publish descriptions of the more colorful assembly programs. A note of warning should be given here against too much of this kind of publicity because of the difficulty of presenting the total picture and the consequent misunderstanding.

In our emphasis upon the need for recognition we are not overlooking the fact that the person's attempt to find satisfaction of this basic wish might easily become morbid. The words of Alfred Adler are helpful: "As long as a person strives for superiority and tempers that striving with social interest, he is on the useful side of life and can accomplish good."[4] And individuals who are on the useful side of life eventually forget themselves in sacrifice for the good of others—the final test of maturity.

---

[4] Alfred Adler, *The Science of Living* (New York: Greenberg, 1929), p. 85.

Providing Recognition for "What the Individual's Family Is"

The maladjustment of children of foreign-born parents often results from the fact that their families are accorded low status in the community. The children suffer because little or no recognition is given to the accomplishments of their parents. To compensate for the feeling of inferiority in these children, situations were planned which made it possible for the parents to acquire some status not only in the eyes of their own children but also in the eyes of others. In several schools foreign-born parents participated in the guest assembly programs. In other schools, the Parent-Teachers' Association initiated a series of nationality and regional suppers and invited parents of the ethnic groups to assist in the choice of songs and of other parts of the entertainment. When such plans are made in conference with leaders of the culture groups in question, as in the planning teas previously referred to, the danger of exploitation of such persons according to what Gabro Karabin calls "sham standards of quaintness"—or thinking of these people as interesting curiosities —will be avoided.[5]

Individuals and groups who are transplanted from one culture area to another often lose their cultural anchorage in the process. They are like children who have lost their parents and with them the security of "belonging."

In illustration, one might mention the Negro boy who could not, at the teacher's urging in private conversation, remember any member of his family who ever had "amounted to anything." Quite casually he mentioned an uncle who had been an itinerant preacher in the South. The resourceful teacher, in this case, quoted Johnson's "Creation" to make the point that these preachers, so often derided nowadays for their lack of erudition, have played a most significant role in the spiritual

---

[5] For a more specific understanding of this problem, see Gabro Karabin, "Honorable Escape" and "Letter" to *Scribner's Magazine,* December, 1937, pp. 40-1 and p. 7.

and artistic rise of the Negro. She gave the boy an emotional tie-up with the culture from which his parents had come, a culture which he, along with all those he knew, tended to despise.

E. Franklin Frazier, in *The Negro Family in Chicago,* lists several sources of pride on the part of Negro families in being descended from those who bought their own freedom, or who escaped from slavery, or who were trusted house servants of distinguished whites. More recently they achieve status by pointing to relatives who have pioneered in some field where Negroes had never entered, or to some unique achievement. The alert teacher will regularly read some Negro newspapers and magazines in order to be of most help to the children under her care.

The importance of what the teacher can do in giving recognition cannot be overemphasized. Thus, for example, while the Polish Americans of Orange County, New York, probably have for many years taken pleasure in the accomplishment of the onion harvest and celebrated it among themselves in old-world style, it was the deliberate effort of teachers and community leaders that made this celebration an annual community festival, designed to give status to the citizens of Polish descent and family pride to their children. The famous all-community Tulip Festival in Holland, Michigan, was also first suggested by a teacher.

Here too, as with every phase of life, there are limiting elements. Perhaps some individuals with their famililies have so changed their names and circumstances that there is no looking back. A free democratic society should accept this. The teacher can help most those cases that are still undecided and therefore are in a state of psychological tension. Louis Adamic's book *What's Your Name?* is especially helpful here. He says that "in secretly discarding their 'foreign labels,' they have buried a good part of their chance for the sense of continuity apparently necessary to a well-rounded-out character." In some cases, however, Adamic approves of an "organic" change of name.

In one of our co-operating communities, into which many Negroes had migrated from the deep South and where relations between whites and Negroes were growing more strained, a more elaborate experiment with conscious tradition-building was made. First, an outstanding Negro sociologist was invited to address the Negro parents. He said, in part, "We do not suffer from persecution so much as from nothingness. We are not proud enough of our group. We need a good dose of ancestors. Many parents tell their children they are nothing anyhow. That is wrong. We need to tell them something to give them pride. After all, tradition even in the 'best' of American families does not go very far back. All such families have had at some time to begin building whatever they now have."

Children of various ethnic groups in these schools were encouraged to look up family festivals, such as German Christmas celebrations, Jewish Seder services, and Japanese tea and flower ceremonies. Parents in the community were asked to look into their pasts for interesting stories of accomplishment and to send to the school objects which they had treasured. One Polish boy of ten could find at home no such treasure, so he bought at a secondhand bookstore a book about Poland and proudly said to a visitor at the school museum, "I'm making a family heirloom out of this and want to hand it down to my children." In one class, which carried on the project for several terms, the same family treasure was brought to school by three different brothers. It should be remembered that acts such as these were purely voluntary on the part of the children, for at no time was pressure brought to force anyone to identify with a culture from which he sprang. Our purpose was not to perpetuate, for example, a Polish group of Americans with a separate Polish culture, but rather to enable the youth to feel so relaxed about his background that he could be a bearer of whatever continuing vitality of Polish culture still remained in America. Because of what has happened to our Japanese-American citizens during the war, however, it may be unsafe for some years for them publicly to identify too closely with even some of the proved cultural values expressed by their parent groups.

There is, of course, a danger that such tradition-building may produce undesirable by-products. This happens when it is insincere and when historically false racial affiliation is maintained or claims to distinction are made. It happens when individual families acquire a sense of self-importance at the cost of their sense of affiliation with a larger social unit, especially their ethnic group. A social teaching that would spread even more widely that false family pride which plays such havoc with a realistic facing of present-day realities in many parts of the United States could only be deplored. But the scope for such conscious exaggeration, fortunately, is limited, even if it were attempted.

Even the poorer homes of immigrant parents often have family heirlooms, modest in money value but rich in associations, that have genuine cultural significance. Or skills have been inherited by members of such families, which may possibly not be of any practical use in our technically more advanced civilization, but which are historically interesting or have their recreational values. Children reading the *Odyssey* may discover that the only person known to them who can spin is an old Slovak peasant woman, the grandmother of one of the boys. To a school exhibit of native arts a Jewish child may contribute a beautiful page of Hebrew calligraphy, a cherished possession of his father who is known to the other children only as a dealer in secondhand clothes. A discussion of family names may reveal that the children of a Polish laborer are likely to be genealogically connected with a Polish king of several centuries ago.

Providing Recognition for "What the Individual's Culture Group Is"

The teachers guiding the projects in intercultural education, then, attempted to help students to feel a justifiable pride in their cultural backgrounds—a pride, however, balanced by appreciation for the cultural backgrounds of other groups and by a feeling of the oneness of the human race. Since the inherent values in these backgrounds are usually expressed by outstanding leaders of the different groups, and since the personalities of young people are influenced profoundly by the process of identification with inspiring leaders, the guests who appeared on the assembly programs were carefully chosen. Italian students who identified themselves with Aurora Unti, a social worker of Italian parentage, or Negro students who identified themselves with Aaron Douglas, the well-known artist, or with the novelist Jessie Fauset, were provided with a basis for a heightened social status. They could be justly proud of belonging to the same group as did these leaders.

After an assembly program on the contributions of the Jews to American life, a girl was overheard to say, "I was obliged to go to Hebrew school but did not want to learn Hebrew. When I heard that girl singing in Hebrew, I was more interested in learning the language." Back of the statement was a conflict which the girl was helped to solve by being enabled to identify herself with a guest whose performance received public recognition in the assembly and in whose honor a tea was given attended by persons of prestige from school and community. The gentile homeroom teacher, who had read such books as Kaplan's *Judaism as a Civilization* and Steinberg's *The Making of the Modern Jew,* seeing the increased interest of this girl in the cultural background of her family, could in a tactful, sympathetic way help her to think through less emotionally the arguments on both sides of a question which disturbs so many modern Jews—that of loyalty to Judaism. It was our aim to help the students to see that in a democracy, which does not insist on uniformity, the problem is transcended.

Students who were able to identify themselves with the German refugee professor, the Negro poet, the dancer of Jewish themes, in many cases gained a greater respect from their fellow students who belonged to those groups. This resulted in a tendency to lessen the feeling of superiority on the part of the former and that of inferiority on the part of the latter.

Homeroom and classroom discussions afforded an opportunity for further identification. As facts were given about contributions made to American culture or world culture by Poles, or Englishmen, or Chinese, student members of those groups felt a vicarious pride in these accomplishments, and other students came to realize that achievement was not the monopoly of any one nationality or race.

Museum trips were also used to develop a justifiable pride in cultural backgrounds. The acting curator and the staff assistant of the American Museum of Natural History in New York report the following reactions to such trips:

> I recall most vividly a class of children, partly Oriental, who came to the museum for a talk on China. As I took the children into the Chinese hall on the third floor and showed them the beautiful Chinese porcelains, silks, embroideries, and carvings, they began to realize the importance of China's contribution to our life.

> I observed how calmly, and yet how proudly, the little Chinese boys in the group heard the exclamations of delight which the beauty of the ancient bronze mirrors brought from some of the Caucasian children. I invited one of the Orientals to describe the design on a piece of brocaded silk he said his mother owned, and another to talk about some porcelain in his home. Each very shyly responded.

> As the group left the hall every child, including the Chinese boys themselves, had a feeling of admiration and respect for the Chinese of old, and also a greater appreciation for this culture and art. But best of all, I felt, was the change in attitude so evident in some of the youngsters toward their Chinese companions. . . .

The same report shows how similar is the reaction to recognition given to cultural backgrounds of members of a very different group—the American Indian.

> Some months ago, a man of uncertain age, attired in clothes typical of woodsmen, came to my desk at the Education Bureau and asked about the location of the exhibit of the work of the Indians of the Canadian Region. The pocket of his mackinaw bore the familiar maple leaf of the Canadian sportsman, so I, in turn, questioned him as to the particular tribe in which he was interested. "I am inter-

ested in the Ojibway," he replied, "I am a Micmac Indian and I wish to show my little granddaughter the work of her people." After directing them to the exhibition hall, I shortly found an excuse to work in the Woodlands Exhibit. It was most interesting to watch this old Indian explain to his grandchild the construction of the conical bark wigwam, the techniques required in working with cedar bark, and the pre-Columbian method of aboriginal writing. The little girl was wide-eyed and thrilled at the display before her.

Later the old Indian came over to me and rather sheepishly explained he was a guide in the North Woods and was in New York as a representative of his group, at the Sportsmen's Show. "But," he further explained, "I wanted my grandchild to see this work of her ancestors—she knows nothing of it and she has never seen a house like this. The schools in Canada do not teach this," and he waved his hand to include the entire Indian display.

The pride shown by this one man and his appreciation of the museum in the preservation of this material was most touching. When I explained to him that we of the museum staff were using this material to vivify history, he was delighted. He questioned me minutely and then proudly turned to his granddaughter and repeated to her what I had told him.

As an attempt was made to help students to identify themselves with inspiring leaders and the cultural heritages they represented, so an attempt was also made to discount the authority of the common expressions of prejudice encountered on every hand in everyday contacts and sometimes, unfortunately, in the writings or utterances of public figures. The words of Dr. Harry Emerson Fosdick were found to be helpful here: "When you hear a man express a collective prejudice against any group, you are listening to a belated mind. He may think himself modern, may ride in motor cars, possess a radio, and take trips around the world, but his mind is properly dated B.C."

An effort was made consistently to help the student feel that there is an intellectual and honorable foundation for his pride in his own cultural heritage—or heritages, if it so happens that he is close to more than one—by pointing out that the theory of cultural democracy is held by a growing number of outstanding leaders. The students collected newspaper clippings, magazine articles, and books related to the subject. In these ways, the individual learnings were merged in an important generalization which it would have been impossible to convey forcefully as an abstraction.

The relation of language teaching to intercultural education has an importance to which it is impossible to do justice in the present study. Nothing, for example, has harmed more the status of the German Americans than the reduced emphasis given in school curricula to German language and literature. More recently, the same may be said of the French Americans. Conversely, nothing tends to give a greater popular support to our country's desire for more neighborly relations with Latin America than the increased teaching of Spanish in the country's high schools and colleges. Some school authorities, while admitting the value of other language studies to offset the cultural alienation between immigrant parents and their American-born children, find themselves in practice impeded from introducing new courses in languages that have little commercial importance, as compared with languages that serve active American intercourse with other nations. With curricula already too crowded, and with the growing importance of a great variety of extracurricular activities, they also tend to be hostile to language study under auspices outside of school hours.

In view of these difficulties, there is now a good deal of support for the introduction of general orientation courses in language which weave linguistics, the main principles of philology, the characteristics of the major language groups, and the like, with a study of the cultural life of the particular language group. This tends to lessen the sense of difference among students from different language groups and the contempt or derision for immigrants whose mastery of the English language is imperfect. In the elementary grades it is possible to introduce children to a few words in several languages as they study particular groups.

Schools were urged to offer courses in the language most widely represented among the parents of the school population. Why, it was asked, should "foreign language" mean only French,

German, and Spanish? Why not Italian, or Hebrew,[6] or Nor-
wegian, or Chinese?[7] Those students who came from homes
where a language other than English was spoken were encouraged
to learn that language. On the other hand, assistance was given
to children to overcome any traces of foreign accent.

Before concluding our discussion of the wish for recognition
in relation to cultural backgrounds, it should be pointed out that
anything which improves the status of the family of the child
of a particular culture group is also likely to enhance his feeling of belonging. The same thing may be said of the position
of a given culture group in the community. If the status of such
a group is high, its members naturally have a sense of greater
security as well as of status. We therefore turn to a brief, discussion of the importance of giving security to the person and the
group as a step toward personality adjustment.

Finding Ways for Satisfying the Wish for Security

In its relation to the problem of social adjustment, the lack
of economic security is important because it sometimes prevents the meeting of other basic needs. The satisfaction of the
wish for response, for example, which comes mainly as a result
of family affection, is sometimes thwarted in families of the
lower economic levels because of insufficient food. The recognition which comes from the ability to put oneself across in a
social situation may be frustrated because of the lack of adequate
clothes. During the depression, school authorities all over the
country fed and clothed many children; else in some places
there would have been no pupils. It may again be necessary to
do this on a large scale. Then the need will be to see that children
do not lose status because the family is on "relief."

---

[6] Write the Jewish Education Association, 1776 Broadway, New York,
N. Y., for information on the teaching of Hebrew in the public schools.
[7] See the small brochure, *Let's Try Chinese,* Institute of Pacific Relations, 1 East 54th Street, New York, N. Y.

A need related to the wish for economic security which the secondary school has a more permanent obligation to fill is that of giving the minority-group students more effective and intelligent vocational guidance. Successful vocational guidance is becoming increasingly difficult, but it is especially difficult for children of minority groups.

Before the war, thousands of Oriental Americans on the Pacific Coast graduated from junior and senior high schools each year more or less equipped for "white collar" jobs, but with the expectation of acquiring such jobs so slight as to be almost negligible. This was true for young people of all groups, of course, during the depression years. For Orientals in the western parts of this country, however, it was always true. An occasional post in a bank, in an insurance office, or in a mercantile house connected with Oriental trade was to be obtained by a few fortunate ones. Dobie says, "In spite of a lip-service affection, which all San Franciscans indulge in when they speak of the Chinese, they will not open their working ranks to receive them."[8]

The same may be said of other minority groups and especially of the Negro. Teachers of mixed classes often ignore this question either because they do not know enough about what professions are open to persons of minority groups, or because they feel that such discussions, if frank, might hurt the feelings of some of their students.

In many Northern schools where Negroes are in the majority, around 75 per cent of the girls would be found pursuing dressmaking and domestic science with only a few taking the academic or commercial courses. Part of the reason for such concentration was found to be that they came from poorly equipped and crowded junior high schools; but the selection was found to be due in the main to the policy of the educational advisors. These advisors discouraged Negro girls from taking such courses on the

---

[8] C. Dobie, *San Francisco's Chinatown* (New York: D. Appleton-Century Co., 1936), p. 325.

ground that "opportunities are not open to Negro girls in the commercial field." The employment needs, especially for office workers, during the war showed the stupidity of those vocational advisors who, by their own counsel to Negro students, made efficient Negro office workers a rarity, thus giving a seeming proof to the contention that Negroes do not make good office workers.

Concerning this problem, the 1936 *Mayor's Commission on Conditions in Harlem* reported:

> The problem of giving vocational guidance to the Negro children of Harlem is especially difficult even for the fair-minded educational advisor. As one seemingly conscientious and intelligent advisor put the problem: Should she direct Negro children to lines of occupations according to their intelligence and interest, although it was known that Negroes were not employed in such occupations; or should she, taking into consideration this fact, direct them into fields in which they would be likely to find employment? While it is true that a conscientious advisor may be conscious of the problem involved, as a matter of fact, it requires more than conscientiousness. Some of these advisors have no knowledge of the occupations in which Negroes have been able to enter in spite of traditional notions and prejudices nor are they concerned with the Negroes' struggle to break down the color barrier in industry. Vocational counsellors who are charged with mapping out the future of Negro children in Harlem should be only such persons as possess a broad knowledge and understanding of the Negro's economic problems and who are in sympathy with his aspirations. No one who is dominated by traditional beliefs concerning the Negro's capacity for intellectual culture or his proper place in society is fit to counsel in his choice of a career.[9]

In one of the schools, a few weeks after a teacher in the author's in-service course had listened to a talk given by a Negro vocational counsellor, she reported on her own change of attitude and its effect on a Negro girl:

> Since our discussion of vocational problems of Negro youth, my attitude toward a Negro girl in one of my classes has changed. Before, I had a hopeless feeling about her because I felt she could not possibly get a job on account of her race. Now I know that she has a chance if she does good work. She has sensed my more encouraging attitude and does better work, no doubt because of it.

---

[9] *Report of Mayor's Commission on Conditions in Harlem, op. cit.*

This lack of information often is at the bottom of hopeless attitudes of teachers or vocational counsellors toward the occupational chances of their pupils of ethnic minorities. They do not know, for example, that obstacles which they find in the way of professional success on the part of such students in their own community may be absent or much less serious in other parts of the country. This was especially true of the chances of Japanese Americans when, under the War Relocation Authority, jobs were found for Nisei in various parts of the country. Or teachers may be uninformed of the opportunities in other parts of the country for professions that are overcrowded in their own community. A striking example of this is the unfilled need for physicians and nurses in many rural areas, irrespective of whether they be Jews or gentiles. Again, teachers may neglect the possibility of avocational choices on the part of students which will help them to secure status as well as other satisfactions even when they are forced to accept vocations that they do not like. This is especially true of literature and the arts. Sometimes an ambition that is liable to be quenched by the seeming impossibility of entering the desired career can be given a slightly different turn, which opens new and unexpected possibilities. This was the case, for example, when a New England teacher, in preprofessional courses in economics, stressed for her Negro students the great need of Negro woman workers for trained leadership in trade-union organization; or when a brilliant Negro student in home economics was introduced into the commercial field instead of being allowed to become discouraged by applying in vain for teaching positions. Sometimes the schools can help change a community pattern, as happened in the nation's capital. At one time Negro students there were not given training as shoe repairers. A teacher with vision gained permission to teach such a course if he could place the pupils so trained. Now not only are Negroes so trained in demand throughout the city, but also many are opening shoe repair shops of their own and thus helping to service the community.

Wounded Personalities 123

The sense of economic security can be strengthened by making students more aware of those trends in American life which emphasize common interests as against competition. In classroom discussions of social security or of the co-operative movement, for example, students are helped to see that a realistic view of their own vocational and economic prospects embraces the prospects of other groups besides their own, as well as of other classes and other regions of the country. Moreover, a resourceful teacher or vocational counsellor has many opportunities, when discussing with individual students their vocational ambitions, to give examples in which inter-group co-operation already has, in recent years, set aside inherited prejudices. This is especially true, of course, of the newer vocations less bound by traditions of discrimination, as, for example, in the vertically organized trades as against those dominated by craft unions, and in such secondary professions as bacteriology, optometry, the new plastic arts, and the like.

More damaging than the ill-informed teacher or vocational counsellor is one who permits his own prejudices to dominate his attitudes toward students of an ethnic minority. In one Pennsylvania city, some years ago, such a situation virtually led to a strike against a particular school which, although situated in a predominantly Negro neighborhood and charged with educating Negro children for a worthy part in American life, did everything, under an unimaginative and unsympathetic principal, to discourage Negro students from preparing for any but manual and servile occupations. Led by a group of purposeful community leaders, both white and Negro, the more ambitious students in that institution insisted on being transferred to other schools. The war, of course, has at least temporarily changed the scene, and everyone knows of the Fair Employment Practices Committee. Now employers are for the most part willing to hire minority-group high-school graduates. Sometimes a recalcitrant employer will give the usual before-the-war answer that his white workers will walk out if Negroes are brought in. Sometimes it has helped when the teacher in charge of placement has naively asked, "Why should they? Those same young people have worked and played together peacefully at school."

In placing minority-group young people in situations newly opened for them, great care must be taken by the school to see that suitable applicants are sent, regardless of race or creed. Care should be taken also to have the young people taking such new positions understand that the future employment possibilities of their whole group rest on their ability not only to do the job well but to get along harmoniously with their fellow workers. Sometimes minority-group workers carry a "chip on their shoulders" and see discrimination on the part of their employers when it is really not intended. If discrimination is not being practiced, and often it is not, such workers should be helped to see both how their attitude is hurting their own professional future and how their lack of emotional maturity is hurting the future of their own group.

Care should be taken, however, not to lay a depressingly heavy burden of social responsibility on members of a minority group. It is not wise to make them especially race-conscious if the situation permits of a less tense personal adjustment. The overwrought individual, conscious all the time of his responsibility to other members of his group, will be handicapped in his contacts with his fellow workers of other groups. This can be avoided if such individuals are instructed in ways of sharing that burden with others: for example, if they are Negro, in making their white fellow workers assume with them a sense of pioneering for better race relations.

Teachers in the schools that were carrying on the experiments in intercultural education were advised to help students to face reality by pointing out to them the historic causes of existing discriminations in employment as well as occupational trends in relation to minority groups. They were also advised to point out that, although there are obstacles in the way, all doors are not necessarily closed to those who have ability, ambition, and the requisite training.

Factual material secured from the National Urban League in New York City, including guides containing the latest information on job placement, were distributed to the teachers after the discussions of such problems and opportunities.[10] Some of the outstanding names used in the sketches but not often mentioned in the usual vocational guidance books were: Jokichi Takamine, the Japanese scientist who, working in the United States, gave us the valuable drug adrenalin; Dr. Joseph Goldberger, the Jewish scientist who conquered pellagra; Lu Gim Gong, the "Luther Burbank of Florida," the Chinese American who created a frost-resistant orange which will hang unchanged on the tree for a long while after it has ripened; Paul Williams, the well-known architect of California, who happens to be a Negro; and Dr. Ernest Just, the Negro American who attained great prominence as a biologist.

Finding Ways for Satisfying the Wish for New Experience

The wish for new experience is often uppermost in the minds of young persons. It expresses itself in curiosity, longing for change, novelty, and adventure. In the experiments reported here efforts were made to satisfy the wish for new experience in order to meet recreational frustrations caused by prejudice and intercultural conflict. Besides seeing to it that the assembly programs were entertaining and instructive, an attempt was made, by a wide use of humor, lively folk dances, music, and dramatic sketches, to offer various kinds of opportunities for new experiences. But most of all, the classroom discussion connected with these programs opened many new vistas of intellectual adventure.

The reader will find it easy to detect the situations offering such opportunities in Chapter III of this book. He will note

---

[10] Write also the Office of Senior Specialists in the Education of Negroes, U. S. Office of Education, Washington, D. C.

that opportunities were often made for individual students to meet leaders of various minority groups. Care was taken, however, that such leaders were not made mere curiosities or "Exhibit A's." Such activities as taking part in an interracial tea, going on trips to Chinatown or Harlem, or visiting a Greek Orthodox Church often receive adverse criticism from leaders of minority groups who consider all this a superficial satisfaction of idle curiosity. Whether such an activity is constructive or not depends upon the spirit of those who go as well as upon their educational preparation and upon the ability of those who guide the activities to see that the experiences, which are often so new that they constitute for the individual a minor crisis situation or shock, are followed by intelligent reading and also by more natural contacts. If this is not done, there is the possibility of students' rationalizing themselves back into their old attitudes.

It will be seen that such new experiences helped to hold the interest in the series of programs of those who participated in them and thus accomplished various purposes. The specific purpose of helping to overcome personality maladjustment, however, was accomplished only in so far as opportunities were provided to give new experiences to persons and groups who had had that desire frustrated on account of prejudice or for some other reason, whether in school or community. The teachers were asked to analyze as far as possible this need on the part of their students. Although it was found that some children came from homes and communities where a sufficient number of new experiences were provided, there were others who lacked such incentives. For instance, in some consolidated small-town high schools, the rural children not only lacked adequate fulfillment of the wish for new experience at home but were also left out of extracurricular activities in the school, either because of snobbishness or because of an inflexible bus schedule. In other schools, it was the minority-group children or those from homes of low economic levels who were so deprived.

Although in some Southern communities mutual understanding is fostered by interschool visitation, in other communities in the South Negro children may not enter libraries, attend the theater, or visit museums. The effect of the whole practice of discrimination against members of such groups as the Mexicans, Italians, Jews, Negroes, Orientals, at bathing beaches, amusement parks, and other recreational centers is to throw these persons upon themselves, to deny them the satisfaction of the legitimate wish for new experiences, and to increase the danger of personality maladjustment. It should be remembered here that it is not the denial as such that rankles, if all are denied the same opportunities. The denial that does rankle is not that of some experience or other; rather it is that of equality in the enjoyment of facilities.

Members of groups such as these were given special attention in the provision, through the school, of opportunities for new experience. Without seeming to single them out, those responsible for the experiments asked them to assist in arranging the special folk-art exhibits, to play the part of hosts or hostesses to outstanding visitors, to attend the teas given in the schools, and when possible to participate in the special functions and trips outside the schools.

These may seem small measures to counteract a humdrum home environment and the exclusion of individuals from ordinary expressions of their spirit of enterprise. But often they are the best the school can take to pave the way for other activities which it cannot directly sponsor. Thus, for example, the public schools of America undoubtedly deserve much of the credit for the large extension of public library services in recent years to previously neglected neighborhoods where particular ethnic groups reside. Created first to satisfy the need of English-reading members of such communities for at least an indirect contact with the world at large through the printed page, such neighborhood libraries often have become specialized in such a way as also to do justice to the cultural interests of the local residents of cultural minorities and, in some instances, have conferred a great deal of status upon them by becoming centers for the permanent display of the contributions of these local groups to letters and to civilization. There should be more co-ordination between the school and the neighborhood library. In one library center, a series of Neighborhood-Home Festivals, attended by some of the faculty and students in the school, resulted in an interesting intercultural and regional folklore treasure hunt and exhibition.

The intercultural school projects here under review often pointed to avenues for adventure that were open before but unused, especially by students or groups that had on occasion found themselves unwelcome. Thus, even in our most cosmopolitan cities, it sometimes requires a school visit before Negro children or those of foreign-language groups will by themselves climb the marble steps and pass the formidable-looking doorman. It may need a visit, with schoolmates of the favored racial group, to a public library or a museum in quest of specific information or to a restaurant in search of foreign food to induce a student of one of the minorities to believe himself welcome there.

Conversely, the student from one of the "better" homes, first introduced by a fellow student to the industrial neighborhood "on the other side of the tracks," in common search for a bit of information on an ethnic minority for use in a dramatic presentation, may afterwards find his way there again and derive considerable satisfaction from his personal observations in a colorful part of the city he had previously regarded as merely dirty and dull. Or a school visit to a social settlement or boys' club in such a neighborhood may be the occasion for new acquaintanceships that bridge the gulf of differences in background and are consciously kept alive for some time afterward.

In these initial face-to-face situations, so important because they are for many the first interracial contacts, Negro young people should be helped to realize that it is their responsibility to take the initiative in creating natural situations that bring about mutual appreciation; that instead of waiting to see how they are going to be treated by a dominant-group person in a given situation, Negroes have the opportunity to set a friendly pattern. This can best be done by remembering that all people are more alike than different. Of course to take such initiative means that one must be ready to accept objectively possible negative responses.

Finding Ways for Satisfying the Wish for Response

The wish for response, we remember, is called out by the desire for love and fellowship of all kinds, and has within it degrees of intensity that range all the way from affection for a pet to love between man and woman. It is not our intention to discuss here the satisfaction of the wish for response in general in school life, but rather to show ways in which response may be gained which compensates, to some extent, for the lack of response resulting from mutual prejudices and intercultural conflicts.

Because of differences in color and customs, it was thought by those conducting the projects in intercultural education that it was legitimate to select as guests of schools physically and mentally attractive individuals from the various culture groups.

It was pointed out to the teachers that the growth of the personality, especially in communities where there are a number of culture groups, depends to some extent on the depth and variety of fellowship *among peoples* of those groups. Teachers as well as young people were encouraged to plan social activities and to form friendships in the light of cultural differences rather than to confine themselves wholly to their own groups.

It was at this point in the discussions with teachers that the question of intermarriage between members of diverse races was inevitably brought up. Although a treatment of this topic is not directly connected with the problem of providing opportunities in schools for satisfying the wish for response, it is introduced here to clarify a subject which always comes up in this connection.[11] In one school, a history teacher refused to give any favorable facts about Negroes to her white students "because that might lead to intermarriage." The opposite of this attitude was expressed by another teacher, who reminded the group that the findings of scientists revealed no chemical differences in the blood of the black, white, and yellow races. She also quoted what she called the most tolerant statement on the matter, that of the first apostle, St. Paul, who said: "God . . . hath made of one blood all nations of man for to dwell on all the face of the earth." The answers which the large majority of teachers worked out for themselves, however, may be found to be of value to others.

Their study of psychology, biology, anthropology, and sociology forced the teachers to agree that racial intermarriage is not a biological but a socio-economic problem. In Latin-American countries there has been a merging of the races because the Catholic Church insists upon the moral and spiritual responsibility of a man for his children, and intermarriage is therefore held to be a normal procedure. In this country, however, there are numerous social reasons why, for instance, members of any two distinct racial groups would find it most difficult to make their marriages successful, and hence there is surprisingly little intermarriage. Youth must learn that crossing the barriers between ethnic or racial groups with a long separate history is not an easy thing; but it is not the teacher's business to exaggerate the difficulty by saying that such crossing, in marriage, is inevitably tragic—because there are examples to show that it is not.

The teachers, then, came to the conclusion that they would not permit the fear of a not too likely possibility to keep them

---

[11] For discussions of race mixture, see the following books: Edward B. Reuter, *Race Mixture* (New York: McGraw-Hill Book Co., 1931); John LaFarge, *The Race Question and the Negro* (New York: Longmans, Green & Co., 1944); Myrdal, *op. cit.*

from making urgent efforts to reduce prejudice among members of our various ethnic groups. They decided that it was much more important to attempt to deepen mutual understanding and to minimize tendencies toward prejudice, which, it was decided, was always at best merely hateful and at worst a hindrance to co-operative effort or full expression of the democratic principle. They did, however, feel that the school has a responsibility for the diffusion of scientific facts. Not so long ago, the reading of adventure stories of all sorts was frowned upon by parents and teachers who feared that this kind of literature might induce some youngsters to go off into the wilderness. There still are parents who would rather not have their children be given chemical laboratory teaching because it might imbue them with a dangerous desire for chemical experimenting. But throughout American pedagogy the opposite principle, generally speaking, has triumphed: the principle that knowledge and not ignorance protects the child.

Participation in a Cause Larger Than Oneself

In the roaring twenties, our American creed had been taken so much for granted that it was almost lost in the rush of acquiring two automobiles in every garage along with a "complex" in every subconscious. And then came the depression, when it was discovered that much of our religion and many of our ideals had been lost. During those years it was difficult to inspire youth to participate in a cause larger than itself. There did not seem to be any causes worth adhering to. Because of the separation of church and state inherent in our American public schools, we teachers were relieved (and felt so), of basing appeals upon any one creed. We made little or no attempt to assist young people to a compelling central conviction. We had been entrusted with personalities young and eager for growth, and too often we had failed to give them experiences which would enable them to organize their lives around a cause—a cause which, as they made their choices through the years, might become more and more meaningful and, therefore, satisfying.

The stimulation of loyalty to the school through appropriate ceremonies, and to the school team through pep meetings, are only beginnings in the direction of helping students to organize their activities around a cause larger than themselves. Quite apart from the question whether these methods are valid, we should not allow the students' loyalty to stop with school and team. To sing a thousand times, "We'll be true to P.H.S.," brings neither comfort nor challenge twenty years afterwards when one needs both.

Superficial loyalties to set or class, however, often play so destructive a part in American life that the school should be interested in fostering loyalties that will encourage students to see themselves as pioneers—not the pioneers of yesterday who reached out for new lands, new liberties, and new inventions, but pioneers of today who can reach up to find new ways of living together harmoniously. Myrdal tells us, after giving high praise to our American ideals (which, he points out, we do not attempt to live up to when it comes to the race problem), that unless we can "check the spread of moral cynicism" and keep alive our "puritan eagerness and courage in attempting to reform ourselves and the world, . . . anything can happen, even a revulsion to fascism and pagan gods." He tells us too that religion is still a potent force in American life.[12]

The question here is whether the schools, public and private, dare use this power, this desire to be part of a cause larger than oneself, to help check the growth of moral cynicism. Of course, the fostering of religion is the main responsibility of the church and the home, as the acquisition of the tools of learning is the main job of the school; but today we realize as never before the danger of fragmentizing the child's social worlds.

---

[12] Myrdal, *op. cit.*

Released time for midweek religious instruction by churches has been tried in some places. It is too early to evaluate its effectiveness, but results seem to be positive or negative according to the social vision and teaching ability of the local leaders. William Clayton Bower, in a challenging little book, *The Church and State in Education,* says that religion at the functional level of being used to give basis and motivation to democracy is unitive and that it only becomes divisive when it is considered on its secular level. He feels that after adequate preparation the public schools should assume the responsibility for the teaching of religion on a functional and nonsectarian basis. It is the belief of the writer that a more direct teaching of comparative religions rather than of creeds, and of the value to mental health of adhering to a religion which is satisfying, can be done in the public schools by teachers who would co-ordinate with the churches much as those responsible for vocational guidance now co-operate with prospective employers of high-school students. There should be no fear on the part of churches of losing their identity or of a merging into one denomination. There are too many differences in ways of thinking and feeling. There will always be the innumerable gradations from the Silence of the Quaker with only the inward voice to the beautiful ritual of the Catholic.

But until the values of a religious instead of those of a mechanistic approach to life can be demonstrated by teachers who themselves have become ex-behaviorists, little can be done, for such truth must actually be experienced in our hearts. Kunkel says it cannot be experienced without confession. At least the schools might start a new list of sins to be confessed. The following might be suggested:

Intolerance must be called an expression of *frustration* and *weakness.*

Thoughtlessness must be called *selfishness.*

Rationalization must be called *lying.*

Fooling oneself must be seen as worse than *fooling others*.
Involuntary segregation and discrimination must be seen as *dehumanizing*.

It is not within the scope of this book to suggest what kind of religious education should be attempted in the public schools. Some good examples of such education are available, but since race relations raise a moral issue, and since hymns are one means of religious education, we may ask whether the assembly period with its opportunity for group singing might not be one place where a start can be made. What songs and music do we find in most of our public school assemblies today? Are they not too often the latest swing tunes and jazz? Of course there is a place in our schools for such music, because it is a part of our American life; but it should not be used at the expense of inspirational song that will tie our loyalties to our American ideals. Religious education, of a formal sort, is not involved when the director of an assembly program chooses the most dignified and tradition-sanctioned modes of expression for the diurnal ritual of the school society as a whole. But modern psychology, through actual experiment, has found confirmation for the contention that a daily elevation of the spirit helps the individual in the performance of his tasks, and that in so far as these tasks bear on personal and group relations, the shared experience of a social rite offers the best guidance.

Hymns and anthems may also carry with them a challenging sense of responsibility to do what it takes to make our values a reality in American life and to give us a sense of historical continuity. It was felt that this was accomplished to some extent in certain schools when the assembly was asked to sing a particular song, not in a routine way, but in spontaneous response to a moving talk or dramatic episode which had just been given. The English departments were asked to use the theme songs of plays and pageants as a basis for discussion and creative writing.

Through the use of such songs, through the speeches made by inspiring leaders, and through the examples given in biographical materials, as well as through the everyday attitude of the teachers themselves, students were helped to see themselves as members of society as a whole, and to devote themselves to the cause of democracy which has as its goal "the life of the common man enriched and ennobled."[13] In some schools it was found easier to use hymns through performances of glee clubs than in the assembly.

Finding Ways of Utilizing the Everyday Classroom Situations for Individual Guidance

In the preceding pages we have described various techniques evolved in our experiments in intercultural education by means of which the frustrations of basic wishes caused by prejudice and cultural conflict were overcome or avoided. These ways of meeting fundamental needs of young people in the schools where our program was carried on were found to be helpful in aiding the victims of race or culture prejudice to overcome its emotional effects on them and to arrive at better adjustments in home, school, and community.

It is important at this point to indicate the opportunities offered by everyday classroom situations to continue intercultural education and to guide young people toward better intercultural adjustment. This individual guidance must take full account of the frustration of the four basic wishes. The following two illustrations of a fifth grade teacher are examples of what may happen to personalities when the teacher is alert enough to seize upon an opportunity for individual guidance. The first shows the change in a boy's personality when his desire for recognition finds some satisfaction.

---

[13] See James Truslow Adams, *The Epic of America* (New York: Little, Brown & Co., 1931), pp. 174, 415-7, for the application of this ideal to the whole of American life.

An eleven-year-old boy with a low IQ was troublesome and indolent. He apparently accepted the verdict of his teachers that he was hopelessly dull. A class activity which began in his fifth-grade year stimulated a latent interest in his cultural background. His mother had come from Russia, and he was able to bring to school several Russian toys, some old Russian paper money, and a blouse embroidered by his mother. He became greatly interested in a study of Russia and was willing to give a talk in assembly on the subject. He wore his Russian blouse as he talked eloquently, if ungrammatically, about the land of his mother's birth. While he did not become a scholar through this experience, he did develop a more responsive and pleasing personality. He made fair progress and ceased to be a "discipline case."

The following case shows similar desirable results when recognition is given the child's culture group.

Louis was not a noticeably maladjusted child. There was no evidence of any persecution on the part of his classmates because he was Jewish, but on one occasion, when he and several companions chose a particular subject for study, the other children in the class laughed scornfully and called them Jews. The teacher seized upon this opportunity to introduce some of the aspects of Jewish culture to the children. Louis, she discovered, was studying Hebrew with the rabbi. He was invited to write the alphabet on the board. The teacher and the boy together explained the symbolism of the Passover feast—the unleavened bread, the bitter herbs, the lamb bone. The gathering prejudice of the other children was dispelled by their interest in the new knowledge. Louis became more of a personality from that time on, and the opportunity to make a distinctive contribution seemed to stimulate all his work. By the end of the term he had shown such improvement over his former moderately good record that he was promoted with favorable comments from his teachers.

Remembering the frustrating experiences which members of minority groups often go through in American life, teachers who grasp these opportunities for individual guidance are careful to see that a student who has come to consider his racial or national background a handicap does not use this as an excuse for inadequacies which may be due to other causes. He is helped to take an objective view of all his personality assets and liabilities, as far as possible, in terms of the social worlds he is facing. Through the use of factual material in literature, science, art, and other subjects, his classroom teachers give him an opportunity to become acquainted with the biographies of great men and women in his own and other culture groups who have overcome real or imagined defects.

The teachers in the schools in which the intercultural experiments were carried on were urged to hold constantly in mind that children of minority groups are basically like all children in their desire for wish satisfaction, but that the students in the minority group may be confronted with prejudice against them in addition to the difficulties of adjustment which all modern youth faces. The difficulties which these students meet are increased in proportion to the amount of prejudice that confronts them. The Negro youth faces discrimination in school, in his occupational life, and in every casual contact in the community. A Negro or a Jewish student who is well-adjusted in his classroom may have the upsetting experience of a sudden change in attitude on the part of a teacher or fellow student. Some factor in the teacher's own experience outside the school may result in a change of attitude. Mere advance in age may break up, through outside influences, friendships that have been constant through the early teens. Or there may be a change in school personnel, and the student may find, instead of his former sympathetic friend, a new teacher who "knows how to keep such a person in his place."

Instead of pointing out their faults to the students, the resourceful teacher analyzes the fears or resentments that come from such situations. She explains in simple language to individual students how fears develop and how they affect the personality. She attempts to show these students that they are like everyone else in having fears of this kind. She points out to them, also, if she truthfully can, that they have enough of some sort of ability to gain recognition and, therefore, do not have to assume attitudes of superiority or become bullies or lie or steal to maintain their self-respect. The best plan, such a teacher makes clear, is not to run away from the situation but to face it and work out a satisfying adjustment.

The simplest treatment, it was found, is to help the student to discover something interesting that he can do, with which he can gain recognition in his own social worlds. If a student displays a persistently rebellious spirit, he is helped to understand why he is rebellious. He is not urged to accept conditions passively. Rather he is encouraged to organize his personality in a constructive way by finding a lifework in line with his ideal to which he may devote himself. Rebellion may be a good sign of a child's initiative and ability to recognize difficulties and do something about solving them. But often a rebellious student, when not able to see quick steps being taken by society toward his goal, becomes bitter and disillusioned. He may then give up all his idealism. In intercultural relations the function of the wise counsellor to help the courageous and somewhat revolutionary student to plan a career is all-important. Such a student, even of high-school age, might very well be asked to function on adult committees in the community. Thus, young and old alike will be co-operating on the educational offensive needed to combat intolerance and to build a better world.

7

THE ROLE OF THE SCHOOL AND THE TEACHERS' OWN ATTITUDES

> Cross-fertilization is as essential as transportation. Bees from other trees, from remote trees, buzz around yours, and the pollen of a different origin and a different habit gets transferred to the stigma—the sticky, open-armed, attentive, eager stigma. New ideas get carried to fresh minds; inbreeding from your ideas is avoided, and you have a new thing and perhaps a very beautiful thing, at any rate a vital thing, growing on your tree.[1]

WISE GUIDANCE for youth demands wise counsellors. Recognizing that most teachers have not themselves been prepared for the most adequate guidance of youth in relation to interracial and intercultural problems, we ask ourselves what the responsibility of the school is in relation to this need and what can be done to aid teachers to prepare themselves.

The responsibility of the school, as this writer sees it, can be divided into its concern for the prejudiced teacher or the merely uninformed teacher and the responsibility of the administrator for these teachers; the need for teachers of all groups to work together in intercultural education; the need for teacher training; the supplying of adequate teaching materials; and the providing for personal contacts between administrators, teachers, and leaders of various cultural groups.

The Problem of the Uninformed and Prejudiced Teacher

From close contact with hundreds of teachers in different parts of the country, the writer would say that most of them, though open-minded on the subject, lack knowledge of the cul-

---

[1] Edward Yeomans, *Shackled Youth* (Boston: Atlantic Monthly Press, 1921), p. 131.

tural contributions of our various groups, of scientific findings concerning racial differences, or of the many subtle aspects of the problem of inter-group relations. Of course, some are indifferent and a few are definitely prejudiced, reflecting the tensions in the community. We should be reminded that communities that cannot or will not pay adequate salaries are more likely to have teachers who have been inadequately prepared and especially those who have not been able to broaden their outlook in intercultural education by courses, trips, or intercultural contacts.

Many teachers throughout the country, however, are sensitive and alert to the need for combating prejudice by the positive approach of intercultural education. Some of these are sacrificing their own time, energy, and money in study of the problem, in securing necessary teaching materials, in sharing their ideas and experiences with other teachers in out-of-school conferences, in taking in-service courses or attending summer workshops, or in writing up their activities for publication.

These teachers should be discovered (some cities have released one or more of them for guiding other teachers)[2] and their experiences and abilities made available for those teachers who may have goodwill but who may be tactless or, through lack of experience, ignorant of the subtleties underlying the relationships between our various groups in American life. Two examples taken from our *Field Notebook* show this lack of tact and knowledge:

> A third-generation girl of Chinese origin told of an experience that she had when in the fourth grade. When her class was studying China, the teacher brought her to the front of the room, pointed out the differences in skin, hair, eyes, and asked, "What part of China did you come from?"
>
> In a senior high-school class of girls in hygiene, with a small percentage of Negro students, the teacher started a discussion with these words: "Many of you know that you do not like to share a locker in

---

[2] Santa Barbara, California, has for several years had a teacher released as co-ordinator of community cultural contacts.

the gym with the colored girls and that you do not like very much their going into the pool." Then she wondered why "none of the colored girls got up and spoke."

The creative teacher is continually successfully handling in her classes discussions involving prejudice, and if given the opportunity could help other less imaginative or less experienced teachers in informal discussions, in-service courses, or school visits. But the release of teachers for such purposes depends upon whether or not the administrator is concerned; and too often the administrator himself has not had enough intercultural experiences to see clearly the problems presented by the presence of children of minority groups in his school. Indeed, his first reaction often is to suppress the subject entirely. One principal thought that nothing should be done in his school in regard to intercultural education, yet he sent special notes and a questionnaire to Jewish and Catholic children who were to be absent because of religious holidays. He knew that Catholic children could return to school immediately after their religious ceremony in the church, but considered the Jewish children uncooperative because they did not do likewise. Evidently he did not know that a Jewish Holy Day lasts from sundown one day until sundown the next.

"This is a public school and we want to ignore backgrounds," said one administrator. But all the while backgrounds are being recognized in negative ways. One administrator showed this when he said, "More than doing anything about cultural backgrounds do we need to do something to counteract the influence of bad movies. Just today three boys were sent to me for having broken some windows, and I said to them, 'Why! your names are all Irish and I see no Irish names on our football team. You ought to be there instead of breaking windows.' " When discipline cases came to him, it was easy to remember backgrounds.

Those who determine the policy of the schools affect the attitudes held therein, and hence it is that the administrator is responsible for the few but extremely prejudiced teachers. The prejudice of these teachers may be too deep for complete eradication short of an emotional catharsis, which can only come about through "depth therapy" or a religious conversion. The following incidents will suffice to make us realize that the teachers responsible are as dangerous in one way as typhoid carriers are in another.

> A teacher in a certain high school asked how many of her home-room group were going to be absent for a Jewish holiday. When a number of students put up their hands she said, "When are you people going to become assimilated?"
>
> "Why do so many of you colored girls come to this school? I should think you'd be happier in . . . school [*naming a school attended almost exclusively by colored*]."
>
> A teacher in a Northern mixed high school was overheard remarking to a fellow teacher as a few Negro students passed them in the hall, "In the South we keep such people where they belong, in the kitchen!"
>
> A New England teacher of "Mayflower" background could see no connection between Tony Bonelli in her class and Italian music and painting; but she did see a close tie-up between all youngsters of Italian background and Al Capone and Mussolini.

It is at least a tentative hypothesis that those who are the most frustrated, for whatever reason, in their own lives are those who are likely to be the most prejudiced; and so it is with teachers.[3] We found some teachers so absorbed in their own interests that they did not give the children a feeling of being accepted. Often the least capable and sometimes the most bigoted teachers were sent to schools in the part of town where most minority-group children were found. Often teachers were unable to take advantage of the situations around them—such as experiences which their pupils participated in during the assembly or the tea in honor of the guests—or to adapt their own plans to the pupils' needs. At one school Dr. Meng was the Chinese visitor. After his assembly talk he was interviewed by a bright ninth-grade boy who had gleaned in his history class that the "backwardness of the Chinese nation has been due to

---

[3] John Dollard, *Frustration and Aggression* (New Haven: Yale University Press, 1939).

its queer pattern of ancestor worship." The guest answered the question in a way which made the boy see similarities instead of differences by reminding the boy that Americans put flowers on the graves of their ancestors whereas the Chinese put food instead. The boy reported the interview in his history class and his teacher was overheard saying later, "It took me forty minutes to get that class back to where it was in Chinese ancestor worship."

Extremely prejudiced teachers should be properly dealt with by the school authorities. This, of course, is easier said than done. Some school systems have made it clear that teachers proved to be prejudiced will be discharged; but proving is difficult, unless the case is an extremely flagrant one. Some systems penalize such teachers for their inadequacies as teachers of youth. Before teachers are allowed to have a hand in the personality development of growing children, their attitudes toward various culture groups should be discovered. Objective attitude tests for such purposes are available, but two or three well-directed questions in the initial interview should be sufficient.

Of course the administrator has a much more positive role to play than disciplining the prejudiced teacher, and many administrators are doing an admirable job. Marian Edman of the Detroit School System has stated this role of the administrator well: "The supervisor needs to orientate herself regarding the importance, the objectives, the scope, and the techniques applicable to the teaching of intercultural education at the various grade levels."[4]

Changing One's Own Attitude

The burden of this book so far has been a discussion of best ways of arranging experiences for others so that attitudes of prejudice may be changed into attitudes of friendliness and

---

[4] Marion Edman, *Americans All—Studies in Intercultural Education* (Washington, D. C.: Department of Supervisors of the National Education Association, 1941), chap. xxiv.

understanding. But can we teachers change our own attitudes? We can if we are open-minded. We have first to admit our need. In the realm of attitudes this is difficult to admit, for our egos always rise up in self-defense—no one wants to admit prejudice. But all of us have been conditioned in early childhood in some way and to some extent. Our egos need not tremble at this knowledge, for it was at such an early age that we cannot be held responsible. We can, however, be held responsible if we, as teachers of youth, have come to this moment and still refuse to put ourselves into broadening experiences. Our knowledge of psychology forces us also to admit, if we are now or have been frustrated (at least in a way that threatens our ego satisfaction), that that frustrated psychic energy may be now finding relief in blaming our own woes on whole groups, races, or religions. Here as individuals we need help to see ourselves as others see us. Barring the extremely prejudiced teacher (and she would not have reached this page), we can ask ourselves and frankly answer the following questions:

> When you are walking through a part of town largely occupied by a group whose culture is strange to you, Negroes or Italians, Jews, or Mexicans or Orientals, do you go tense across the middle?
>
> Is it impossible for you to eat without discomfort in a restaurant largely patronized by Negroes?
>
> If you are riding in a crowded conveyance and a person of obvious membership in a derogated group sits next to you, do you tend to draw into yourself, to try to make yourself as small as possible physically?
>
> Do you do the same thing if an individual not so obviously marked sits next to you?
>
> If you are jostled in a crowd by someone recognizably Jewish or Negro or Italian, do you react with just a little more rancor than if a similar act involved one of "your" group?
>
> In your contacts with all people not of your immediate culture or religious creed, do you feel somewhat ill at ease, a little stiff, insecure, walled off?
>
> Do you still laugh at so-called jokes that make a butt of Negroes or Jews or Italians or Chinese?
>
> Do stories in dialect strike you as very funny?[5]

---

[5] *Pi Lambda Theta Journal*, March, 1944, pp. 84-5.

Honesty then will make us admit our need, if we do no more than recognize that, prejudiced or not, we need to extend our circle of fellowship. Our experiences in the past, our concern for others, have been confined mainly to those of our group: our own club, church, professional or social clique. We are to that extent group-centered—the sociologists call it ethnocentric. What broadening experiences can we give ourselves so that we shall feel at home with any group—so that our liberated personalities will the better guide and inspire the children under our care to build a better world?

Let us imagine a self-centered person with few friends—a person callous to other people's needs, lonely and full of distrust for others, full of anxiety for himself because he has so few contacts. Suddenly he begins to build a friendship. Perhaps he falls in love or undergoes a conversion. What happens? He changes from thinking only of himself to thinking of the needs of the other person. He spends time with his new friend. He sees life through his eyes. Then he feels less anxious about himself because (though he may not know why) he has now experienced what Kunkel calls the "we-group feeling."[6] His own creativity is released and he really is a new person.

Let us now try to put this process into terms that will help us to help ourselves identify emotionally with members of different cultural, racial, and religious groups. We can arrange experiences for ourselves under the three headings which described the kinds of experiences we arranged for students—the emotional, the intellectual, and the situational. Take it gradually if you wish, for this is a matter of growth. Here is a list that has guided the growth of many individuals:

1. Read biographies and autobiographies of heroes and heroines in the groups toward which you feel your attitudes need changing—stories involving people of great courage, those

---

[6] Fritz Kunkel and Roy Dickerson, *How Character Develops* (New York: Charles Scribner's Sons, 1940).

who in all humility have found the strength to sacrifice themselves for others.

2. Read the mythology and folklore and experience the art of the out-group, in order to experience how similar to your own are their group images.

3. Read sympathetically written novels, poems, plays, about and by members of various groups.

4. Read the best magazines, newspapers, and periodicals of those groups.

5. Read books and articles which in a general way depict the cultural contributions of those groups to our common American life.

Participate in social situations similar to the following:

1. Attend church or other culture group meetings or ceremonies—a Jewish Seder, a Catholic Mass, a Quaker Meeting, a Buddhist Temple.

2. Visit nationality centers; learn some folk songs and dances.

3. Attend a regional or national convention of a group.

4. Join the local branch (if this is possible) of some group's national organization and volunteer to work on a committee for social betterment.

5. Evince a friendly curiosity in the religious backgrounds and home customs of the children in your class. You will learn much.

6. Attend and help to arrange inter-group contacts through Home Festivals, teas, forum discussions, and the like.

7. Build inter-group friendships, visiting back and forth in homes.

8. Form an intercultural committee in your club or church. Join with others who are motivated by the same desire to square their everyday actions with their American ideals.

While finding that group in your own community, correspond with those who can help.[7]

But no list is of any value unless the seeker starts the adventure in all honesty and sincerity. Even then the novice is as bound to make mistakes in something said or left unsaid, in a mere gesture, as is one who first starts to play the piano. Here our minority-group friends need to blend patience with frankness. If they are sure of the sincerity of the seeker, they should tell him when and why he has erred. The seeker should not be shocked into inactivity if an oversensitive member of a minority group snubs his first attempt at building inter-group friendships. These minority-group people are human too and have their own frustrations to deal with. Forgive them and try again.

But no outside help can fight our own inner battles. Do not be afraid of what "they say," for that is the voice of our egos resisting any change. Sit down and have a good talk with your ego. "What do you and I want most out of life? To be popular and comfortable with a higher and higher salary?" Can we honestly ask that we be singled out for such exceptional treatment? Knowing the world as we know it now, do we really want that? When there is blood in the streets from race riots led by Jew-baiting and Negro-baiting youth whom we have taught in our own schools, is there not also blood on our own hands? Have we not now found our own battle front within our own souls? Is this not the place where the problem of race, culture, and religious conflict is to be lost or won? Once we recognize this in a spirit of humility, then our better selves will come to our rescue and we shall find that "our most genuine interest is the welfare of our fellow men rather than our individual wel-

---

[7] Subscribe to *Common Ground*. The editor offers a service whereby readers and like-minded people in the same community may be put in touch with one another.

fare."[8] Then our own battle and the battle of mankind is won, for we have "reached a higher level of consciousness, the person being individually conscious and responsible for the whole group to which he belongs."[9] This whole group includes the white, Negro, and Oriental, the Jew, Catholic, Mohammedan, Buddhist, and all others. We are conscious now of a new feeling of belongingness. We now feel ourselves belonging to a larger, stronger, more worth-while "set"—a real community of which we may be proud to be members. And with that feeling, we become relaxed in a feeling of security of a higher sort, because now we know we are not our constricted little selves but a part of the Whole Self. With that feeling of release comes greater creativity; we are now more interesting to ourselves and to others. We are new persons. We are better teachers.

The Importance of Having Teachers of All Culture Groups Work Harmoniously Together

Perhaps the quickest and surest way to give the teacher in service an understanding of any particular cultural or racial group is to adopt the policy of the mixed faculty. Racially mixed faculties have been successful for many years in such cities as New York, Cleveland, Chicago, and Los Angeles. Springfield, Massachusetts, is taking advantage of the increased interest in a fairer attitude toward minority groups and is employing a few well-trained Negroes and members of other racial groups. The relocation of the Japanese Americans has resulted in the placing of some of them as language teachers in several colleges and universities in different parts of the country.

Results prove on the whole that such experiences of working together on the job, whether in factories or on faculties, tend to develop confidence and trust. There is too often a tendency even on the part of minority-group leaders to overlook the value

---

[8] Kunkel, *In Search of Maturity, op. cit.,* p. 216.
[9] *Ibid.,* p. 285.

of this working together. Thus we find that in the Negro colleges and schools in the South, which have been under various church boards, there is now a tendency toward an all-Negro faculty. It should be remembered that our common American culture cannot develop through a system of more and more isolated cultural islands. Keeping the ideal of the interculturally mixed faculty before us has its value. Sometimes the mores of a given community are too much against it; sometimes gradual steps forward can be taken. The fact that a Northern community may contain no Negro citizen may be a good reason why a few well-trained Negroes should be given positions on the faculties of its schools. George School, a Friends' private school in Pennsylvania, has taken a first step by each year having a visiting Negro spend a few weeks with the faculty and students while he teaches a particular unit. It must be kept in mind, however, that there is a danger involved in first-step gestures of this sort. The sense of difference between Negroes and whites may be heightened rather than lessened by giving Negro teachers a conspicuously distinct status on the faculty. This is outweighed by giving the students the chance to meet an educated Negro; but the limitation to their learning is firmly established along with the learning.

During the carrying out of our projects in the New York City schools, teachers of various groups planned and worked successfully together; but in the New Jersey school across the river, the mores of the community upheld the practice of having teachers only from the dominant group. The New Jersey schools were willing to invite able leaders of minority groups for particular needs, however, such as lectures and discussions on the backgrounds and history of these groups, and a series of enjoyable folk-song sessions. This was a practical step in the right direction. It suggested the possibility of co-operation among several schools in a vicinity to secure the services of such talent more continuously for a definite period.

The racially mixed faculty plan, if carefully worked out, would, we feel, help to solve many of the problems of the administrator, since there would result from it a feeling of trust toward the dominant-group leaders on the part of the minority-group children and their parents. Of course, the representatives of different racial or nationality groups on such a faculty should always be carefully selected on the basis of personality and training.

Not only the right attitude but also a certain skill in the management of intercultural relations is needed on the part of the administrator in a school with a mixed faculty. Recently, for the first time, two Negro teachers were added to the faculty of a high school, the student body of which is 70 per cent Negro. The selection of these two personalities was fortunate; the attitude of the principal was sympathetic; but one sensed a certain lack of skill on his part in handling situations. This lack seemed to be attributable to the fact that neither he nor the Negro teachers had had enough inter-group experience to know how members of the other group would be likely to feel in certain social situations. Experience is the best teacher in the handling of such situations; and many of our inter-group problems will solve themselves when it becomes the normal and expected thing to see teachers of all our culture groups working harmoniously together.

Courses in Intercultural Education

Should special courses in intercultural education, both in-service and in-training, be offered to teachers? The answer would seem to be in the affirmative, at least until the regularly established courses in American history, literature, art, science, psychology, and sociology in our colleges and teacher-training institutions include sufficient information and training in that area. Some school systems are already offering in-service courses in intercultural education.

However, in our eagerness to get started, we sometimes arrange for the type of lecture courses for teachers in which each week a different outstanding speaker gives his views on the subject. Such lectures should be considered as first steps to introduce the teachers to the subject and to some of the personalities in the community who are interested in the problem; but they should not take the place of, or at least they should be followed by, lecture-discussions and inter-group social experiences planned to meet more specifically the teachers' needs.

Sometimes a lecturer may be outstanding in his particular field but yet so unfamiliar with inter-group relations that he may say or leave unsaid something that will alienate some of the minority-group people who hear him. Race relations in our country is a complex subject and has many subtleties which one begins to understand only after years of experience, so that at least a sincere attitude of humility should be required of any speaker. A patronizing air can so easily slip into a phrase or into the bearing of a white leader. For instance, he may use when speaking to a colored teacher some such stilted term as "your people." Perhaps the teacher's resentment is evidence of the chip-on-the-shoulder attitude common to most minority-group people; but this is a part of the picture which those who profess to be leaders in intercultural education must understand.

What, then, should be included in courses in intercultural education? First it seems necessary that all teachers, regardless of what subject or grade they teach, should have some command of the facts regarding the cultural heterogeneity of this country and the important contributions that have been and are being made by people of varied backgrounds to our country's life and growth.

Teachers need also to be encouraged to think through the history of immigration and Americanization in relation to the cultural life of the country, in order to work out their own philosophy and thus be able more adequately to plan their classroom activities. In our courses we include a series of lecture-discussions on cultural democracy, comparing it with past theories of Americanization; this is followed by an overview of the latest findings of anthropology in regard to race differences and of the technique of organized propaganda which is aimed at instilling hatred.[10]

During the courses the teachers plan their own classroom activities and school projects in intercultural education. This requires that some attention be given to the principles of social psychology in relation to the formation of attitudes. Projects which have been conducted in other schools are reported on and analyzed as to their application of such principles. Mimeographed factual materials on the different culture groups, lists of classroom aids, book lists for various age levels, films, recordings, pamphlets, magazines, and newspapers are furnished or presented to the teachers. Every school system, if not every school community, should start its own intercultural workshop by collecting such materials now being prepared by various organizations so that the teacher can use them from day to day to help her to counteract the many untruths which can still be found in most textbooks about the Negro, the Jew, the Oriental, and the recent immigrant.

Another important area examined in our courses is that of mental hygiene as it is related to the problems of personality needs of minority-group children. Usually we bring to the class leaders of such groups to discuss the problems. What peculiar demands, if any, are made upon the child in his home and community group life? Why, for instance, do some parents, as Jewish, Oriental, Armenian, want their children to learn the language of their ancestors, and why do they feel that this adds

---

[10] These courses were offered in Boston University; Temple University; the University of Northern California; Teachers College, Columbia University; Newark and Paterson, New Jersey, state teachers colleges; and for several years at New York University.

to rather than detracts from their development into good American citizens? These visitors are asked to tell us something of the home and community ceremonies and festivals of the groups from which they come. What problems of adjustment do children in each group have to face because of discrimination, and what traditional ways of reacting to that discrimination have been employed by the various groups? How similar are those reactions? How different?

The possession of such intimate knowledge of home backgrounds is of inestimable value to the teacher; but for the most part it cannot be found in books. A few studies have been made on the relation of color to personality development within the Negro group.[11] But even these studies mean much more to the teacher if they can be interpreted by a Negro who has attained an objective attitude toward the problem.

The teachers taking the courses are encouraged to visit in the homes of their pupils and occasionally to attend churches, synagogues, or other kinds of meetings in which the parents regularly engage. Some have found, after such visitation, that difficult problem children suddenly become co-operative. This happened in one case when a Jewish boy saw his gentile teacher attending his synagogue at a Channukah Festival.

Of course, all this takes time and energy; and while there is no substitute for home visitations, we have found our P.T.A. Neighborhood-Home Festivals,[12] attended by both parents and teachers, a quick and interesting way for the teachers to get better acquainted with home backgrounds. Sometimes teachers have said, "I wish my whole class had been here to learn about these customs and to see the lighting of the candles by the Jewish refugee while she sang 'Rock of Ages' in Hebrew."

As for Negro homes—they are like those of the white people on the same economic level. But most white teachers have never

---

[11] See Appendix for list in the series published under the American Council on Education.

[12] See chap. viii.

been in the homes of Negroes of their own cultural level. It
has been our privilege, while giving these courses for teachers
in different parts of the country, to arrange for meetings in the
homes of both white and Negro leaders so that mixed groups
of teachers could come to know one another better. Some people
feel that interracial teas are unnatural and therefore ineffective.
Any new experience has in it an element of unnaturalness. It
depends on the sincerity of the people involved as to whether.
they will pursue their initial experience until it becomes natural. Here again the group conversation method developed in
our Neighborhood-Home Festivals has been found to be of inestimable value in helping people quickly to get over the feeling
of unnaturalness. One teacher said, "Usually at teas one gets
to talk with only one or two people, but tonight I feel that I
have learned to know at least fifteen people."

It is the opinion of the writer that nothing will take the place
of thinking, feeling, and acting on a basis of co-operative effort
with individual members of the groups one is attempting to
understand. To follow such a path takes not only time and
energy, but also absolute sincerity and sometimes courage. Such
co-operative effort with people of various cultural backgrounds
is possible in most communities because of our country's heterogeneous composition. But usually one finds teachers and culture
group leaders moving in lines which never, or rarely, meet.
We have, therefore, found it necessary to help the teachers to
start these inter-group contacts by arranging social experiences
as a part of the courses. Later they make their own contacts.
From several attitudinal histories written as a result of such
experiences we select a typical one:

> Growing up with no special prejudice against the Negro, neverthe-
> less I shared with the majority of the white race a smug, unquestioning
> sense of benevolent superiority. One should be kind to them, of course,
> in the manner of Lady Bountiful. Vaguely I knew that there were
> Negroes who were educated in the arts and sciences, but I suppose
> it all seemed a little like child's play—imitating the white people—
> they were so amusing that way. Possibly they were capable of develop-

ment if there was a bit of white blood in them. All in all, I wished them well and even resented things that were said against them by my friends. One young teacher of my acquaintance walked out of a Chautauqua tent because Negro singers were about to appear on the platform. "When they stick to spirituals they're all right, if you like—that sort of thing," she explained, "but the absurdity of trying to sing operatic arias! I know for a fact that their vocal cords are by nature unfitted for anything of the sort. My voice teacher said that had been proved!"

In our town there were two families of Negroes who were our neighbors. They were people of taste, their homes were well kept. However, one had only to ride through the slums of Philadelphia to see how Negroes "really" lived. It never occurred to me to examine this great guilt of my country, and of the white race in this matter. In common with those of most white people, my sensibilities were not shocked by the cruelties, the injustices visited upon these people for three centuries. Frequently one hears, "Of course slavery was wrong, but they are free now; and look at the problem we have!" Common sense made one aware of an absurdity, however, in the objections of white people to Negroes. Here is a public-school teacher who says contemptuously, "You should see the fine clothes and the manners of those colored people who board the No. 6 car on X Street! Tsst! Tsst! Tsst! And the nice neighborhood they live in!" But somewhat later she will make horrified comments upon the degraded living conditions among Negroes in certain other sections of the city. To aspire to have ambitions is to be "uppity." To be indifferent or resigned to a low standard proves the "cultural laziness of the race."

In a school which I attended in Boston, a committee of girls went to the Dean to protest against the indignity of being obliged to sit in the same classroom with several Negro girl students. The Dean could do nothing about it and the white girls had to share Goethe and Shakespeare with the Negro girls!

Throughout these years my attitude had been shaped by a sense of fairness. I did not like to see people treated unkindly. I had not had positive experience until I became a member of this class. I had not met in social situations Negroes of my own cultural level. One day, at a tea in the home of a friend, I met a girl who possessed beauty, personal charm, education, and a family pride equal to that felt by any white girl. But, of course, I could see that she had white blood! That accounted for her attitude and gifts. A Negro man born and educated abroad was later a guest at this home. He, too, was obviously partly white. And so my pet theory found support—that white blood works all the marvels.

I was to have this ideal destroyed, however, not only by hearing a noted anthropologist declare that there is no ground for this belief, but also by meeting in New York Negroes from Africa and from America whose strain is pure, who are proud of their color and who have achieved magnificently in many fields of endeavor. I have enjoyed the hospitality of a Negro artist and his wife in their attractive home. I have been a guest at a Sunday evening musical in a colored musician's home. I have talked with Negro writers, physicians, teachers, business people, and I blush to think how blind we white people have been.

We do not, of course, limit such experiences to contacts with the Negro; each teacher needs to understand several American groups, the members of which are too often confined mainly to their own social worlds.

This need for widening our circles of fellowship leads us to the realization of the need for better school-community co-ordination, which can only be mentioned here. To find ways for the home, church, school, and other community groups to co-operate so that all the child's social worlds will be pulling in the same direction is especially urgent when one is working on the problem of intercultural relations. Those who have studied the 1943 Harlem and Detroit riots have said that rioting seemed to take place mainly because Neogroes and whites had not had experiences of working and living together in community life.[13]

In the last analysis, the success of any plans for intercultural education depends upon our ultimate values. In our more discerning moments, we sense the truth that humanity is basically one in its fundamental needs and activities, and that the reason we are constantly striving to put ourselves in the place of others is that harmony with others satisfies one of our basic human wishes. To co-operate on such a basis of mutual acceptance with persons who have come from various backgrounds is to develop and to complete ourselves. It was Emerson who quoted an elderly Quaker as saying, "It is the not-me in thee which makes thee valuable to me."

---

[13] A. M. Lee and N. D. Humphrey, *Race Riot* (New York: Dryden Press, 1943).

8

INTERCULTURAL EDUCATION ON A
COMMUNITY BASIS

The wider and more numerous contacts of the present day
need not destroy community traditions, but may make possible
the conscious creation of greater traditions. The community
can be a reservoir for the preservation and transmission of basic
culture on a higher level than at any time in the past.[1]

Some First Steps

I T IS well known that schools cannot be successful in changing
and developing the attitudes of young people unless they
work with regard for the attitudes of the parents and others in
the community. Such co-operation is necessary for ordinary educational objectives, for instance the establishment of good health
habits. In the realm of social attitudes it is equally necessary to
co-ordinate all of the child's social worlds. Conflicts of all sorts
may and do arise between the school and the home when those
institutions are not pulling in the same direction on matters that
deeply involve the emotions. This is especially true in the realm
of race and culture conflict.

It is not our aim, however, to report on such disharmony, nor
is it within the scope of this book to present a complete picture
of what is being or could be done in an all-school-community
project in intercultural education. That is a study in itself. Although we have participated in many intercultural activities in
schools, clubs, churches, and community centers, and have with
others made extensive and intensive plans on an all-school-

---

[1] Arthur E. Morgan, *The Small Community—Foundation of Democratic Life* (New York: Harper & Bros., 1942), p. 113.

community basis in intercultural relations, we have not as yet
been part of an attempt to carry through such comprehensive
community planning.

We present here only those plans in the formulation and execution of which we have had a part. As community groups
throughout the country, mobilized into action because of riots
between races and motivated by a sincere desire to build a postwar world based on co-operation, begin to weave intercultural
activities into their group and community life, they may find
these plans of value. If an all-community project seems too big
an undertaking for a given community, then at least the various
organizations should attempt to synchronize what they plan to
do, for too long our community life has been fragmentized. We
offer these plans for what they are worth to planners, and not
with the idea that they constitute a blueprint. The needs of each
community should determine the nature of the intercultural
education project developed in it.

The Role of Teacher-Training Institutions

For the blind to lead the blind is dangerous only for those involved; but for the ignorant to lead the ignorant in the realm of
race and culture conflict is to invite national disaster. Leadership
training, then, becomes a paramount problem. An observing
teacher, one who, after years of leadership and much study in
the field of intercultural relations, returned to the classroom,
writes of this need as it was exhibited in his own school: "We
have had two speakers at faculty meetings this year who dealt
with the problem of intercultural education. In each case discussion on the part of the faculty was cut short. The speakers
were all right, but they showed little background of knowledge
of the subject. The only practical suggestion was that the social
studies classes that meet the last period in the day devote one
afternoon a week as an intercultural club. No preparation for
teachers—just things thrown at them. From my observation, each

of the social studies staff needs a series of experiences to get him ready for such an undertaking."

The following activities, which were carried on by those responsible for teacher training in certain cities, are suggestive of what might be done in almost any town or city:

A. A Series of Lectures for Teachers and Community Leaders[2]

The Making of American Culture

I. *America, the Inheritor of Culture:*
   1. The origin and nature of folk culture.
   2. Folk culture which has come to America.
   3. Life enriched by sharing cultural values: The future.

II. *Rich Strands in the Fabric of American Living:*
   1. Our heritage in music.
   2. Our heritage in the dance.
   3. Our heritage in the drama.
   4. Cultural heritage opens the door of science.
   5. Our heritage in art.
   6. Group action in solving our common economic problems.

III. *Threats against a Community of Cultures in America:*
   1. Is there such a thing as race?
   2. Race prejudice and its implications.
   3. Economic and other influences which stultify cultural expression in America today.
   4. The social pyschologist looks ahead.

The Sources of American Culture[3]

1. Cultural treasure from China.
2. Japanese gifts to American culture.
3. Cultural riches from India.

---

[2] Adapted from San Francisco State Teachers College's series of lectures in 1936, Mary L. Kleinecke, chairman, Faculty Committee. The lecturers in this series were members of the faculty.

[3] The lecturers in this second-semester series were distinguished representatives of cosmopolitan San Francisco's community of peoples.

4. The heritage of America from Mexico.
5. England, Scotland, and Wales: Their contributions to America's cultural inheritance.
6. French and Belgian influences in American culture.
7. Irish culture in American living.
8. Latin American contributions.
9. Italian inspiration in American culture.
10. Spanish influence in American culture.
11. Cultural contributions of the American Jew.
12. Germany's gifts to American life.
13. Russian heritages in American culture.
14. Cultural contributions of the American Indian.
15. The American Negro and his cultural contributions.

B. Institutes and Panel Discussions

A series of American Unity Institutes for school administrators, teachers, and community leaders was given in April, 1942, by the Newark State Teachers College (Tuesdays—April 14, 21, 28, May 5), and the Paterson State Teachers College (Thursdays—April 16, 23, 30, May 7). They were sponsored by the State of New Jersey Department of Public Instruction, the State of New Jersey Goodwill Commission, and the Intercultural Education Workshop in New York City.

First Session
Subject: National morale and culture group problems:
  I. The foundation of American democratic unity.
  II. Civilian morale and ethnic-group relationships:
      a. Problems of adjustment of children of Jewish background.
      b. Color and personality—a report on the studies brought out by the American Council on Education.
  III. Behavior problems arising from war tensions:
      a. Employment discriminations and morale.
      b. Giving recognition to minority-group children.
      c. The role of the classroom teacher.

Second Session
Subject: Civilian morale and the scientific attitude toward race:
  I. Popular misconceptions about race in time of war.

II. The teacher interprets anthropology—some classroom units.

III. The dance and intercultural relations:
    a. Interpreting culture groups through the dance.
    b. Dance recital.

Third Session

Subject: The feeling of "belonging" in American life—some school experiences:

I. The function of intercultural education in the elementary schools of New Jersey.

II. The function of intercultural education in the secondary schools of New Jersey.

Fourth Session

Subject: The development of national unity through inter-group relations:

I. The influence of religion.

II. The function of the home.

III. The community as a whole.

IV. The role of labor.

C. Courses in Intercultural Education for Teachers in Training and in Service[4]

The following is a general outline of the first term of an in-service course given by the author under the New York City Board of Education in 1939 and 1940:

National Unity through Intercultural Education[5]

First Meeting   *Get Together Americans*

Overview of term's work and self-introductions of class members as to regional or cultural backgrounds and professional interests. (This "defrosting" experience sometimes is provided

---

[4] A similar course, going into each phase of the subject more deeply, was given by the author at New York University School of Education, 1936-1942.

[5] Outside culture group speakers are sometimes brought into the course to cover a particular topic, as cultural anthropology, or to present pertinent facts about particular groups.

for in an especially arranged social in a person's home with special guests invited who are of the culture groups represented in the schools.)

SECOND MEETING
Americans All—Immigrants All
An overview of our many cultural and racial groups and why they came here. The first script of the radio program "Americans All— Immigrants All" is used.

THIRD MEETING
American "Melting Pot"
A review of various theories of Americanization and a presentation of the theory of cultural democracy.

FOURTH MEETING
Cultural Democracy
Class discussion of cultural democracy as a major educational objective. Formation of committees according to professional interests of teachers, church workers, social workers, etc.

FIFTH MEETING
National Morale and the Scientific Attitude Toward Race
An overview of the latest findings of cultural anthropology is presented by an outstanding authority on the subject.

SIXTH MEETING
Cultural Anthropology
Class discussion of cultural anthropology with special emphasis on how such findings should be used in schools, group work agencies, etc.

SEVENTH MEETING
Psychological Insecurities Arising from Culture Conflicts
Wish frustration as a cause of personality maladjustment. Effects of ethnic-group prejudice in family life; among minority groups; among dominant groups. Problems of adjustment of minority-group youth.

EIGHTH MEETING
Negro Americans
Pertinent facts about the participation of the Negro in American life. Color and personality, and the role of the parent, the social worker, and the church worker.

NINTH MEETING
Jewish Americans
Pertinent facts about the participation of the

Jew in American life. The roles of the school and home in overcoming psychological insecurities.

TENTH MEETING *Reports*

Reports of committees.

ELEVENTH MEETING *Creative Discussions*

The use of the creative discussion method as a democratic process in the classroom, the homeroom, school clubs, church groups, etc.

TWELFTH MEETING *School and Community Co-ordination in Morale Building*

School and community co-ordination through intercultural education. The school assembly project and the creative theater method in intercultural education are presented. Report of the School and Community Committee.

THIRTEENTH MEETING *Evaluation*

Evaluation: (a) Clear statements of objectives on various age levels. (b) Checking on real-life practices. (c) Attitude testing.

FOURTEENTH MEETING *Open Meeting*

Open meeting for discussion of whatever phase of the subject is pertinent at that time.

FIFTEENTH MEETING *Final Meeting*

Other Types of In-Service Teacher Training

The Philadelphia school system, in co-operation with the Intercultural Education Workshop, then of the Service Bureau for Intercultural Education, in 1940-1941 arranged the following kinds of experiences for some of their teachers:

I. *A Week-End Retreat with Dr. William Kilpatrick*
   General Theme: The Problem of Human Relations in Education for Democracy.

   Subjects for the five sessions:
   1. General education and American democracy.
   2. The problems of racial, religious, and cultural minorities in a democracy.
   3. Toward "cultural pluralism" in our schools.

4. Inter-group prejudices and antagonisms in our schools.

5. Education for improved inter-group relations.

Teacher Evaluation:

"We were oriented to a similar philosophy—a philosophy based on respect for human personality."

"It made me feel that it was possible to introduce a definite curriculum into the schools."

"I came back with a broader outlook—a short- and long-term planning."

"The living together—the retreat idea—was beneficial."

All felt that this type of experience should be continued. Three said that it should be expanded to larger groups of teachers.

II. *Experiences with Settlement Houses*

Because most teachers lived away from the communities in which they taught, arrangements were made for groups of twenty-five teachers to spend an afternoon and evening (including dinner) in settlement houses near the schools.

Teacher Evaluation:

"We ought to do more to reach the parents of our own school children."

"These experiences increased my knowledge and understanding of both ethnic and social groups."

"This was a new experience for many of our teachers."

"It gave us an opportunity to see our children in other than classroom situations."

"It gave contact with persons we rarely meet."

III. *Neighborhood-Home Festival with Parents of the Community*

An evening social with group conversation after the manner reported in *Get Together Americans.*

Teacher Evaluation:

"Parents were especially enthusiastic and conversant."

"Our P.T.A. received some new members of Italian background."

"I shall never forget that moment when I think I saw a prejudice die. The Italian woman had moved away from me in the circle dance, but when we all joined hands, I felt she accepted me." (A Negro school principal.)

"Parents find teachers just human beings when they enter into activities with them."

"I've always felt teachers are not too willing to meet parents

halfway. The St. Martha's House activity was a good example
of what can be done."

"The feeling of harmony and satisfaction among members of
the various groups was an almost unbelievable situation."

IV. *Lecture Discussions with Teachers at Their Regular Faculty
Meetings*

With the teachers who did not attend special courses or meetings on the subject, it was thought to be a necessary first step to
discuss not mere generalities about intercultural education but the
relationship to community problems of what happens in their
everyday classes and school situations: discrimination in housing
and industry, and juvenile delinquency, for example.

Teacher Evaluation:

"It stimulated discussions among members of the faculty for
days after the meeting."

"To me it was one of the best methods of reaching teachers.
The groups are small, and questions about definite school
problems are brought up for discussion."

"There was more open talk and discussion about attitudes."

V. *Weekly Discussions with Key Groups of Teachers around the
Following Topics*

1. Sociological picture of South Philadelphia.
2. Popular misconceptions about race.
3. Personality maladjustments and ethnic-group prejudice.
4. Social processes involved in changing attitudes.
5. Practical applications in elementary grades.
6. Classroom materials and audio-visual aids.

The group agreed that key materials should be placed in each
school in the hands of a representative teacher and that a City
Intercultural Education Workshop should be established.

During the school year 1939-1940, the Service Bureau for
Intercultural Education offered a regular weekly consultation
service in intercultural education to the teachers of the New
Rochelle, New York, school system. This was done to test the
value to any school system of providing for such regular guidance. The service was put on a voluntary basis. Any teacher
throughout the system who desired to do so could discuss with
the Bureau's field secretary whatever themes her children were

currently interested in, with the idea of securing guidance and help in weaving into her activity units educational experiences likely to develop more appreciative attitudes. Several school systems are now releasing one or two teachers to serve as what might be termed *Supervisors in Intercultural Education.*

New York University Intercultural Education Workshop

A report of summer activities in the Workshop held at New York University during 1940 to 1942 follows. Although New York City is exceptional in the variety and number of intercultural resources in exhibits and personalities, yet enough such resources may be found in any community to make such a Workshop a success. Paralleling the following reported exhibits, weekly socials were held during the summer featuring guests from different culture groups and followed by spontaneous discussion on whatever topic was desired. The Workshop staff of two was available for interviews with people taking summer work in New York City. Assistance was given (1) in developing units for school work in the fall; (2) in preparing graduate-school theses; (3) in giving special advice on how best to work with minority-group children. The professor of one student wrote: "You not only gave Miss M. a vision of what she might do with those Mexican children and tools to work with, but you also gave her courage to start. She had been overwhelmed with a feeling that she might not be able to handle her new position."

List of exhibits

1. Service Bureau materials and "Americans All—Immigrants All" recordings.
2. An exhibit of original textiles of various countries showing the influences of Near and Far Eastern designs, borrowed from the Metropolitan Museum of Art.
3. An exhibit of reproductions of American painters selected with a view to show regional approaches (e.g., Thomas Benton and Missouri), Oriental and other influences, (e.g., Whistler), or the work of artists of foreign backgrounds (e.g., Kuniyoshi, Lucioni, etc.), from the Metropolitan Museum of Art.

4. An exhibit of books about Jews in America, Palestinian folk tales, songs, plays, etc., plus an exhibit of Jewish ceremonial objects— e.g., menorahs, scrolls, etc.—from the Bloch Publishing Company, Palestine House, Inc., and the Jewish Welfare Board.

5. An exhibit of books, teaching pictures, cut-outs, maps, plays, and other teaching materials relating to various groups in this country —Orientals, Mexicans, etc.—and also relating to the American Negro, from the Friendship Press.

6. An exhibit of Japanese pottery, lacquer ware, porcelain, bamboo ware, and other domestic art objects designed for use in American homes, and inexpensive Japanese prints, graphs, and books illustrating the block-print process.

7. An exhibit of art work done by adults and children from the Harlem Community Art Center.

8. An exhibit of sculpture and painting by outstanding Negro artists, including a painting by Aaron Douglas and a plaster head by Richmond Barthe.

9. A temporary exhibit of books for children on and about the Negro, divided according to different age levels and accompanied by an annotated bibliography, from the Schomberg Collection, the largest and most important library on the Negro, at the 135th Street Branch of the New York Public Library.

10. An exhibit on racism, with pictorial statistics on the theme that "No nation has a monopoly of Nordics," from the American Committee for Democracy and Intellectual Freedom.

11. An exhibit of anti-Semitic propaganda in circulation in the United States, borrowed from the American Jewish Committee.

12. An exhibit of anti-Negro propaganda in American textbooks, borrowed from the N.A.A.C.P.

13. An exhibit of original modern Chinese paintings, water colors, paper cut-outs, etc., from a member of the staff of the China Institute; also some art objects from the China Traders.

A New Pattern for Enlarging Our Circles of Fellowship

There are many ways of approaching the problem of intercultural education with adult groups. Churches, libraries, community centers, P.T.A.'s, Y.M. and Y.W.C.A.'s, International Institutes, labor groups, classes for English to foreigners, and refugee committees throughout the country, all have been conducting various interesting projects in this field. From our own experience we report on a type of project, fitted for adult groups, which developed as an outgrowth of our earlier work in inter-cultural education in the schools.[6]

The American people are ready for new ways of coming together in small, face-to-face, emotionally satisfying experiences. For the most part, the meaningful experiences of life go on behind the closed doors of homes, churches, synagogues, and culture group associations, with more social isolation than inter-group confidence and trust resulting. Yet all groups are more alike than they are different. It is time for all sorts of people to discover this for themselves. What more pleasant and therefore memorable way to fill the need for relaxing together than for neighbors to meet during our American holidays, which, for most people, have become emotionally sterile affairs?

The Neighborhood-Home Festival was created by a group of teachers and community leaders in collaboration with artists and social psychologists to meet this emotional need of adults. It was started in 1941 in one of the author's New York University classes. The overcoming of prejudice has been a by-product. In small, mixed-group, face-to-face contacts, brought together in homes, P.T.A.'s, churches, or community centers, led by a group conversation leader (the only one who needs any preparation), the participants (there is never an audience) introduce themselves by telling in a spontaneous way what they remember from their youth (or from what the older people tell them) about the particular holiday or season of the year which they are then experiencing. The group conversation is not always about the season, however; any all-embracing, noncontroversial topic will serve.

From 1941 to 1944 a total of some six thousand people came together in city, small-town, and rural communities for such mutual and joyous experiences of fellowship. Such meetings give individual hostesses, Women's Club leaders, church and parent groups, a legitimate reason for inviting people from various cul-

---

[6] See Rachel Davis DuBois, *op. cit.*

ture groups, and thus they help to develop friendly understanding so that all can work together more easily toward the solution of their common community problems. The experiences have also been a means of motivating parents to become more interested in the similar but more formal intercultural education projects in school, church, and community center. The method minimizes differences and shows likenesses, yet does not cut people away from an emotional tie-up to their cultural pasts.

IN A METROPOLITAN CHURCH CENTER

The Neighborhood-Home Festival method of bringing together mixed groups of people is one answer to the need of churches to increase their circles of fellowship. An outline of what one metropolitan church has done to increase its circle of fellowship follows:

The church invited to meet with its own young people of mixed cultural backgrounds Jewish, Negro, Nisei, Italian, and Irish-background young people from nearby churches and synagogues. Letters to the pastors, rabbis, and other leaders explained the purpose of the Neighborhood-Home Festival and invited them to send representatives to a planning meeting. It was then decided that each group should take its turn in being host to the others in celebrating together each season, allowing the in-between contacts to develop as the needs and desires arose. Some of the outcomes as evaluated by the leaders are:

a. It gave several very enjoyable social evenings to a large number of people of different faiths, races, or cultural antecedents.

b. It gave opportunity for the members of the particular church to become personally acquainted with congenial young people of other groups.

c. Firsthand acquaintance with Negroes and other minority-group individuals stimulated discussion of the problem of minorities in the young people's societies and provided "documentation" for it. The discussion was thus lifted out of the realm of abstract argument and made real. The Young People's Society of the church, as a result, began to study with their Negro friends the problem of employment discrimination in their own community.

d. The experience was culturally enriching, as members of different groups told one another of their customs, their legends, their great men and women, or taught one another their songs and dances.[7] The superintendent of the Sunday School said that the planning of inter-group worship and other social processes had been enriched because of the ceremonials which were often a part of the Festival experience: the sharing of Jewish prayers and candle-lighting, of the purposed silence of the Quakers, and similar experiences. At the same time that the young people gained an appreciation of the religious and cultural values of other groups, they became more profoundly aware of the values in their own inheritance. This was especially true of the minority-group young people.

e. The experiences yielded occasions for the participants to understand how prejudice can greatly increase personality difficulties. In discussions following their Festival experiences, the dominant-group young people were led to place the blame partly on the discriminatory situations in which members of minority groups have to function and for which the dominant-group people must share a certain responsibility.

There are many ways in which the churches can co-operate with the schools and P.T.A.'s. In fact they must begin where the public school leaves off, for we cannot expect goodwill attitudes to withstand the emotional tensions of war and its aftermath, unless they are strengthened by a religious motivation.

---

[7] The church groups used the excellent graded booklets in the Friendship Press Series, *The Church and America's Peoples.* See Bibliography.

In Americanization Classes

One of the problems facing the teacher of Americanization classes is to help the members to "warm up" to one another. Too often old-country antagonisms are held onto and planted in this country, adding even more competitions and fears to our crowded cities. Perhaps the class simply takes on a cold, formal character. The warm friendliness which starts growing where adults from different cultural backgrounds begin to share their happy memories of youth with old-stock Americans, who give them the feeling of belongingness they need, is the kind of social cement badly needed in our too fragmentized social worlds.

At Labor Temple in New York City the members of the various English classes regularly come together to welcome each change in the season. Such occasions give a reason for inviting old-stock Americans from churches. The leader has found that the members of her classes have become more relaxed, more adjusted, and more friendly with their neighbors. In some instances, it was noticed that the experiences helped to bridge the gap between the American-born children and their foreign-born parents, and thus resulted in better family relationships. The classes are now exchanging visits with evening classes in Harlem to their mutual interest. They use the group conversation method of the Neighborhood-Home Festival, choosing various topics which have a universal appeal.

In a Suburban Town—A Women's Club

In Plainfield, New Jersey, a series of such "get-together" parties, held in several homes over a period of eight weeks, culminated in a public choral speaking and dance program, "The Four Freedoms," in which groups of many backgrounds participated. As a result, the Plainfield Council for World Fellowship became intercultural in scope and included Negroes among its officers.

In a Rural Community—Parent-Teachers' Association

In Woodstown, New Jersey, the P.T.A. gathered together neighbors originally from six different countries and from several parts of this country, and including both white and Negro citizens, around their common interest in the December Feast of Lights. Experiencing together the lighting of the Channukah candles and the Christmas carols was a good introduction for a series of more formal discussions the following month on the topic: "How can majority and minority groups contribute to democracy?" These were held under the auspices of the New Jersey Education Association's state plan for better co-operation between parents and teachers called "Democratic Discussions." The fact that a few high-school students, both Negro and white, and some of their teachers were present gave an opportunity to follow this experience in the school by reports and other activities in the high-school English classes.

The Library, School, and P.T.A. in a New York City Neighborhood Co-operate

In a crowded and culturally very diversified New York City neighborhood the branch library held two Neighborhood-Home Festivals, one around spring memories and one around work memories. Special book displays suggesting related readings accompanied these socials, which inspired the P.T.A. to hold a Lullaby Festival. It had been difficult to get parents or more than one group to attend. The principal sent a special invitation to all the mothers of the first three grades to come to the school to see their children in a short assembly program. One hundred mothers came. After the assembly they were divided into two groups for the Festival. They began by introducing themselves, telling how many children they had, what songs they sang to their children or what had been sung to them by their parents, and where they had grown up. Lullabies were sung in seven different languages, with the whole group humming if they did not know the song. The conversation which accompanied the songs centered around "How we came to name our babies." The women were pleasantly surprised to realize that naming ceremonies in the different religions were more alike than different. This brought forth the comment, "I guess we all just want to dedicate the child to the good life." That reminded one member of the group of the Old Testament story of Hannah and Samuel, whereupon an Italian-American mother in broken English held the group's attention as she told the story.

Comparing superstitions about the coming of babies added to the humor, so that at the end of the hour and a half the mothers felt that they had really become acquainted. After such a "defrosting". experience, the officers of the P.T.A. felt that they could plan their future programs with more assurance of attendance, and the teachers who were present found suggestions for motivation and content which they could use in their activity units. Thus a small step was taken in co-ordinating the home and the school.

Further Suggestions for P.T.A. and Women's Clubs' Co-operation with Schools

a. *Sponsor a series of progressive "cover-dish" suppers celebrating each of the four seasons.* Have foods of different regional or national groups that are appropriate to the season. A Neighborhood-Home Festival can precede or follow the dinner. (See Appendix for list of helpful books, and see *Get Together Americans* for more detailed suggestions on how to lead a discussion.)

b. *Sponsor a series of "Home-Sweet-Home" evenings.* Interspersing the seasonal Festivals, there can be a series of "Home-Sweet-Home" evenings in which are shared such experiences as family songs, jokes, lullabies, kinds of table grace, favorite foods, home treasures, marriage and birthday customs, "tall tales" of how the family came to this country or migrated within our country, old folks' tales of how things used to be—such as sleigh-ride parties. It would be valuable to have parents and children spend such an evening together. The school might see that several children are prepared to participate, but, if their teacher leads the group conversation, such participation could be woven in with the spontaneous participation of the parents. Follow some of these Festivals with discussions of whether our common American life would be enriched if some of the customs from various culture groups in our midst could be more generally adopted. (*Bruderschaft,* for example, is an interesting European custom celebrating the cementing of friendship.) Especially encourage newcomers in the community from other regions or countries to tell of their customs. In the larger communities, in order to reach a greater group of people, several such festivals can be held simultaneously in different homes during a period of weeks. These affairs might culminate in a large all-community meeting in the school.

c. *Sponsor a community forum.* Interspersing the Neighborhood-Home Festivals, other meetings should be held to discuss vital topics related to the recognized issues in the community. This can be correlated with the work of the social studies department in the school. Your State Department of Education no doubt has a division of adult education which will help. Often such discussions are divisive, since, of course, opinions differ. If the same people experience the warm friendliness of a Neighborhood-Home Festival three or four times a year, they should be able to discuss controversial issues with less rancor.[8]

----

[8] See Justus Lane, "Our Town—An Adventure in Co-operation," *Common Ground,* Summer, 1943, for suggested ways to get your whole town co-operating. For discussions, use wisely such tools for learning as movies, recordings, and the radio. For catalogues describing such aids, write New Tools for Learning, 7 West 16th Street, New York, N. Y. One of the best reports of discussions on postwar problems is the one described in *The People Are Ready,* New York Adult Education Council, 254 Fourth Avenue, New York 10, N. Y., 25¢.

CULTURE GROUP ORGANIZATIONS

In some of the larger communities there are such organizations as Italian welfare societies, associations for the advancement of colored people, or Irish historical societies; but in most communities one must look for outstanding leaders who know their people. Often they and their group center around a church or synagogue. They should be asked to supply the school with a list of men and women and young people who might represent their groups at school assemblies or Neighborhood-Home Festivals. This list should be composed of persons who can tell about some interesting folk, religious, or family custom, and demonstrate or lead others in some easy folk song, work song, or dance. Often this can be done with the greatest effectiveness by very simple people.

If it happens that people of a particular background are not familiar with their own folk culture, and there is a sincere desire to revive some of it in order to share the best of it with others in the Neighborhood-Home Festival or other intercultural activities, then the culture group organizations or leaders should sponsor a series of meetings for the purpose. If a group is or becomes proficient in song or dance, it might represent the community at the National Folk Festival held each year in Philadelphia under the auspices of the *Evening Bulletin*. Regional and cultural folk song and dance groups gather from all over the country to participate in this week of fun and festival. The National Folk Festival Council encourages also local and state folk festivals.

All groups will find it easy to co-operate with the schools in planning for special days. Race Relations Sunday (Federal Council of Churches, 289 Fourth Avenue, New York, N. Y.) ; Brotherhood Week (National Conference of Christians and Jews, 387 Fourth Avenue, New York, N. Y.) ; Negro History Week (Associated Publishers, 1538 Ninth Street, N. W., Washington, D. C.) all take place some time in February. "I Am an American Day," formerly World Goodwill Day, May 18, would be a good time to end the year's work. (For a suggested program for this day, send for special handbook to Immigration and Naturalization Service, United States Government Printing Office, Washington, D. C.)

ALL-COMMUNITY FESTIVAL

All forces in the community can co-operate in holding an all-community festival, perhaps around one of the special days. Large cities will gain much from studying the methods of the St. Paul International Institute. (Write to the International Institute in that city.) What marks this festival as different from other community international festivals is the fact that its preparation goes on for a year beforehand, during which time mixed groups of people meet regularly to make decisions together.

Some Suggestions for Amateur and Professional Use of Motion Pictures and Radio in Intercultural Education

Since the spread of the "candid camera" and amateur motion pictures, schools need not necessarily wait for a Hollywood production on the subject of America's culture groups. Motion picture and camera clubs may find interesting and profitable activities in showing how cosmopolitan their own home town, city, state, or section of America is. The subjects that they may "shoot" are legion. Among some of the more simple but colorful culture items which may be found in our American communities are: the artistic homemade cart of the Greek flower vendor, and the hurdy-gurdy of the Italian playing a bit of opera; activities of the Negro orange pickers and the Greek sponge divers of Florida; the beautiful potteries and textiles of the Spanish and Indian elements in the Southwest; the great red barns of the Pennsylvania Germans; the white, steepled churches and the old town halls of the New Englanders; the colorful influence, in several American industrial and agricultural communities, of Negroes from the Caribbean islands; the revived pageantry of folk dancing, singing, and festival in many parts of the country. Such pictures, when studied in the light of the more socially significant contributions of those same groups to American life, might well become the backgrounds for local historical motion pictures which would show the impact of one wave of immigration upon another, and the ways in which the peoples who made up those waves became or are becoming adjusted and assimilated.

The radio, also, lends itself easily to intercultural education. The music and song, both folk and classical, of our various culture groups may be heard on the air at almost any hour, while the educational sustaining programs of the broadcasting systems often offer series related in some way to the subject.[9] Radio programs of which permanent recordings have been made are the series "Americans All—Immigrants All" (CBS) and "Freedom's People" (WEAF), both sponsored by the United States Office of Education; and the program "The Melting Pot Boils" in the series "Here's to Youth" (WEAF), sponsored by the leading youth organizations. Local radio stations are usually eager to co-operate with schools wishing to experiment with the educational value of creating their own radio programs.

An Evaluation

We have presented these outlines of activities which, in the past few years, have had a measure of success, with the hope that other groups and communities may find some of the suggestions useful in planning their own intercultural activities and thus be able to start farther ahead.

The experiences herein described extended from the "thin" contact of *a series of formal lectures* on "The Making of American Culture," which, we feel, have a certain but limited value,

---

[9] See L. D. Reddick, "Educational Programs for the Improvement of Race Relations: Motion Pictures, Radio, Press, and Libraries," *Journal of Negro Education*, Summer, 1944. See also Appendix for list of organizations offering radio and film aids.

through the *institutes and panel discussions* of several days' duration, involving the coming together for common decisions of leaders from many groups, to the "thicker" contacts of *courses in intercultural education,* which gave salary increment and university credit; through the less formal but more intensive *in-service training,* where selected groups of teachers studied their own school-community needs under expert guidance; the *regular weekly guidance of teachers in the classroom;* the formation of a permanent *Intercultural Education Workshop,* provided with reference books and audio-visual aids, to which teachers and community leaders could come for guidance; to the new pattern for enlarging our circles of fellowship, the *Neighborhood-Home Festival.*

We must ask ourselves, as others are bound to ask, how valuable for other communities are such experiences in dealing with the critical situations of the postwar years when our disrupted institutions will be attempting to find balance and stability. Only further experiment on a community-wide basis can answer that question. Good advice and suggestion, at this point, may be obtained from the keen analyses of the Detroit race riots made by Lee and Humphrey.[10] These authors state that any effective program must contain three points:

1. Constant fact-finding.
2. Constant integration and analysis of facts.
3. Constant translation of analyses into *things to do*.[11]

It is this last function, the authors continue, "on which we are most likely to fall down. . . . This step is likely to fall short of real implementation in any effective sense. It usually amounts to nothing more than passing a resolution or writing a memo. . . ." The authors then present what seems to us to be the core of the whole problem:

Let us never lose sight of the great lesson of the Detroit tragedy!

---

[10] Lee and Humphrey, *op. cit.*
[11] *Ibid.,* pp. 125 ff.

People who had become neighbors in mixed Negro and White communities did not riot against each other. [Italics ours.]

It is our firm belief that merely living in the same block—at least in our larger cities, and too often in our smaller towns—does not mean that we have become neighbors. Only through *experiences of neighborliness* do we begin so to care about other persons of a different race, culture, or class that we shall be moved to translate that feeling into action in time of crisis. When city people leave their apartments, it is not to meet their neighbors but to avoid them. The Neighborhood-Home Festival (we should like to offer a prize for a better name!) described on page 168 has been effective in producing the kind of experiences which does make people care about one another as persons. Whether its use as a prophylactic on an intensive community-wide basis would aid in preventing riots, no one knows. We do know that in one community its positive effect is still being felt four years after the method was used rather extensively. Whether that method can be used for healing purposes after a community has suffered conflict is another conjecture. Those who have experienced the Festival point to instances in which adults have testified to their change in feeling. "The war had made me feel bitter toward these foreigners, but I can see now that a person shouldn't feel that way," was a recent comment.

Nor can we say how effective the wider use of the integrated assembly project would be in preventing or relieving critical situations in school or community. Some five hundred student statements from a few of the schools and numerous letters from teachers and principals written at the time the projects were being conducted testify to pupil interest in and to faculty appreciation of this kind of intercultural education. However, all educational projects must be an adventure of faith.

The five hundred student statements gathered in the English classes were, of course, quite subjective; but the teachers felt that the pupils reported what they really believed. The comments from the faculties were unsolicited.

What has been far more rewarding is the chance meetings with young men and women, now community leaders devoting much of their time to the betterment of inter-group relations, who, upon closer scrutiny, turn out to have been students in the high schools in which the projects were conducted.

APPENDIX

A WORKSHEET FOR THOSE CONDUCTING THE PROJECTS IN INTERCULTURAL EDUCATION

I. *Preliminary Survey*

    A. The community is to be studied. This is to be done by visiting parents association meetings and community councils to discover

        1. the racial and cultural make-up of the community;

        2. what recent conflicts or tension situations, if any, have occurred in it;

        3. possible resources to be drawn upon. This is to be done by interviewing heads of

           a. religious agencies;

           b. boys' clubs;

           c. civic societies;

           d. settlement houses, etc.

    B. The school is to be studied. This is to be done by

        1. interviewing the principal and meeting the faculty committee in order to

           a. gain an idea of the time available for the project, the nature of student government, the kinds of clubs and extracurricular activities, etc.,

           b. obtain information as to the cultural and racial backgrounds of students,

           c. determine what culture groups the school wishes to study;

        2. visiting classes to determine types of teaching and also the spirit and caliber of students;

        3. visiting assemblies to determine school spirit;

        4. obtaining judgment of teachers as to shortages in attitudes of students;

5. giving preliminary tests: home background and attitude tests;

6. obtaining copies of all courses of study so that factual content material supplied may fit particular class situations and units.

II. *Preliminary Procedure*

A. Faculty co-operation is to be solicited.

1. Hold conferences with members of the faculty, especially those who have charge of assembly program. Thus

  a. the teachers' ideas will be included in the policy decisions;

  b. they will be made aware that one aim of the project is to help them save time rather than to add burdens;

  c. problems of integrating activites of the various departments will be worked out with the teachers.

2. Hold a minimum of six special weekly conferences in which there will be presented to the teachers

  a. the underlying philosophy of cultural democracy;

  b. the latest findings of science in regard to race prejudice, race differences, etc.;

  c. as much of the principles of social psychology as shall be thought applicable to the project;

  d. some emotionally satisfying experiences with people of various cultural backgrounds in the community.

III. *The Conducting of the Project*

A. Organizing student and teacher project committees. (Arrange for regular meetings to plan the program a month in advance and keep adequate records of activities.)

1. The Committee on Assembly

  a. makes arrangements with outside guests;

  b. makes arrangements for student follow-up activities;

  c. invites local culture group leaders to help plan the program concerned with their group;

  d. plans early for the large combined pageant or program at end of term.

2. The Committee on Social Affairs

  a. plans the school tea or forum to follow the guest assembly;

b. sees that various student groups have their turn in being represented;

c. limits number at each social affair to thirty or forty;

d. invites a few community leaders.

3. The Committee on Preparation of Discussion Outlines for Homeroom, Class, or Club

a. sees that discussion groups have adequate factual material. (For materials write to national and local agencies concerned with the problem of intercultural relations.)

B. Planning each assembly

1. General objective: To provide motivation for the study of the cultural backgrounds of the ethnic groups chosen by the student-faculty committee.

2. Points to keep in mind

a. Organize the work so that it does not appear to be a program extraneous to the regular part of school work but rather an enrichment of the curriculum;

b. avoid isolation of groups; as far as possible, mix people of various backgrounds on both guest and student programs;

c. provide an entertaining and æsthetic program and aim to present attractive personalities of the culture groups.

3. Method of building assemblies

a. Establish contacts with organizations and institutions within each culture group;

b. invite five or six leaders of the group to be studied to meet with the school's planning committee;

c. enlist their guidance in the preparation of programs, supplying of materials, and procuring of books and possible necessary financial aid;

d. procure through these contacts speakers, singers, dancers, instrumentalists, or others with distinctive contributions for an assembly program;

e. enlist the co-operation of some of the national and local agencies concerned with the problems of immigrant welfare, Americanization, character education, folk arts, etc. For example: churches and synagogues, P.T.A.'s, culture group organizations, settlement houses and community councils, National Institute for Immigrant Welfare, International Institutes of the Y.W.

C.A. and parallel units in the Y.M.C.A., the Y.M. and
Y.W.H.A.'s, foreign language newspapers, Common
Council of American Unity, women's clubs, race relations committees, refugee committees, and War Relocation Authority.

C. Follow-up activities

  1. Informal gatherings

     a. Immediately after the assembly, in order to provide
        an opportunity for social contact between pupils and
        guests, give a tea or luncheon or have a general social
        and discussion period;

     b. give an exhibition of handicrafts, books, etc.;

     c. to these gatherings invite a few interested community
        leaders.

  2. Classroom activities

     a. Give guidance to teachers in supplementing the regular
        course of study with facts not usually found in text-
        books;

     b. present teachers with suggested mimeographed factual
        materials to supplement the regular studies of the
        curriculum.

  3. Homeroom activities

     a. Have the committee in charge of homeroom activities
        make out suggested monthly outlines for discussion;

     b. discuss these outlines with the homeroom or section-
        room teachers.

  4. Club activities

     a. Dramatic clubs: Study the drama of different culture
        groups; experiment with the use of documentary plays
        and folk plays.

     b. Language, music, and art departments clubs: Gear into
        growing interest throughout the country in regional and
        national folk arts, songs, dances, stories, poetry, drama.
        Reach out toward a study of these arts on an inter-
        tional scale.

     c. Social clubs: Co-operate with Hi-Y, Co-Y, etc. in
        arranging informal discussions with people of various
        cultural backgrounds. Study the methods used by the
        Play Co-op.

     d. Athletic teams: Arrange games and outings with teams
        of various cultural backgrounds.

e. Camera clubs: Take stills and movies of evidences of interesting cultural diversity in school and community.

D. Student-planned assembly

a. Bring the period given over to a study of each culture group to a close with a student-planned assembly— thus giving an opportunity for vicarious living through drama;

b. teachers should be assigned or given the opportunity to choose at the beginning of the term the student assembly for which they are to be responsible;

c. make arrangements for the co-operation of several departments in the school;

d. provide when possible for the students of one cultural background to act the parts of persons of other cultural backgrounds;

e. in situations where praise of a particular culture is to be given, see that it is done by someone of another group.

E. Establishing an Intercultural Library-Workshop

a. Collect, even on a small scale, materials such as books, magazines, audio-visual aids, and folk art examples;

b. if possible, use the Workshop as a place for planning groups to meet.

II

A BROTHERHOOD DAY PROGRAM

JUNIOR HIGH SCHOOL

In order to close fittingly the work of the term, and as an inspiration for future work, the students of the Englewood, N. J., Junior High School presented an assembly program based on attitudes acquired during the project.

1. Announcement of significance of the day.

2. Bible reading.

3. Prayer:

"Almighty God, we who are members of different races and faiths desire together Thy Fatherhood and our kinship with one another. In our difference we find that many of our hopes, our fears, our aspirations are one. Thou art our Father and we are Thy children.

"We are heartily sorry for the mists of fear, envy, hatred, suspicion, and greed which have blinded our eyes and thrust us asunder. May the light that comes from Thee scatter these mists, cleanse our hearts, and give health to our spirits. Teach us to put away all bitterness and walk together in the ways of human friendship.

"Open our eyes to see that as nature abounds in variation, so differences in human beings make for richness in the common life. May we give honor where honor is due, regardless of race, color, or circumstance. Deepen our respect for unlikeness and our eagerness to understand one another. Through the deeper unities of the spirit in sympathy, insight, and co-operation may we transcend our differences. May we gladly share with one another our best gifts and together seek for a human world fashioned in good under Thy guidance. Amen."[1]

4. Song: "America the Beautiful."
5. Salute to the Flag. (Used before World War II as a flag salute in Hawaiian schools.)

CIVIC CREED

God hath made of one blood all nations of men, and we are His children, brothers and sisters all.

We are citizens of these United States, and we believe our flag stands for self-sacrifice and for the good of all the people.

We want, therefore, to be true citizens of our great country, and to show our love for her by our work.

---

[1] Prayer composed by the Rev. John A. O'Brien, Rabbi Benjamin Frankel, and the Rev. James C. Baker, Urbana, Ill., 1927.

Our country does not ask us to die for her welfare: she asks us to live for her, and so to live, and so to act, that her government may be pure, her officers honest, and every corner of her territory shall be a place fit to grow the best men and women who shall rule over her.

6. Sketch: "What Makes an American?" (*See page 190.*)

7. Student Talk: Religious Freedom and Equal Opportunity are American Ideals.

8. Responsive Reading: "The Land Where Hate Should Die."

(Denis A. McCarthy)

LEADER.

> *"This is the land where hate should die"*—

RESPONSE.

> No feuds of faith, no spleen of race,
> No darkly brooding fear should try
> Beneath our flag to find a place.
> Lo! every people here has sent
> Its sons to answer freedom's call;
> Their lifeblood is the strong cement
> That builds and binds the Nation's wall.

LEADER.

> *"This is the land where hate should die"*—

RESPONSE.

> Though dear to me my faith and shrine,
> I serve my country best when I
> Respect the creeds that are not mine.
> He little loves his land who'd cast
> Upon his neighbor's word a doubt
> Or cite the wrongs of ages past
> From present rights to bar him out.

LEADER.

"This is the land where hate should die"—

RESPONSE.

This is the land where strife should cease,
Where foul, suspicious fear should fly
Before the light of love and peace.
Then let us purge from poisoned thought
That service to the State we give
And so be worthy as we ought
Of this great land in which we live.

WHAT MAKES AN AMERICAN?

by FLORENCE BRUGGER[2]

(Two students are talking together.)

1ST STUDENT. You know, you and I live in the United States of America and so we call ourselves Americans, don't we?

2ND STUDENT. Yes, what of it?

1ST STUDENT. Well, I've been thinking. Are the people who live in South America, Americans?

2ND STUDENT. No, they are South Americans.

1ST STUDENT. Then why aren't we just North Americans?

2ND STUDENT. Because North America includes Canada and Canadians aren't Americans.

1ST STUDENT. Well, you live in Vermont (*Whatever state skit is given in can be substituted here*), why aren't you just a Vermonter?

2ND STUDENT. I am, but I'm also an American.

1ST STUDENT. Then you're two things.

2ND STUDENT. Yes, I suppose so.

---

[2] Of the staff of the Y.W.C.A. International Center, New York, N. Y.

1ST STUDENT. But if you move to New York then are you three things—a Vermonter, a New Yorker, and an American?

2ND STUDENT. You're funny. I guess I'm a Vermonter because I was born there and a New Yorker because I live there and an American because, because—

1ST STUDENT. Because why?

2ND STUDENT. Well, I don't know, what does make a person an American?

1ST STUDENT. I'm asking you.

2ND STUDENT. Gee, I guess Americans are the people whose ancestors have been here the longest. That's what my mother says. She says our family is real American because my great-great-great—I don't know how many greats—grandfather came over in the "Mayflower." So it wouldn't make any difference in what state we lived—we'd be Americans because we were the first! (*Smiles with superior satisfaction.*)

(*American Indian boy appears, dressed in American clothes, of course.*)

1ST STUDENT. Oh, hello. Who are you?

INDIAN. Oh, I'm an American.

2ND STUDENT. You are? You don't look like one.

INDIAN. No? Why not?

2ND STUDENT. Well, your skin is dark and your hair and eyes are different.

INDIAN. Different from yours, yes. But is it color of skin and kind of eyes and hair that make an American?

2ND STUDENT. No—o—o.

INDIAN. I just heard what you were saying about what makes an American and according to your definition I'm the most real American of all because my ancestors were here long before any of yours.

2ND STUDENT. How's that?

INDIAN. I'm an American Indian and your forefathers crossed an ocean to come to take our land away from us.

2ND STUDENT. No, that's not true. They came for religious freedom.

1ST STUDENT. Maybe that's what makes an American—a person who comes to this country for religious freedom.

2ND STUDENT. Yes, that's it.
(Jewish boy appears.)

JEWISH. That's what my people thought when they heard about America.

1ST STUDENT. Who are you?

2ND STUDENT. *(Pokes first boy.)* I know—he's a Jew.

JEWISH. *(Proudly.)* Yes, by religion, I'm Jewish, but I'm also an American, by your own definition. My people lived in ghettos in Europe and were persecuted because of their religion and so they came to this country for religious freedom.

2ND STUDENT. Maybe—but most Jewish people came here because they were poor in the old country and thought here was a good chance to make some money.
(Irish boy appears.)

IRISH. Even so—that doesn't keep them from being Americans, I guess. That's why my people came to this country. They got sick of eating only potatoes in Ireland. And believe me, I'm an American.

1ST STUDENT. Oh, you're an American all right because your folks all speak English and—and—you're the same race and religion as we are.

2ND STUDENT. He is not. He's a Catholic. My mother says— well, she says Catholics can't be good Americans.

IRISH. Why not? I guess no one believes more in liberty and freedom than the Irish.

1ST STUDENT. Is that what makes an American?

2ND STUDENT. Sure, that's right—liberty and freedom—it's in the Constitution. An American is a person who believes in the Declaration of Independence and the Constitution of the United States.

CHORUS (*except* 1ST STUDENT). Sure, that's right!

1ST STUDENT. That's what lots of people say but they don't act according to what the Declaration of Independence and the Constitution state.

(*Negro boy enters.*)

NEGRO. I'll say they don't.

2ND STUDENT. How do you happen to be here? We're talking about Americans.

NEGRO. I know, that's why I am here. I'm an American, too.

1ST STUDENT. Why? Your ancestors didn't come here for religious freedom or economic opportunity.

NEGRO. No, they were brought here as slaves.

JEWISH. That's funny—when America was supposed to be a place for liberty.

NEGRO. Yes, that's what some people thought who really believed in the Declaration of Independence.

2ND STUDENT. Just what is in that famous Declaration?

NEGRO. I know it. We Negroes still have to remind people: "We hold these truths to be self-evident, that all men are created equal, that they are endowed by their Creator with certain unalienable Rights, that among these are Life, Liberty and the pursuit of Happiness."

IRISH. It sounds swell—but what does it really mean? Liberty? We Irish fight for it but I wonder whether we know what it's all about.

2ND STUDENT. Say, don't get us into another mix-up. We haven't figured out yet what makes an American.

1ST STUDENT. Perhaps liberty and being an American have something to do with each other.

2ND STUDENT. How?

1ST STUDENT. Well, now, an American isn't the person whose family has been here the longest?

INDIAN. No.

1ST STUDENT. And he isn't a person of a certain religion.

JEWISH. And he isn't a person with a certain amount of money.

CHORUS. No!

1ST STUDENT. Then, he must be a person who believes in certain things.

2ND STUDENT. Yes—yes.

NEGRO. Don't you think it isn't enough just to believe in certain things—aren't the real Americans the ones who are willing to *do* something about what they believe?

IRISH. You bet. A man has to act like an American to be one.

1ST STUDENT. How does an American act?

2ND STUDENT. Gosh, I never thought of acting according to the Declaration of Independence.

1ST STUDENT. No, it's easier to act as though people who go to a different church are queer and to think that people from a different country or race are not so good as we are.

2ND STUDENT. Then, if I'm an American I'll give the other fellow a chance to be what he wants to be.

1ST STUDENT. Certainly—give him a chance for education, a job, and some fun in this life and, of course, the right to worship God as seems right to him.

2ND STUDENT. I never thought of it before but I can see now that an American is something bigger than a person born in one place, believing in one religion, being of one race. It's sort of like being born in Vermont and living in New York state. A person is a bigger person—more interesting—

if he's been around a bit. So I guess an American that includes more than one thing can be a bigger person in this little old world.

JEWISH. Yes, just think what America has stood for—Liberty for all kinds of people.

NEGRO. And think what real Americans are—men and women of all kinds who give justice to all.

IRISH. I wonder, am I an American?

(*All the participants turn to one another and finally to the audience.*)

INDIAN. Am I an American?

2ND STUDENT. Am I an American?

JEWISH. Am I an American?

(*To the audience.*)

2ND STUDENT. Are you?

NEGRO. Are you?

IRISH. Are you?

JEWISH. Are you?

INDIAN. Are you?

1ST STUDENT. Are you?

III

A GUEST PROGRAM
THE CHINESE
JUNIOR HIGH SCHOOL

1. Guest Program.
   a. Selections from Chinese Opera: Dorothy Yow.
   b. Talk on China: Tennyson Chang.
   c. Dialogue: "Who is an American?" Louise Chin and Florence Brugger.

The part of the Chinese girl was taken by a young Chinese student of Barnard College who was a third-generation American; her partner was a fellow student who considered herself "a true American" though she had immigrant parents. The dialogue was based on the real life of these girls and very clearly presents the predicament in which descendants of Chinese immigrants find themselves at present, directly challenging the listeners to consider the important question, "Who is an American, anyway?"

WHO IS AN AMERICAN?

(A CHINESE GIRL [C. G.]. ANOTHER GIRL [O. G.].)

THE OTHER GIRL. Oh! are you Chinese?

THE CHINESE GIRL. I—why, yes, I suppose so.

O. G. What part of China are you from?

C. G. I'm not from China.

O. G. Oh! where *were* you born?

C. G. I was born in New York City.

O. G. Well, was your father born in China?

C. G. No. He was born in San Francisco.

O. G. How about your mother?

C. G. She was born in Philadelphia. She's never even been in China.

O. G. That's interesting.

C. G. Do you mind if I ask you some questions?

O. G. No, of course not.

C. G. Are *you* an American?

O. G. Why, of course! I was born in Nebraska.

C. G. Was *your* father born in this country?

O. G. No, he was born in Switzerland.

C. G. And your mother?

O. G. Well—she was born in France.

C. G. Then why are you American—and I Chinese? My parents were born in this country and yours weren't.

O. G. I don't know. It *is* funny, isn't it? Do you read and write Chinese?

C. G. Oh, yes, I *had* to learn Chinese.

O. G. Why, I didn't learn French or German. Why did you learn Chinese?

C. G. Because I intend to go to China some day to find work. There's no work in this country for me—because I'm a Chinese.

O. G. That doesn't seem fair. You were educated here, and you and your parents were born here; won't you seem awfully strange and different from people born and raised in China?

C. G. I'm afraid I shall.

O. G. Do you live in Chinatown now?

C. G. Oh, no. I live on Long Island.

O. G. Then, *why* are you a Chinese? I can't see. Do you do anything differently than we do? How do you spend your leisure time?

C. G. Oh, I swim and dance and go to the movies, and read.

O. G. Do you read English books?

C. G. Of course! and, of course, I'm doing a lot of required reading now for my university work.

O. G. Oh, where do you go to college?

C. G. At Barnard.

O. G. Well, it seems just a shame you should have to go to China to work. Aren't you afraid it will be difficult to get used to everything there?

C. G. Yes, I'm afraid it will be—but you see—I'm Chinese— and America is just for Americans.

O. G. But it doesn't seem fair—you were born and educated here just as the rest of us Americans.

C. G. But finding a *job* isn't the *only* thing. We want a chance to *be* Americans.

O. G. Well—what *is* an American?

C. G. I wish I knew (*She turns to the audience.*)—don't you?

2. School Tea.

3. Homeroom Discussion.

4. Student Program: "The Thrice Promised Bride," by Cheng-Chin Hsiung. A modern Chinese play published by The Carolina Playmakers, Inc., Chapel Hill, North Carolina.

IV

AMERICANS ALL—IMMIGRANTS ALL RADIO PROGRAMS

In 1938-1939, twenty-six dramatic radio broadcasts, spotlighting the contributions of various cultural groups to the economic, social, and political development of the United States, were presented by the United States Department of the Interior, Office of Education, and the Columbia Broadcasting System, with the co-operation of the Service Bureau for Intercultural Education, and assisted by the Works Progress Administration. The programs, designed to promote a more appreciative understanding of our growing American culture, dramatized the contributions made by the many groups which are a part of American life, and dealt with the question: What brought people to this country from the four corners of the earth? What gifts did they bear? How did they together build our country? What were their problems? What problems remain unsolved? The titles of the programs follow.

1. **Opening Frontiers.**—New trails are blazed, frontiers are

pushed westward, and foundations of our great democracy are laid by newcomers from across the seas.

2. Our English Heritage.—Rich experiences in self-government and basic liberties are introduced by the English in colonizing the northern Atlantic seaboard.

3. Our Hispanic Heritage.—The Spaniards build missions and bring Andalusian cattle and horses into the Southwest.

4. Scots, Scotch-Irish, and Welsh.—Sturdy Scotch-Irish and Scots, vanguard of march to the West, settle along frontiers. The Welsh, lovers of song, discover coal and develop our mines.

5. Winning Freedom.—Through co-operation and willingness to sacrifice both wealth and life, colonists win independence and preserve priceless principles and ideals.

6. The Negro.—From early colonial days, the Negro, who composes one-tenth of our population, plays a large part in our economic and artistic life.

7. The French and Netherlanders.—French fur traders and missionaries pioneer the Mississippi Valley; Netherlanders settle on Manhattan Island; French Canadians work in lumber camps and mills of New England; diamond cutters come from Belgium; and French-speaking Swiss build up our cheese industry.

8. Upsurge of Democracy.—Frontiersmen and newcomers unite to bring about decline of aristocracy. Eastern wage earners march in the ranks of the new democracy.

9. The Irish.—Sons of old Ireland develop canals, railroads, and factories, enter the ranks of public service, and bring song, humor, and literature of a high order.

10. The Germans.—The Germans—Protestant, Catholic, and Jew—push frontiers westward, fashion the Kentucky rifle, build "Switzer" barn and Conestoga wagon, and develop agriculture, forestry, music, art, education, and science.

11. The Scandinavians.—Swedes, Norwegians, and Finns settle in Delaware and North-Central states, introducing log cabins, co-operatives, progressive dairy methods, social consciousness, gymnastics, and folk high schools.

12. Closing Frontiers.—When there is no more good free land to settle, immigrants crowd into our cities to supply demand for unskilled labor.

13. The Jews.—Participating in American life since early colonial days, the Jews make significant contributions to science, industry, music, literature, theater, law, medicine, and philanthropy.

14-15. The Slavs.—The Slavs—northern and southern— succeed in making abandoned farms productive and work in our mines, steel mills, automobile factories, packing houses, and forests.

16. The Orientals.—Chinese and Japanese bring artistic sensitivity of Far East. Chinese answer call of railroad, ranch, and factory. Japanese reclaim California swamps and develop farms.

17. The Italians.—Early explorers and artisans come from Italy, help to build grape and wine industry, work in our marble quarries, raise vegetables, and help to build railroads, bridges, and highways.

18. Near Eastern People.—Armenians, Greeks, and Syrians bring philosophy, poetry, medical skill, manual skills, and unique artistic sense.

19. Other Peoples.—Hungarians, Rumanians, Portuguese, Bulgarians, Lithuanians, Estonians, and Latvians bring ideas, labor, fine traditions, and aesthetic values.

20. Contributions in Industry.—Each wave of immigration contributes brain and brawn to American life. Group co-operation makes the United States leader of world industry.

21. Contributions in Science.—Our country is in the forefront of scientific progress, due to brilliance and inventive genius of individuals of divers racial and national origins.

22. Arts and Crafts.—Cultural value of artistic gifts by immigrant groups since early colonial days is a priceless gift enriching the United States of today and tomorrow.

23. Social Progress.—Champions of human freedom, drawn from many groups, preserve and develop ideals for which the founding fathers fought and died.

24. A New England Town.—The New England town, founded by early settlers, changes and develops as new groups participate and function in its life.

25. An Industrial City.—A panorama of a rapidly expanding industrial city, peopled by groups drawn from many nations, who learn the American way of democratic life.

26. Grande Finale.—In a thrilling climax, outstanding people of various cultural backgrounds, from different parts of our country, summarize the story of "Americans All—Immigrants All."

It is suggested that excerpts such as the following from the "Americans All—Immigrants All" scripts be used for assembly programs. Scripts may be obtained from the Office of Education, Washington, D. C.

SCRIPT NO. 21—CONTRIBUTIONS IN SCIENCE

NARRATOR. We bring you the contributions which immigrants to the United States have made to the foundation of all our wealth, our comforts, our progress in understanding the world we live in—their contributions to science. These contributions have affected your health, your relation to your fellow men, and the satisfaction you have in life.

Music. (Chorus: Fanfare.)

2D NARRATOR. The first Nobel prize in physics ever given to an American goes to . . . Albert Abraham Michelson, Jewish immigrant from Germany, for . . .

READER. Determining the speed of light . . .

Music. (Chorus: Fanfare.)

NARRATOR. The first Nobel award in chemistry to an American goes to F. W. Richards, descendant of . . . Netherlanders and English, for . . .

READER. The most accurate determination of atomic weights.

Music. (Chorus: Fanfare.)

NARRATOR. The first Nobel award in medicine to an American goes to Alexis Carrel, immigrant from France, for . . .

READER. Success in suturing blood vessels and for transplantation of human organs . . .

Music. (Chorus: Fanfare.)

NARRATOR. Later Nobel awards, the highest international recognition scientists can win, have gone to Robert A. Millikan and Arthur Compton in physics, to Karl Landsteiner, once an Austrian, in medicine, and to Albert Einstein, once a citizen of Germany, a citizen of Switzerland when the prize came to him, later an immigrant, and now a citizen of the United States.

Music. (Chorus: Fanfare.)

NARRATOR. But European recognition of American scientists begins long before the Nobel prizes. In the summer of 1752, the son of an English immigrant was flying a kite in a thunderstorm—for a specific purpose . . .

Sound. (Thunder.)

READER. Just as he was beginning to despair of his experiment, he observed some loose threads of the hempen string beginning to stand erect . . .

FRANKLIN. Look, my boy, these threads . . . they are avoiding one another . . . Pull down the kite so that I can touch the key we tied to the string . . .

YOUNG MAN. Is it safe?

FRANKLIN. Perfectly . . .

Sound. (*Clap of Thunder.*)
    Now, observe closely . . . I touch my knuckle to the key. (*Pause.*) Ah!

YOUNG MAN. The spark . . . I saw it . . .

FRANKLIN. Yes, an electric spark . . . (*Fade on Thunder.*)

NARRATOR. So Benjamin Franklin brought the lightning down from the Heavens, as the French said when they paid honor to him . . . and a recent biographer has said, "He found electricity a curiosity and left it a science." Within a year, the Royal Society in London awarded him a medal and all Europe rang with his praise. And, like many other Americans, he instantly found a practical use for his discoveries . . . for he announced the lightning rod in the same year.

2D NARRATOR. Contributions to science! Oliver Evans, of Welsh descent, anticipating both the railroad train and the motor car by his application of the use of steam . . . John James Audubon painting the birds of America . . . Dr. Edward Trudeau dreaming a mountain-slope haven for the victims of tuberculosis, opening the windows of the United States, indicating the importance of pure air in the treatment of this disease . . .

3D NARRATOR. And, in other fields of medical service, the work of scientists rises to supreme importance . . .

NARRATOR. To the Japanese, Jokichi Takamine, we owe the drug adrenalin, potent stimulant of heart action and, at the same time, most useful to stop bleeding in the course of surgical operations. To Karl Landsteiner, of Austrian descent, we owe scientific study of blood groups, without which transfusion in desperate cases was always a matter of chance and guesswork, and significant work in infantile paralysis . . .

Sound. (Sneeze.)

1ST WOMAN. God bless you!

2D WOMAN. It's coming on again . . . every year at this time . . . hay fever . . . I'd rather be dead . . .

Sound. (Sneezes.)

NARRATOR. From a Chinese herb, Dr. K. K. Chen, himself of Chinese birth, developed ephedrin, used in hay fever and in the commonest of all ailments, the cold in the head. Whether it is a slight cold or a desperate illness, somewhere in the course of your treatment, you owe much to those men and women who came to the United States to find free opportunity to study, liberty to devote themselves to research . . . A few generations ago, diphtheria was like a plague . . .

Music. (Orchestra.)

MOTHER. Diphtheria! Oh, doctor, what can we do?

DOCTOR. There isn't very much . . . But she's a strong child . . . she'll pull through . . .

MOTHER. But she's stifling . . . she can't breathe.

DOCTOR. It'll get better. If we had only known that she might catch it . . .

MOTHER. She's choking, Doctor . . . do something . . . do something . . .

Sound. (Fade on Sobbing.)

NARRATOR. Something was done . . . While he was still living in Hungary, Béla Schick worked out the famous test called by his name, which determines in advance whether an individual is susceptible to diphtheria, and doctors estimate that hundreds of thousands of lives have been saved by this foreknowledge . . . And Joseph O'Dwyer, born in Cleveland of Irish descent, perfected a new method of treatment, and after years of experiments, found the way to introduce a breathing tube into the larynx, so that the victims of diphtheria escaped asphyxiation and had the chance to fight off the disease.

Music. (*Orchestra Up.*)

Other plagues of mankind have also been checked. There was pellagra—ravaging the South—its cause unknown until a scientific commission declared . . .

VOICE. Pellagra is an infectious disease . . .

NARRATOR. (*Continuing.*) . . . And Joseph Goldberger, a Jewish immigrant from Austria, was sent by the United States Public Health Service to check the infection . . .

GOLDBERGER. But I tell you it's not an infection . . . there's no proof . . . Listen . . . I admire Walter Reed . . . I worship him . . . yes, and Jesse W. Lazear and these unknown soldiers who exposed themselves to yellow fever . . . but they didn't prove that every disease is carried by an insect. They were scientists . . .

FRIEND. What do you propose to do?

GOLDBERGER. What can anyone do? I'm going to find out where pellagra happens . . . to what kind of people . . . in what conditions . . .

FRIEND. Look, Goldberger—you've given yourself typhus and yellow fever already in all your looking around . . . do me a favor . . . don't give yourself pellagra . . .

GOLDBERGER. I won't unless I have to . . .

NARRATOR. Did he have to? The story of Goldberger's tracking down pellagra as a disease of malnutrition is well known. He proved that pellagra came when diet was wrong; that pellagra could be prevented by proper diet. But for final proof . . .

GOLDBERGER. Apr. 25, 1916. Today, I made an injection into my veins of blood from a woman suffering from advanced pellagra . . . April 26 . . . Further injections today . . . April 30 . . . My wife also exposed herself to pellagra infection— *if it exists . . . (Pause . . . Triumph)* June 1 . . . There can be no question whatever, neither of us has shown the slightest trace of infection. Pellagra is not a bacterial infection— that much is certain . . .

ORATOR. *(Fading In.)* . . . And in view of Goldberger's discoveries, I move that we, the members of the American Society of Biochemists give the initial of his name to the pellagra-preventive vitamin—vitamin G—so that Goldberger's great achievement may always be remembered.

Sound. (Fade on Applause.)

NARRATOR. Goldberger's work was not done alone. In 1914, when he was just beginning to investigate pellagra, an announcement was made—very cautiously . . .

VOICE. *(Hesitant.)* . . . A yet unidentified dietary factor—fat soluble . . . *(Rising.)* vitamin A . . .

NARRATOR. So Elmer McCollum of Scotch-Irish descent first spoke of the revolution in our knowledge of diets . . . faithfully, he pushed his work on . . .

2D VOICE. Meanwhile Holst discovers vitamin C—against scurvy . . . and Goldberger makes his discoveries in pellagra . . .

3D VOICE. McCollum isolates vitamin D—the protection against rickets . . . and Evans isolates the vitamin which protects fertility . . .

NARRATOR. And these discoveries were matched by the creation, in the chemical laboratory, of the pure vitamins . . . so that where proper diet could not be had, medicine might be effective. And . . .

4TH VOICE. 1924 . . . Harry Steenbock, of Netherlands descent, turns over to the University of Wisconsin his patented process for increasing vitamin D in food by irradiation with ultraviolet ray . . .

NARRATOR. In this field, as in every other scientific work, men of many racial strains collaborated. But it is also notable that many different approaches were made . . . the experiments with human beings made by Goldberger; experiments with rats by McCollum; experiments in the laboratory by the creators of synthetic vitamins; finally, experiments with the ultraviolet ray by Steenbock. Where did the basic knowledge for all these experiments come from? So far, we have spoken of direct practical science—of electricity and engineering and medicine. Now let us look for a moment at pure research . . . let us start with a group of British scientists— meeting informally a few years ago—taking a straw vote . . .

ENGLISHMAN. We are now ready to announce the vote. Let me remind you, gentlemen, of the conditions. We have been trying to select the names of the twenty greatest men of science since the Renaissance . . . regardless of their field . . . . Your votes have been tabulated and . . .

Sound. (*Rattle of Paper.*)
Oh . . . it will no doubt be a matter of patriotic satisfaction to you to note that several of the leading names are those of our own countrymen . . . first, Sir Isaac Newton . . . (*Murmur after each name.*) second, Charles Darwin. In third place, two names are bracketed, Michael Faraday and Albert Einstein. Fifth, Willard Gibbs . . . Let me say, gentlemen, that the name of Willard Gibbs, the first American on our list, occurs in high place in every single one of your ballots . . . Though little known to the world outside of science . . . (*Fade.*)

NARRATOR. Willard Gibbs, of English descent, has been called the father of physical chemistry . . . He worked obscurely at Yale University and the details of his accomplishments are far too complicated to be casually explained. But this can be said—wherever chemistry enters modern industry—which is almost everywhere—the work of Gibbs has been of supreme importance.

NARRATOR. It doesn't matter to the scientist that the practical result should come at once . . . it matters only that the search for truth should continue . . . the search for truth about nature—and about man—and it goes on . . .

1ST VOICE. Ales Hrdlicka . . . born in Bohemia . . . of the Smithsonian Institution . . . student of ancient man in North America . . .

2D VOICE. Franz Boas, student of the races of man, enemy of all racial tryanny . . .

3D VOICE. Menas Gregory, of Armenian descent, student of the mind of man, for over twenty years head of the psychopathic department of Bellevue Hospital in New York.

NARRATOR. These men, and many others, contributed to our understanding of ourselves . . . others to our mastery of the world around us . . .

Sound. (*Mule Team Plodding Along.*)

DRIVER. Want a ride, boy?

CARVER. (*Negro.*) Thank you, sir. You needn't stop . . . I'll hop in behind.

DRIVER. Where you going?

CARVER. Fort Scott . . . if I can make it . . .

DRIVER. What's the matter? Tired?

CARVER. No . . . just broke . . . might have to stop and work a couple of days to get some money.

DRIVER. I'll take you into Fort Scott. What are you aiming to do there?

CARVER. Go to school. It's hard for a colored boy to get a good schooling, but I think at Fort Scott I could get a job.

Sound. (*Fade on Wheels.*)

WOMAN. Yes, I can give you a job . . . but if you want to go to school . . .

CARVER. I'll go to school nights when you don't need me . . . and I'll work nights if you do need me.

WOMAN. Well, it's pretty hard work . . . you'll have to do a lot of washing . . . and work around the place.

CARVER. Just my meals and a place to sleep . . . and a little money for books . . .

WOMAN. All right . . . suppose you start raking the leaves.

CARVER. Yes, ma'am . . .

NARRATOR. George Washington Carver, born right after the War between the States, in Missouri, learning to read out of an old blue-backed speller, as Booker T. Washington had done, working for nine years as a servant, going into laundry work to make his way through high school, slowly prepared himself for scientific research . . . and, presently, tackled the basic problem not only of the Negro in the South, but of the South itself . . . and a few years ago, was called before a Congressional Committee . . .

CARVER. (*Fading In.*) And that's all I can tell you in ten minutes. Thank you very much, gentlemen . . .

VOICES. No . . . no. Go on! Go on!

CHAIRMAN. It seems to be the unanimous opinion of the Committee, Mr. Carver, that our rule of ten-minute speeches should be suspended in your case. I agree with that opinion. We've had hundreds of experts here and most of them we wish had stopped after five minutes . . . But you go ahead . . . as long as you like . . .

CARVER. Thank you. It seems strange to be talking about the ordinary peanut as if it were so important, but it is, gentlemen. The South has had one product in the past—cotton; now it has cotton and tobacco—but it needs more. But we don't know how to use our own products—and that's been my work. If we can use the peanut, the pecan—the potato—whatever we have—if we can bring them into industry—and make useful things out of them—can't you see what a difference it would make? New factories . . . new machines making things we need . . .

(*Overlap.*)

NARRATOR. The Negro, George Washington Carver, told the committee about the 115 products he had extracted from the peanut . . . and other native sources . . . breakfast foods and a type of coffee, flour, lard, axle grease, face powder, ink, soap, and linoleum. So one patient scientist in his laboratory turns all his thoughts to the benefits of his fellow man—but the knowledge he uses goes back to the researcher whose work may never seem practical at all. There was once a Yugoslav immigrant, Michael Pupin, who made some of the basic inventions for long-distance telephone and the radio . . . and who said at the end of his life . . .

PUPIN. But best of all were my pupils. The greatest thing was to start others on their way . . . There was Millikan . . . Millikan's people must have come over here when the first Scotch-Irish were invited to settle on the Indian frontier. He wasn't planning to study physics, but somehow physics got hold of him . . . and, when he wanted to go abroad and study more, when he was through with what I could give him, I helped him to go, and Michelson sent for him to come to the University of Chicago . . .

NARRATOR. So Pupin, the immigrant inventor, and Michelson, the immigrant scientist, both helped along the career of Millikan, who won the Nobel prize for his researches into the great mystery of the cosmic ray . . . and it may be centuries before the knowledge we have of cosmic radiation is put to practical use . . . but that doesn't matter in science.

VOICE. What is important in science?

NARRATOR. To keep alive the free spirit of investigation . . . to recognize that the search for truth knows no boundaries of politics or race or creed.

VOICE. Consider the names of those who created the telephone as we know it today . . . Alexander Graham Bell of Scottish birth; Thomas Alva Edison, of Netherlands descent; Emile Berliner, a Jewish immigrant from Germany; Michael Pupin, immigrant from Yugoslavia.

2D VOICE. Consider those who made the radio as we know it to-day . . . Nikola Tesla, immigrant from Yugoslavia, Lee de Forest, Alexanderson and Werner, Swedes . . .

3D VOICE. Consider the single study of the scourge of cancer . . . Leo Loeb . . . Ludvig Hektoen . . . Alexis Carrel . . . Felix Bernstein . . . Cey . . . McDonald . . . Sigerist . . . and the notable figure of Dr. Maud Slye of Chicago . . . following different lines of research . . . disagreeing in method perhaps, but never kept apart by any consideration that they represent half a dozen racial and national stocks.

NARRATOR. It is impossible to say which man or woman did most . . . since all have given the one thing which is above all measure . . . complete devotion to finding out the truth. The knowledge they have given is to be turned into power by ourselves and by the Americans of the future. To that knowledge, every nation which has sent immigrants to the United States has contributed in full measure . . . and our lives are safer and better for the work in science by these Americans All.

Music. (Up and Under.)

NARRATOR. Nothing is ever done by one group alone. The making of the United States goes on—today as always—by endless co-operative effort.

Music. (Up and Out.)

V

A SAMPLE HOMEROOM DISCUSSION[1]

MRS. ECKERSEN. Doubtless by this time you have connected me
with your Human Relations project, and it's about that
project that I want to speak to you. So far we have had
three culture groups: the Chinese, the Japanese, and the
Jewish, and you will have the Mexican and the South
American in May.

Before I take up the Jewish culture group in particular,
I'd like to say a few things about human relations in general, and mention at least three things which I'd like to
have you get from this work.

First, we must learn not to generalize in regard to groups
of people. By that I mean that because the only Chinese
whom you may have known was a laundryman, you must
not think that all Chinese are laundrymen. Or if you have
had an unpleasant experience with an Italian or Polish
child, you must not think that friendship with all Polish
and Italian children will give you a similar experience.

You may ride in the subway, and think you are jostled
by a person who you are sure is a Jew. He may not be a
Jew, but you may come home and talk about the aggressive
and pushing New York Jew. Is it fair to attach such a
characteristic to any other Jew you may meet? In other
words, would it be fair for you to feel that all teachers are
ogres because you have had one teacher who seemed unfair
or tyrannical? I wonder now if you understand what I
mean by *generalizing,* that is, attaching to a group of people
characteristics you have found in one of that group.

The second thing that I'd like to have you get out of
the project is to learn to look at things positively, not negatively. You have all heard of the optimist who looked at

---

[1] From the *Field Notebook.*

the doughnut, while the pessimist looked at the hole. In other words, the optimist is looking for something real, tangible, something to take hold of, something meaty and useful, and the pessimist sees only the negative, the nothingness, the unpleasant side. To illustrate: When you first came into this room, your teacher may have stood in the front of the room and, as she looked at the class, without meaning to, she may have thought, "What a terrible-looking class! I'll bet I have some awful rascals here. They certainly look dumb, and I'm sure I won't be able to trust them. I'll just have to play policeman all the time." Now if she merely thought this, it would be only a minute before you would all realize that here was a teacher with whom you would have difficulty working, and without meaning to, you would doubtless begin living up to her conception of you. And the personal equation would be so poor that the class would be most unsuccessful. But she does *not* do this. Instead, like any other good teacher, she thinks as she looks at you, "What a nice-looking class this is! I'm going to have a good time working with them. I presume some of them may be only average, but I may have some geniuses here. At least I'm sure they're going to be trustworthy, and so I shall trust them." In other words she is looking at the class positively, not negatively, is looking for good qualities, true qualities—in other words, the doughnut. And immediately you like her and you feel her interest, and the class bids fair to be a success.

Now the same thing can be applied to your everyday life, in the way that you look at your friends. If you look for the good qualities, the positive qualities, in other words the doughnut, you will be a whole lot happier than if you look for the bad traits, the negative qualities, or the hole.

Applying this to our Human Relations Project, let us look for those same positive qualities in people of other cultural backgrounds, other races, other religions.

Now the third thing: learn to appreciate peoples' differences. Because the Chinese read from what we call the back of the book toward the front whereas we read from what they call the end toward the beginning is no reason why you should feel that they are queer. I recall hearing some young children of German and Italian background taunting and ridiculing one another with "You eat barrels of sauerkraut!" and "You eat barrels of spaghetti!" As if that were a basis of separation. As if both foods were not now a part of the American menu! If we stop to think of it, people from all over the world do the same thing for the same reason, but in different ways. They eat when they are hungry; they laugh when they are happy; they dance when they want to celebrate; they play games when they want to exercise. They do all of these things differently. So it makes no difference how people do these things when they all do them for the same reason.

While we're talking about appreciating differences, let me plead with you to appreciate your own background, and never to be ashamed of it. Don't be like the two little boys I had in class who, because their names ended in "vich," changed their names when they first came to the town and for the next six years went under what they presumed was a more American name. When their father discovered it he raised Old Ned, and I could hardly blame him. These boys were made to realize that Yugoslavia was a country to be proud of; that her people possessed courage and a love of liberty; that they possessed a culture which had added much to American life. And so, the boys were no longer ashamed of their background. If your parents speak Italian or Polish, or any other foreign language, don't answer them in English; learn to speak the language yourself just as your parents are learning English. Learn what it stands for, and what the people from that country have brought to America, which makes her the country she is. In other words don't cheat yourselves out of the opportunity to enrich your knowledge and experience by being able to understand people of other culture groups. Through this understanding you will become a better American. Be like the man who, standing on a mountain, looks off into the valley and sees approaching him, at a distance, a beast. As it comes closer he sees that it is a man, and as it comes still closer, he sees that it is his brother. Through understanding and appreciation of the other fellow, you will find that he will become your brother.

Now today I want to speak particularly about the Jewish culture group. For here we live next to the city which has the largest Jewish population of any city in the world. In fact, there are more Jews in New York City than in Jerusalem. I wonder if you know just what they have contributed to our common life, to America, to civilization. Can anyone tell me a contribution of the Jews?

PUPILS. Business methods.

The Bible.

Our religion.

The recording of thoughts.

MRS. E. All right. Let's stop for a minute and consider these four. The first we'll leave till the last, and we'll take up first the religious contributions. Just how did the Jews contribute to religion, to Christianity?

JEWISH PUPIL. They were the first to believe in one God.

MRS. E. And from that belief what two other religions have grown up?

PUPIL. Christianity and Mohammedanism.

MRS. E. Why Christianity?

PUPIL. Because they gave us the Bible.

Mrs. E. Any other reason? (*No responses.*) Who was the founder of Christianity?

Pupils. Christ.

Mrs. E. And from what people did Christ come?

One or Two Pupils. He was a Jew.

Mrs. E. That's right. So, naturally, having been brought up in Judaism, He was familiar with its laws and prophecies and with the Jewish home customs and temple services. He took part in the celebration of Passover, we know, because the Last Supper was a Passover feast. So from Judaism sprang Christianity. Mohammedanism has its roots in Judaism, too, because Mohammed acquainted himself with all the Jewish writings and accepted all of them and all the prophets and all the teachers, and added only himself as the greatest prophet.

Now for the second contribution, that of the Bible. Who can tell me the name of the Jews' sacred book?

Pupil. The Torah.

Mrs. E. Can anyone tell me what "Torah" means? (*No response.*) "Torah" means Law, and the first five books of the Bible comprise the Jewish Torah. It is the Law which has bound the Jews together and caused them to survive these thousands of years of persecution, for these laws are not only religious, but they contain laws of health and sanitation. The orthodox Jew still lives up to these implicitly, whereas the conservative and reformed group are not so strict. In the Bible the Jews have given us the first recorded history, contained in such books as I and II Kings, I and II Samuel, Esther, Ruth, and so on, and the first written poetry, the Psalms. Perhaps that's what you meant when you spoke of the Jews' recording thought.

Now for the contribution of business methods. Before we go into this, we'll have to know what this boy has in mind by the expression "business methods."

PUPIL. Well, the Jews always charge more for a thing than they think it's worth, and then as you start to walk out of the store, they go down in the price until you buy it, and even then you've probably paid more than it's worth.

ANOTHER PUPIL. I can't see why the Jews buy something for a nickel and sell it for a quarter, when they oughtn't to charge more than a dime.

MRS. E. But if a person really did that, would anybody buy from him? And if you did buy for a quarter what you could buy for a dime, at a five-and-ten-cent store, we'll say, wouldn't *you* be the foolish one? If it were possible to do what you describe, not only Jews would do it, but everyone.

PUPIL. Yes, but nobody else would try it.

MRS. E. You know enough about human nature and greed as a human instinct to know that many who could get away with such a thing would probably do it, and that if you bought such an article, you yourself would be responsible for the man's being able to get away with it. But don't we have to examine our whole system of producing and distributing goods before we can discover what practices are the fairest to all concerned?

We might, however, take up the custom you spoke of—that of asking more than you expect to get. That is an Eastern custom, which all good Oriental traders have used for centuries. In fact, if you ask an Arab first to pay you what a thing is worth, he thinks you are insulting his intelligence, and feel that he is incapable of bargaining. It is only the Jews—and others of Oriental background—who are most recently from Europe who continue to practice this custom, and it is one which they must and do slough off after they've been here a little while. People the world over have different customs of trade, as they have different customs of eating, dancing, and so on.

Are there any other questions you have to ask about Jews,

or any ideas you have about them which you would like
to talk about?

PUPIL. Well, the Jews killed Christ.

MRS. E. Did they? Who was in authority in Palestine when
Jesus was preaching?

PUPIL. The Romans.

MRS. E. Yes, and the hierarchy of Temple priests had great
authority with the people. They with some exceptions
wanted to hold on to their privileged position. Jesus was
to them a disturbing influence as He was to the civil authorities. Jews in power and Romans in power contributed
to His condemnation, but you must remember that the vast
majority of the common people who were His followers
were Jews. Now let us look at the Gospels. In all four of
them we find that Jews were tried by *Pilate,* the *Roman*
governor, and turned over to the soldiers for execution.
The soldiers of course were Roman. The mob that followed,
which was mostly Jewish, was partly for Him and partly
against Him, that's true, but that is true of mobs everywhere. And then we must remember that Jesus was at that
time important only to a handful of people. By the others
He was looked upon as queer and odd, teaching a simple
doctrine of brotherly love, which somehow or other always
gets under peoples' skins. For instance, look how the world
looks at Gandhi, and yet he is far better known than was
Jesus; for in all the histories of the time there are only two
tiny mentions of Jesus, and in those He is called a political
leader who led a revolt against the Romans. You see the
teachings of Christianity might have died out entirely, because He had such a small following, had it not been for the
first Christian press agent and missionary, Paul. And it was
really Paul who exaggerated and emphasized the crucifixion
of Jesus, for he taught "Christ Crucified," and brought out
that because of the crucifixion and then the resurrection,

Christ proved His sonship with God. And Paul, the Roman citizen, was himself a Jew.

Do you see what errors we fall into when we attempt to generalize? I should like to leave with you today, for your further consideration, the three ideas you were asked to examine when we began this talk. First, learn not to generalize in regard to groups of people; second, learn to look at things positively, not negatively; third, learn to appreciate peoples' differences; for underneath, we are all alike.

VI

COMMENTS AND OUTCOMES

SOME COMMENTS OF STUDENTS[1]

1. "I have learned to call all people—my neighbors. I have learned to love their ways of living and to respect them more for what they have done. I think these programs have opened my eyes to the fact that each country and each set of people has its own beautiful music, colors, and many other things."—9B girl.

2. "I have learned that hatred between different races of people is mostly caused by propaganda."—9B boy.

3. "I haven't changed my mind because I never had any real jealousy." —8B girl.

4. "I have changed my attitude toward most of the groups. For instance, I've always considered Italians as outcast people but the programs have changed me. Probably a colored program would change my attitude toward the colored race."—9A boy.

5. "I learned that other people have contributed just as much to the world as we have."

6. "I go to Hebrew school and did not want to learn Hebrew, but when I heard that girl singing Hebrew, I was more interested in learning the language."

7. "I have changed my attitude toward the Mexicans and now I regard them as one of us."

8. "I have learned that the Scottish people are not all stingy; Italians are not all dirty; Polish are not all sullen; Jews are not all money

---

[1] Made by students of Englewood, N. J., Junior High School.

hogs; Germans are not anxious to start wars with the United States; Mexicans are not bandits and do not play guitars all day; Latin Americans are not half-naked in a very hot country; Chinese are very prosperous sometimes and are not all laundrymen or bandits or pirates; and Negroes—well, I've always felt as though they were like me, being around them all my life."

9. "My feeling toward the Jewish people has changed because of Miss Ephraim's visit to us in English class."

10. "I find that every country or nationality has its good and bad people. Most of the people are just like us."

11. "I have changed my attitude toward the Jews—partly because of the study and partly because I enquired most in the way of religion and found some resemblance between mine and theirs." (This from an Italian American of Roman Catholic faith.)

12. "I have changed my attitude toward the Chinese. I never used to go to a Chinese laundry because I was told that if you smile or laugh they would stab you with a knife. But now I even go to see Lee Poy in the afternoon to talk with him."

13. "I believe I have learned to realize that you can't judge a country by one person in it."

SOME COMMENTS OF TEACHERS

1. "The contact with lecturers of other races has given the pupils a sense of their 'similarity' to us. The project has given teachers as well as students a greater knowledge of cultural backgrounds and alertness to cultural and racial matters, with a feeling of understanding and appreciation."—Head of Literature Department.

2. "The informal lecture of Mr. Aaron Douglas, Negro artist, was applauded with much enthusiasm. An interchange of ideas in art in our various races is necessary. Art is a particular expression, which differs and remains the same in all countries."—Head of Art Department.

3. "At least we can say that teachers, students, and community leaders had several very pleasing and satisfying experiences with people who represent various culture groups. This in itself is bound to affect our attitudes and may lead us into the habit of acting in a more tolerant way in our own real-life situations."—Head of History Department.

4. "Personally, I have gained a great deal. I must have been a biased person because I can now see many mistakes in my life where I have not given the foreign-born a fair chance simply because I thought America must come first in all things. I had a particular dislike for Negroes and Jews simply through misunderstanding them.

I wish every public-school teacher might have the opportunity of being a part of such a project. The mental transformations are amazing."—Head of Music Department.

5. "One of the greatest benefits of the project is that the students have been led into a much wider field in their own reading—*not assigned reading*. They are reading of China, Mexico, and Italy in particular, and finding great pleasure in something besides fiction."—Teacher of English.

6. "The Intercultural Relations project has made our students more alert in the matter of the great need for peace and friendly understanding among the nations of the world. It has helped to make vivid the realization that all people contribute to our world." —Head of English Department.

7. "The course is of great educational value from both the cultural and the informative factors of real education. I believe we should have more of this sort of thing in our schools."—Head of Science Department.

SOME COMMENTS OF PRINCIPALS

1. "This is what our schools need. It is vital, alive, real. It makes the students think and reason. It should be a part of the activity of every school in the city."

2. "May I once again express to you my appreciation for the worthwhileness of the program in education for a better understanding of relations to our fellow men? The program which was put on in the Englewood School last year was not only a success, but was of great value to us; and in a similar way I feel that we are deriving increased benefit from the program that is being put on this year. I have faith that the outcome of all of this will mean a better understanding and a more sympathetic attitude on the part of our students toward the peoples of other races and nationalities.

"May I assure you of our desire to continue to co-operate with you and your group in the splendid work you are doing."

3. "We are exceedingly well pleased with the programs. The pupils' reaction has been beyond our expectations. A consciousness of other cultures is being established in an admirable manner."

4. "This morning we had the second of our programs on 'Education in Human Relations.' The first was on 'China.' With the follow-up materials which Mrs. Eckersen furnished, in addition to the personal interest which she has shown in the work, it was a splendid success. It has proven to be a very valuable asset in our teaching. From the way in which the program this morning on 'Great Britain' was presented, I feel that it will be as great a benefit as was the one on 'China.'

"I sincerely hope that your committee will be able to continue the work which, judging from its results, seems to be so excellent."

5. "We were more than pleased with the results from this program which you supervised in our school last year. The little flurry over the colored question has subsided and I think that the net results even with them has been good. I am sorry that we will not be able to continue the program as we had it last year, due to the Bureau not having a field secretary; however, many of the teachers who were in your class are enthusiastically speaking of the work and will undoubtedly continue it upon their own initiative."

VII

AN OVERVIEW OF THE GROUPS THAT CO-OPERATED IN BUILDING OUR COUNTRY[1]

A little more than three hundred years ago, from a land three thousand miles across the sea, the handful of people who began to build our country came and settled upon a narrow, wooded frontier that faced the Atlantic Ocean. Today that frontier has disappeared. Today our country—three million square miles of it, occupied by 133,000,000 people—stretches up and down and across the whole heart of the North American continent.

Beginnings. In the year 1565, forty-two years before the coming of the English to Jamestown, the Spanish founded St. Augustine, Florida; and in 1598 the Spanish from Mexico established the first capital of New Mexico. Through all the early years, Spanish adventurers and missionaries explored and settled the southern expanse of our country. They irrigated its deserts and built up the beginnings of our great cattle industry. They planted California's first vineyards and fruit orchards, and developed there an American architecture—a blend of Spanish and Indian types—of which we are today very proud.

In 1607 the English came and slowly—moving by inches, as James Truslow Adams says—planted their towns up and down

---

[1] Ruth Edwards Davis, "Yet All One People," *Junior Red Cross Journal,* Washington, D. C.

the Atlantic seaboard. They came in larger numbers, filling the seaboard and thus pushing the later comers westward. They founded our fisheries and floated our merchant marine. They wrote our first school laws and established our language, our form of government, and our fundamental law. They and their children pushed westward, settling here, there, almost every· where; quietly, surely establishing, by reason of their numbers or their prestige or both, their language and their institutions.

Early in the 1600's the French came. They passed up the St. Lawrence River and down the Mississippi Valley to New Orleans. Missionaries, explorers, fur trappers, and traders, they made friends with the Indians and settled here and there in nine of our present middle states. French Huguenots (Protestants) came and settled among the people of our seaboard colonies. From Priscilla Mullens to the LaFollettes, their names dot our history books; and wherever they settled, their influence upon the manners and the food of the people may still be traced.

Netherlanders, too, came early and made New Amsterdam, even in 1643, "the common city of all cities in the world." They gave us delicious foods, our first windmills, our New Year's Day celebration, our Santa Claus, and some of our early public elementary schools.

In 1638 the Swedes and the Finns came. They bought land from the Indians and settled along the lower banks of the Delaware River. They gave us the house of horizontally laid logs, which was soon to become a familiar part of life on our expanding frontier.

In 1619 the Negroes came. As individuals they had taken part in early discoveries and explorations. Now, removed forcibly from their homeland, they came into Jamestown unwillingly, and continued so to come for more than two hundred years. During that time they helped to transform the Southern wilderness into prosperous plantations and developed the song, music, and dance that were to become the Negro spirituals and the work songs— real American folk music.

In the 1700's the Scotch-Irish and the Germans, because of political, economic, and religious persecution, and at the invitation of the English, began to come in large numbers. They settled the frontiers in Massachusetts, Pennsylvania, Virginia, and the Carolinas, thus protecting the earlier comers from the Indians. Together they formed the courageous vanguard of the westward movement, developing as they went—especially the Scotch-Irish—an aggressive democracy. Like the Negro, many of these people, as well as people of other countries, were sold to masters as redemptioners or bonded servants. In Pennsylvania, many of the Germans remained in their original settlements and preserved their language and their folkways. These people are today known as the "Pennsylvania Dutch," or, more properly, the "Pennsylvania Germans." Examples of their art are today finding important places in museums throughout the country.

In the 1800's and 1900's. Toward the end of the 1700's the United States emerged, and time passed swiftly into the 1800's. Canals were dug; old buffalo and Indian trails were widened into transcontinental roads; railroads were built. And the immigrant played always an important part in this development of our country.

Toward the middle of the nineteenth century mass immigration—impelled by the Irish famine and the German revolution—began again. Irish filled the factories of our Northeastern towns and cities, built canals, roads, railroads, and passed on to easier and better-paying jobs. Germans helped to build up the farming states of the Middle West. They brought music to our communities and educational methods to our schools. They gave us the Christmas tree and educational toys.

Austrians and Hungarians came, and they too became givers and sharers in American life. Scandinavian farmers built up the great farming sections in our upper Mississippi Valley and took part in the logging and lumbering industry. Finns established our first co-operatives, took on the cranberry bogs of our New England states, and became leaders in the fishing industry on the Pacific Coast.

Greek sponge divers developed our sponge industry in Florida, and Portuguese became leaders in our fishing industry off the New England coast. Welsh, English, Scotch-Irish, Scots, Irish, and later Slavs, Lithuanians, and Italians, entered our mines and mills and built and serviced our railroads. They made possible the development of some of our largest industries, among them the iron and steel, the meat-packing, textile, and building-trades industries.

Poles took over abandoned farms, and immigrants from Russia helped to make us the greatest grain-growing nation in the world. Italians came in large numbers and took the place of the Irish on our roads and railroads. They, too, transformed wastelands and abandoned farms into flourishing gardens. They brought us music, song, color, and an appreciation of beauty for its own sake.

Chinese, drawn at first by the discovery of gold in California and later by invitation from our industrialists, came to our Pacific seaboard and performed most of the work of building our Western railroads. Japanese followed the Chinese and helped California to attain an important place as provider of fruits and vegetables to the country.

Jews from Spain and Portugal had taken part in the discovery, explorations, and early settlements of America. Now they came from Germany, Poland, Russia, and other countries in large numbers and became complete participators in American life.

Armenians became rug merchants and factory workers in our Eastern cities, professors in our colleges and universities, and workers in various enterprises and industries on our Pacific Coast. Hindus studied and taught in our universities, and, loving the land, became agriculturists in our Western states.

After the First World War, large numbers of immigrants from Mexico, the Philippines, and Hawaii came and helped to develop the industries of our Southwest and our Middle states.

Today, people from many countries are among us—new immigrants fleeing, as in the old days, from political, economic, and religious persecution; ready, as in the old days, to contribute their best to our developing American culture.

VIII

SOME "DO'S" AND "DON'T'S"

Don't use such terms as "your people," "we Protestants," "we Jews," when speaking in a mixed group. Such terms seem to connote the idea of feelings of separateness on your part, and sometimes of condescension.

Do say, "those of us of Negro background," or "of Jewish (or Protestant) faith."

Don't use words like "Negress," "pickaninny," "darky." They carry with them a hangover of slave days.

Avoid all derogatory terms about any group, as "kike," "dago," "greaser," "squarehead."

Don't say "Chinaman." Say "Chinese." *Don't* say "Scotch." Say "Scots" or "Scottish."

Don't say "half-breeds" when speaking of some American Indians. Do say "mixed bloods."

Be careful to know when the term "Jew" indicates a religion, a culture, or a nationality. Remember that it *never* indicates a race.

Beware of considering all people in any group to be alike. Not all Negroes sing or dance; not all are cooks or laborers; not all Chinese are laundrymen.

Remember that only non-citizens can be considered a "nationality group." People born here or naturalized are American citizens and therefore have no other nationality. One can use such a term as "Americans of Italian origin." *Don't* call such people "Italians" but "Italian Americans." *Don't* hyphenate the words unless they are used together as an adjective modifier, as "Italian-American girl."

Overcome any confusion about who are the first and second generation. The immigrants themselves are the "first generation"; their children are the "second generation."

Remember that those whose ancestors have been here for several generations may be called "old-stock Americans." *Remember also that,* although these are mainly of British stock, many families of Spanish, Negro, and various kinds of Jewish and other backgrounds are also "old-stock Americans."

Don't forget that Puerto Ricans are American citizens although they have a Spanish culture, and that Spanish is their mother tongue as it is that of many people living in at least four of our states.

Don't confuse the terms "interfaith," "interracial," and "intercultural." The first has to do with relationships among people of various religions; the second with relationships among people of the racial groups (anthropologists generally agree on only three large major racial groups: the "Mongolian," the "Caucasian," and the "Negro"); and the term "intercultural," the latest to be coined, concerns relationships among all the various groups in American life and could also refer to such relationships on an international level. (The term "culture," as used by most sociologists, refers to the typical ways of thinking or acting of a group of people.)

The term "Negro," since it refers to one of the three races, is capitalized, as are the other two. One does not capitalize "colored," however, for that is comparable to "white."

Be careful not to tell jokes that deride any group. Remember that laughing *with* people unites; laughing *at* them separates.

A guiding principle to remember is that one's ego is deflated when the group one feels a member of is maligned in any way, and, conversely, one's ego is inflated when one's group receives praise or recognition.

If a member of a minority group, *try to overcome* the natural tendency to be supersensitive by taking second thought before condemning. If a member of a dominant group, *try to overcome* callousness and indifference toward minority-group people "by putting yourself in the other person's shoes."

IX

"MUST" READINGS IN INTERCULTURAL RELATIONS

1. Adamic, Louis. *From Many Lands.* New York: Harper & Brothers, 1940.

2. Alland, Alexander. *American Counterpoint.* New York; John Day Co., 1943. A photographic story showing the cultural diversity of our schools, churches, and other institutions.

3. Benedict, Ruth. *Race: Science and Politics.* New York: Viking Press, 1943. Distinguishes between the scientific study of human differences and race propaganda.

4. Brown, Francis J., and Roucek, Joseph (eds.). *One America: Our Racial and National Minorities* (rev. ed.). New York: Prentice-Hall, Inc., 1945.

5. *Common Ground.* Common Council for American Unity, 222 Fourth Avenue, New York, N. Y. A quarterly magazine.

6. Department of Supervisors and Directors. *Americans All: Studies in Intercultural Education.* Washington, D. C.: National Education Association, 1942. Reports from schools in different parts of the country describing what and how they are developing for programs in intercultural education.

7. DuBois, Rachel Davis. *Get Together Americans.* New York: Harper & Brothers, 1943. A tested method for bringing people of various groups together in an atmosphere of friendly understanding, used in P.T.A.'s, churches, homes, and schools.

8. DuBois, W. E. B. *Black Folk. Then and Now.* New York: Henry Holt & Co., 1939. The best one-volume history of the Negro from ancient Africa to modern America.

9. Duncan, Ethel M. *Democracy's Children: Adventures in Intercultural Education for the Elementary School.* New York: Hinds, Hayden & Eldredge, 1945.

10. Embree, Edwin R. *Brown Americans*. New York: Viking Press, 1943. Probably the best single introductory volume available.

11. Holt, Rackham. *George Washington Carver*. New York: Doubleday, Doran & Co., 1943. The life story of a great scientist.

12. Janowsky, Oscar (ed.). *The American Jew*. New York: Harper & Brothers, 1942. The role of the Jew in American life with chapters written by several authorities.

13. Kunkel, Fritz. *In Search of Maturity*. New York: Charles Scribner's Sons, 1943. Since prejudice is partly due to personality maladjustment, this book should be read by those who attempt to guide the prejudiced.

14. LaFarge, John. *The Race Question and the Negro*. New York: Longmans, Green & Co., 1944. A notable study of the Catholic doctrine on interracial justice.

15. Lee, Alfred McClung, and Humphrey, N. D. *Race Riot*. New York: Dryden Press, 1943. Points the way to riot prevention: a careful analysis of the Detroit riot.

16. McWilliams, Carey. *Brothers under the Skin*. New York: Little, Brown & Co., 1943. Deals with the past history of our discrimination against the Negro, Indian, Mexican, Japanese, Chinese, Hawaiian, Puerto Rican, and Filipino. Proposes a national solution.

17. Mangione, Jerre. *Mount Allegro*. Boston: Houghton Mifflin Co., 1943. An entertaining but sympathetic story of some people of Italian background becoming "the life blood of a new nation."

18. Ottley, Roi. *New World A-Coming*. Boston: Houghton Mifflin Co., 1943. Urbane, entertaining, and highly informative. A "best seller."

19. Plant, James S. *Personality and the Cultural Pattern*. New York: Commonwealth Fund, 1937. The importance to mental hygiene of giving youth a feeling of pride in cultural backgrounds and a sense of belonging in American life.

20. Saenger, Gerhart. *Today's Refugees, Tomorrow's Citizens*. New York: Harper & Brothers, 1940. Real-life stories of some of the immigrants who are leaders in American life today.

21. Sargent, Daniel. *Our Land and Our Lady*. New York: Longmans, Green & Co., 1939. A scholarly book interestingly written showing the role of Catholicism in the building of America.

22. Wittke, Carl. *We Who Built America*. New York: Prentice-Hall, 1939. One of the best overviews of the coming of all groups to America.

X

BIBLIOGRAPHY

INCLUDING SOURCES OF MATERIALS[1]

The following bibliography is by no means exhaustive, and often newer books are listed at the expense of older books. The older books may be found in many already prepared bibliographies. Book lists can be obtained from most of the organizations listed under "Sources of Information and Material," and from magazines such as *Common Ground* and the various culture group periodicals.

Anthropology

Benedict, Ruth. *Patterns of Culture*. Boston: Houghton Mifflin Co., 1934.

————. *Race: Science and Politics*. New York: Modern Age Books, 1940.

————, and Weltfish, Gene. *The Races of Mankind*. New York: Public Affairs Committee, Inc., 30 Rockefeller Plaza, 1943.

Boas, Franz. *Race, Language, and Culture*. New York: Macmillan Co., 1940.

Herskovits, Melville. *The Myth of the Negro Past*. New York: Harper & Brothers, 1941.

Hooton, Ernest Albert. *Up From the Ape*. New York: Macmillan Co., 1931.

Howells, William. *Mankind So Far*. New York: Doubleday, Doran & Co., 1944.

Huxley, Julian, and Haddon, A. C. *We Europeans*. New York: Harper & Brothers, 1936.

Journal of Negro Education. "The Physical and Mental Abilities of the American Negro." Washington, D. C.: Howard University Press, July, 1934.

Klineberg, Otto (ed.). *Characteristics of the American Negro*. New York: Harper & Brothers, 1944.

————. *Race Differences*. New York: Harper & Brothers, 1935.

Linton, Ralph. *The Study of Man: An Introduction*. New York: D. Appleton-Century Co., 1936.

---

[1] Prepared with the assistance of Ruth Edwards Davis.

Mead, Margaret. *And Keep Your Powder Dry.* New York: William Morrow & Co., 1942.

————. *Growing Up in New Guinea.* New York: William Morrow & Co., 1930.

Montagu, M. Ashley. *Man's Most Dangerous Myth: The Fallacy of Race.* New York: Columbia University Press, 1942.

Powdermaker, Hortense. *A Study of Prejudices.* New York: Harper & Brothers, 1944.

Sumner, W. G. *The Folkways.* Boston: Ginn and Co., 1907.

Taylor, Eva. *Men Are Brothers.* New York: Viking Press, 1937. (For young people.)

Wissler, Clark. *Man and Culture.* New York: Thomas Y. Crowell Co., 1923.

Bibliographies

American Association of University Women. *A Selective List of Books for Building International Attitudes in Childhood.* Washington, D. C.: The Association, 1937.

American League for Peace and Democracy. *A Bibliography on Anti-Semitism.* New York: The League.

Board of Public Education. *Orientals Are People, Too.* Philadelphia, 1944.

Carman, Harry J. *Guide for the Study of American Social Problems.* New York: Columbia University Press, 1942.

Council Against Intolerance in America. *An American Answer to Intolerance.* New York: The Council.

Crisis Book Shop. *Selected Titles By and About the Negro.* 69 Fifth Avenue, New York, N. Y.

Department of Supervisors and Directors. *Americans All: Studies in Intercultural Education,* "Bibliography." Washington, D. C.: National Education Association, 1942.

East and West Association. *Peoples East and West.* New York: The Association, 1944.

Lomax, Alan, and Cowell, Sidney R. *American Folk Song and Folk Lore: A Regional Bibliography.* Progressive Education Association Service Center pamphlet.

Mitchell, Lucy Sprague, and Boetz, Johanna. *The People of the U.S.A.: Their Place in the School Curriculum.* New York: Progressive Education Association, 1942.

National Conference of Christians and Jews. *A Goodwill Booklet for Each Year.* New York.

New York City Association of Teachers of English. *Readings on Tolerance and Democratic Ideals for Teachers and Students.* New York:
Committee on Tolerance Assembly Programs, 1939.

New York Public Library. *The Negro: A Selected Bibliography.* New
York: 1940.

————. *Books About the Negro for Children,* by Augusta Baker. New
York: 1944.

Ramsey, Eloise. "The Calendar in Books," *Childhood Education,* September, 1939.

————. "Making Festivals," *ibid.*

Rollins, Charlemae. *We Build Together.* Chicago: The National Council
of Teachers of English, 1941.

State Department of Education, Nashville, Tennessee. *The Negro, A
Selected List for School Libraries of Books By or About the Negro
in Africa and America.* Nashville, Tenn.: The Department, 1941.

Biography and Autobiography

Adamic, Louis. *My America.* New York: Harper & Brothers, 1938.

————. *The Native's Return.* New York: Harper & Brothers, 1934.

Agresti, Olivia Rossetti. *David Lubin.* Boston: Little, Brown & Co.,
1922.

Antin, Mary. *The Promised Land.* Boston: Houghton Mifflin Co., 1912.

Beard, Annie S. *Our Foreign-Born Citizens.* New York: Thomas Y.
Crowell Co., 1939.

Bok, Edward. *The Americanization of Edward Bok.* New York: Charles
Scribner's Sons, 1920.

Bridges, H. J. *On Becoming an American.* New York: Jones Publishing
Co., 1919.

Browne, Waldo R. *Altgeld of Illinois.* New York: Huebsch, 1924.

Buck, Pearl. *What America Means to Me.* New York: John Day Co.,
1943.

Bullock, Ralph W. *In Spite of Handicaps.* New York: Association
Press, 1927.

Cahan, Abraham. *The Rise of David Levinsky.* New York: Harper &
Brothers, 1917.

Carnegie, Andrew. *Autobiography.* Boston: Houghton Mifflin Co., 1920.

Chase, Mary Ellen. *A Goodly Heritage.* New York: Henry Holt & Co.,
1932.

Christowe, Stoyan. *This Is My Country.* New York: Carrick & Evans,
Inc., 1938.

Cohen, Anne N. *The Man Who Stayed in Texas.* New York: McGraw-Hill Book Co., 1941.

Cohen, Rose. *Out of the Shadow.* New York: Doubleday, Doran & Co., 1918.

Conrad, Earl. *Harriet Tubman,* New York: Associated Publishers, 1943.

Cooper, Alice C., and Palmer, Charles A. *Twenty Modern Americans.* New York: Harcourt, Brace & Co., 1942.

Cross, Wilbur L. *Connecticut Yankee.* New Haven: Yale University Press, 1943.

Damrosch, Walter. *My Musical Life.* New York: Charles Scribner's Sons, 1923.

De Jong, David Cornel. *With a Dutch Accent.* New York: Harper & Brothers, 1944.

Douglass, Frederick. *Life and Times of Frederick Douglass.* New York: Pathway Press, 1944.

Driscoll, Charles B. *Kansas Irish.* New York: Macmillan Co., 1943.

DuBois, W. E. B. *Dusk of Dawn.* New York: Harcourt, Brace & Co., 1940.

Duffus, Robert L. *Lillian Wald: Neighbor and Crusader.* New York: Macmillan Co., 1938.

Embree, Edwin R. *13 Against the Odds.* New York: Viking Press, 1944.

Fast, Howard. *Citizen Tom Paine.* New York: Duell, Sloan & Pearce, 1943.

———. *Haym Salomon, Son of Liberty.* New York: Julian Messner, 1941.

Ferber, Edna. *A Peculiar Treasure.* New York: Doubleday, Doran & Co., 1939.

Gag, Wanda. *Growing Pains.* New York: Coward-McCann, Inc., 1940.

Garbedian, H. G. *Albert Einstein: Maker of Universes.* New York: Funk & Wagnalls, 1939.

Gompers, Samuel. *Seventy Years of Life and Labor.* New York: E. P. Dutton & Co., 1925.

Hammond, J. W. *Charles Proteus Steinmetz.* New York: Century Co., 1924.

Handy, W. C. *Father of the Blues.* New York: Macmillan Co., 1944.

Harrison, Juanita. *My Great Wide Beautiful World.* New York: Macmillan Co., 1936.

Helm, MacKinley. *Angel Mo' and Her Son, Roland Hayes.* Boston: Little, Brown & Co., 1942.

Holt, Rackham. *George Washington Carver: An American Biography.* New York: Henry Holt & Co., 1942.

Hughes, Langston. *Not Without Laughter*. New York: Alfred A. Knopf, 1930.

Hurston, Zora Neale. *Dust Tracks on a Road*. Philadelphia: J. B. Lippincott Co., 1943.

Johnson, Henry. *The Other Side of Main Street*. New York: Columbia University Press, 1943.

Johnson, James W. *Along This Way*. New York: Viking Press, 1933.

Lewisohn, Ludwig. *The Island Within*. New York: Harper & Brothers, 1928.

Lowe, Pardee. *Father and Glorious Descendant*. Boston: Little, Brown & Co., 1943.

McClure, S. S. *My Autobiography*. New York: Frederick A. Stokes Co., 1914.

McKay, Claude. *A Long Way from Home*. New York: Lee Furman, Inc., 1937.

Mangione, Jerre. *Mount Allegro*. Boston: Houghton Mifflin Co., 1943.

Mann, Erika and Klaus. *Escape to Life*. Boston: Houghton Mifflin Co., 1939.

Meade, Robert D. *Judah P. Benjamin: Confederate Statesman*. New York: Oxford University Press, 1943.

Muir, John. *The Story of My Boyhood and Youth*. Boston: Houghton Mifflin Co., 1913.

Mukerji, Dhan Gopal. *Caste and Outcast*. New York: E. P. Dutton & Co., 1923.

Pagano, Jo. *The Paesanos*. Boston: Little, Brown & Co., 1940.

Patri, Angelo. *A Schoolmaster of the Great City*. New York: Macmillan Co., 1917.

Peattie, Donald C. *Singing in the Wilderness: A Salute to John James Audubon*. New York: G. P. Putnam's Sons, 1935.

Pupin, Michael. *From Immigrant to Inventor*. New York: Charles Scribner's Sons, 1925.

Ravage, M. E. *An American in the Making*. New York: Harper & Brothers, 1917.

Redding, J. Saunders. *No Day of Triumph*. New York: Harper & Brothers, 1942.

Rihbany, A. M. *A Far Journey*. Boston: Houghton Mifflin Co., 1914.

Riis, Jacob. *The Making of an American*. New York: Macmillan Co., 1903.

Rizk, Salom. *Syrian Yankee*. New York: Doubleday, Doran & Co., 1943.

Santayana, George. *Persons and Places: Memories of Childhood and Youth*. New York: Charles Scribner's Sons, 1944.

Shaw, Anna Howard. *The Story of a Pioneer*. New York: Harper & Brothers, 1915.

Shridharani, Krishnalal. *My India, My America*. New York: Duell, Sloan and Pearce, 1941.

Sikorsky, Igor S. *The Story of the Winged S*. New York: Dodd, Mead & Co., 1938.

Smith, Ellen Hart. *Charles Carroll of Carrollton*. Cambridge: Harvard University Press, 1942.

Stern, Elizabeth. *My Mother and I*. New York: Macmillan Co., 1917.

Sugimoto, Etsu. *A Daughter of the Samurai*. New York: Doubleday, Doran & Co., 1927.

Sullivan, Louis. *Autobiography of an Idea*. New York: Press of American Art Institute of Architects, Inc., 1924.

Wright, Frank Lloyd. *An Autobiography*. New York: Longmans, Green & Co., 1932.

Children's Books

Albert, Edna. *Little Pilgrim to Penn's Woods*. New York: Longmans, Green & Company, 1930. Germany in 1750, the journey to the New World, and the settling in Pennsylvania.

Angelo, Valenti. *Golden Gate*. New York: Viking Press, 1939. The writer, a famous designer, decorator, and illustrator, tells and illustrates this story, based on his own immigrant boyhood in California.

Brown, Jeanette Perkins. *The Family Goes Traveling*. New York: Friendship Press, 1936. Text about and photographs of a Negro family.

Bullock, Ralph W. *In Spite of Handicaps*. New York: Association Press, 1927. Biographies of celebrated Negroes. Secondary level, but excellent as a reference in the elementary school.

Coe, Douglas. *Road to Alaska*. New York: Julian Messner, 1943. Shows the part the Negro played in building the Alcan Highway.

Cuthbert, Marian. *We Sing America*. New York: Friendship Press, 1936. A study of Negro Americans. Suitable for fourth, fifth, and sixth grades. Excellent material for classes in citizenship.

Davis, Lavinia. *Americans Every One*. New York: Doubleday, Doran & Co., 1942. Brief stories of thoughts and feelings of children from other lands.

De Angeli, Marguerite. *Henner's Lydia*. New York: Doubleday, Doran & Co., 1936. Story of a present-day Amish girl in the Conestoga Valley of Pennsylvania.

Evans, Eva Knox. *Key Corner*. New York: G. P. Putnam's Sons, 1936.

Life of Negro children in present-day Georgia, presented without condescension or caricature. Also other books by this author.

Fauset, Arthur. *For Freedom.* Philadelphia, Pa.: Franklin Publishing Co., 1928. A history of the Negro, told through biographies.

Gedo, Leopold. *Who Is Johnny?* New York: Viking Press, 1939. Translated from the Hungarian. Hungarian Jani, a Negro boy, becomes American Johnny.

Harris, Joel Chandler. *Uncle Remus, His Songs and His Sayings.* New York: D. Appleton-Century Co., 1908. Classic American folklore.

Hughes, Langston. *The Dream Keeper.* New York: Alfred A. Knopf, 1932. A collection of poems for young people, selected from two former volumes of the author.

Judson, Clara I. *They Came from France.* Boston: Houghton Mifflin Co., 1943. French immigrants in Louisiana.

————. *They Came from Sweden.* Boston: Houghton Mifflin Co., 1942. Swedish immigrants in the Middle West.

Levinger, Elma E. *The New Land.* New York: Bloch Publishing Co., 1920. Stories of Jews who took part in the making of America. Based on important events in American history.

Lockwood, Myrna. *Macaroni: An American Tune.* New York: Oxford University Press, 1940. The Americanization of Gasperino, son of an Italian violin maker. For ten-year-olds.

McLean, R. N., and Crawford, M. L. *Jumping Beans.* New York: Friendship Press, 1929. Stories and studies about Mexicans in the United States. For junior boys and girls.

Means, Florence C. *Children of the Promise.* New York: Friendship Press, 1941. A sixth-grade teacher and her Catholic, Protestant, and Jewish children. For both adults and children.

————. *Shuttered Windows.* Boston: Houghton Mifflin Co., 1938. A novel about a young Negro girl who goes to the South. See also other books by this author.

Melbo, Irving R. *Our America.* Bobbs-Merrill, 1937. The story of our country through the stories of its men and women. From Lief Ericson to Julius Rosenwald and Walt Disney.

Moon, Grace. *Magic Trail.* New York: Doubleday, Doran & Co., 1929. Indian life in the Southwest.

Peck, Anne Merriman, and Johnson, Enid. *Young Americans From Many Lands.* Chicago: Albert Whitman & Co., 1935. Narratives of children of foreign parentage, telling of their food, customs, and holidays in America.

Saroyan, William. *My Name is Aram.* New York: Harcourt, Brace & Co., 1940. Fourteen delightful stories of the Garoghlanians from Armenia, and of the American-born Aram in particular.

Seyfert, Ella Maie. *Little Amish Schoolhouse.* New York: Thomas Y. Crowell Co., 1939. A story of the Amish of Pennsylvania.

Shakelford, Jane D. *The Child's History of the Negro.* Washington, D. C.: The Associated Publishers, 1938. Biographies of famous Negroes, folk tales, stories of Africa.

Singmaster, Elsie. *Bred in the Bone.* Boston: Houghton Mifflin Co., 1934. Ten connected stories describing the lives of the Pennsylvania Germans.

Weilerstein, Sadie R. *Adventures of K'Ton Ton.* New York: Women's League of the United Synagogue, 1935. For small children.

————. *What Danny Did.* New York: Bloch Publishing Co., 1928. Stories of the Jewish festivals for small children.

Cook Books

Around the United States on a Cook Stove. Board of National Missions, Presbyterian Church of the United States of America.

Berolsheimer, Ruth. *The United States Regional Cook Book.* New York: Garden City Publishing Co., 1939.

Brown, Cora. *The European Cook Book for American Homes.* New York: Farrar & Rinehart, 1936.

Fergusson, Erna. *Mexican Cook Book.* Santa Fe: Rydal Press, 1934.

Frederick, George. *The Pennsylvania Dutch and Their Cookery.* New York: Business Bourse, 1935.

Greenbaum, Florence Kreisler. *Jewish Cook Book.* New York: Bloch Publishing Co., 1918.

Greenberg, Betty D., and Silverman, Althea O. *The Jewish Home Beautiful.* New York: Women's League of the United Synagogue, 1941.

Morphy, Countess Marcelle. *Recipes of All Nations.* New York: Wm. H. Wise & Co., 1936.

What's Cooking in Your Neighbor's Pot. New York: Common Council for American Unity.

Wood, Bertha. *Foods of the Foreign-Born.* Boston: Whitcomb Barrows, 1922.

Works by Culinary Arts Press, 14 N. Sixth St., Reading, Pa.: *Chinese Cook Book, Pennsylvania Dutch Cook Book, 'Round the World Cook Book,* and *Western Cook Book.*

Creative Discussion

Bowman, Leroy. *How to Lead Discussion.* New York: Womans Press, 1934.

Clarke, E. H. *The Art of Straight Thinking*. New York: D. Appleton-Century Co., 1921.

Elliot, H. S. *The Process of Group Thinking*. New York: Association Press, 1926.

Hubbard, Ursula P. (ed.). *Handbook for Discussion Leaders*. New York: Carnegie Endowment for International Peace, 1940.

Jones, Sylvester. "Group Discussions—The Quaker Way," *Friends Intelligencer*, Twelfth Month 2, 1939.

Judson, Lyman S. and Ellen. *Modern Group Discussion: Public and Private*. New York: Wilson Co., 1937.

Laughlin, S. B. (ed.). *Beyond Dilemmas*. Philadelphia: J. B. Lippincott Co., 1937. Chap. v, "The Quaker Method of Reaching Decisions."

McBurney, James H., and Hance, Kenneth. *Principles and Methods of Discussion*. New York: Harper & Brothers, 1939.

Sheffield, Alfred Dwight. *Creative Discussion*. New York: Association Press, 1930.

Slavson, S. R. *Creative Group Discussion*. New York: Association Press, 1937.

Thouless, R. H. *How to Think Straight*. New York: Simon & Schuster, 1939.

Cultural Democracy

Agar, Herbert. *A Time for Greatness*. Boston: Little, Brown & Co., 1942.

Berkson, Isaac. *Theories of Americanization*. New York: Teachers College Publications, Columbia University, 1920.

DuBois, Rachel Davis. *Get Together Americans*. New York: Harper & Brothers, 1943.

Follett, M. P. *Creative Experience*. New York: Longmans, Green & Co., 1924.

Frank, Waldo. *Our America*. New York: Boni & Liveright, 1919.

Hunter, Allan A. *Secretly Armed*. New York: Harper & Brothers, 1941. Chap. ii.

Tillich, Paul: "Migrations Breed New Cultures," *Protestant Digest*, February, 1940.

Van Kleek, Mary. *Creative America: Its Resources for Social Security*. New York: Covici Friede, 1936.

Vickery, William, and Cole, Stewart G. *Intercultural Education in American Schools*. New York: Harper & Brothers, 1943.

Wieman, Regina Westcott. *The Family Lives Its Religion*. New York: Harper & Brothers, 1941. Chap. i.

Willkie, Wendell L. *One World.* New York: Simon & Schuster, 1943.

Wissler, Clark. *Man and Culture. New York:* Thomas Y. Crowell Co., 1923.

Festivals and Festival-making

Achelis, Elisabeth. *The Calendar for Everybody.* New York: G. P. Putnam's Sons, 1943.

Apperson, G. L. *English Proverbs and Proverbial Phrases.* New York: E. P. Dutton & Co., 1929.

Auld, W. M. *Christian Traditions.* New York: Macmillan Co., 1931.

DuBois, Rachel Davis. "American Home Festival," *Classmate,* June 20, 1934.

———. "Sharing Cultural Loyalties Through Festival-making," *Childhood Education,* April, 1940.

———. *Get Together Americans.* New York: Harper & Brothers, 1943.

———, and Greenbie, Marjorie, "Give a Neighborhood Party," *Parents' Magazine.* September, 1943.

Diener, Thelma D. *United We Grow.* New York: Friendship Press, 1943.

Douglas, G. W. *The American Book of Days.* New York: Wilson Press, 1937.

Edinin, Ben M. *Jewish Holidays and Festivals.* New York: Hebrew Publishing Co., 1940.

Eichler, Lillian. *The Customs of Mankind.* New York: Garden City Publishing Co., 1937.

Frazer, Sir James. *The Golden Bough* (one vol.). New York: Macmillan Co., 1940.

Gillilan, Elizabeth. "Sharing Backgrounds," *International Journal of Religious Education,* February, 1943.

Greenbie, Marjorie Barstow. "Parties Go Global," *Coronet,* April, 1943.

Hazeltine, M. E. *Anniversaries and Holidays.* Chicago: American Library Association, 1928.

Hottes, Alfred C. *1001 Christmas Facts and Fancies.* New York: A. T. De La Mare Co., 1937.

Kerr, Annie B. *So Gracious Is the Time.* New York: Womans Press, 1940.

———. *Strangers No Longer.* New York: Friendship Press, 1943.

Levinger, E. E. *Jewish Holiday Stories.* New York: Bloch Publishing Co., 1918.

Oakes, Grace Mayer, and Kuebler, Ernest. *Life Goes On and On.* Boston: American Unitarian Association, 1942.

Patten, Helen P. *The Year's Festivals.* Boston: Dana Eestes, 1903.

Patten, Marjorie. *The Arts Workshop of Rural America.* New York: Columbia University Press, 1937.

Peattie, Donald Culross. *Almanac for Moderns.* New York: G. P. Putnam's Sons, 1935.

Schauffler, Robert H. *Our American Holidays.* New York: Dodd, Mead & Co., 1930.

Schauss, Hayyim. *The Jewish Festivals.* Cincinnati: University of American Hebrew Congregations, 1938.

Scherer, Margaret. *Thanksgiving and Harvest Festivals.* New York: The Metropolitan Museum of Art, 1942. Pamphlet.

Schibsby, Marian. *Foreign Festival Customs.* New York: Common Council for American Unity. Mimeographed.

Secrist, Elizabeth. *Christmas Everywhere.* Philadelphia: Roland Swain, 1931.

Spicer, Dorothy Gladys. *The Book of Festivals.* New York: Womans Press, 1937.

———. *Folk Festivals and the Foreign Community.* New York: Womans Press, 1923.

———. *Holiday Parties.* New York: Womans Press, 1940.

Steiner, Rudolf. *Festivals of the Seasons.* New York: Anthroposophic Press, 1928.

Wilson, Frank E. *An Outline of the Christian Year.* New York: Morehouse-Gorham Co., 1941. Pamphlet.

Works in *Festival Series.* New York: Friendship Press:
Fun and Festival from Africa.
Fun and Festival among America's Peoples.
Fun and Festival from India.
Fun and Festival from the Other Americas.
Fun and Festival from Moslem Lands.

Zeligs, Dorothy. *The Story of Jewish Holidays.* New York: Bloch Publishing Co., 1942. Activities and program suggestions.

Folk Arts and Folkways

Botkin, B. A. *A Treasury of American Folklore.* New York: Crown Publishing Co., 1944.

Carmer, Carl. *The Hurricane's Children.* New York: Farrar and Rinehart, 1937.

Clark, Thomas D. *The Rampaging Frontier.* New York: Bobbs-Merrill Co., 1939.

Appendix 241

Eaton, Allan. *Immigrant Gifts to American Life.* New York: Russell Sage Foundation, 1932.

Eichler, Lillian. *The Customs of Mankind.* New York: Garden City Publishing Co., 1937.

Frazer, Sir James. *The Golden Bough* (one vol.). New York: Macmillan Co., 1940.

Frederick, George. *The Pennsylvania Dutch and Their Cookery.* New York: Business Bourse, 1935. "Introduction."

Greenbie, Marjorie. *American Saga.* New York: Whittlesey House, 1939.

Harrison, Jane. *Ancient Art and Ritual.* New York: Henry Holt & Co., 1913.

Hurston, Zora Neale. *Of Mules and Men.* Philadelphia: J. B. Lippincott Co., 1935.

Langdon, William C. *Everyday Things in American Life: 1607-1776.* New York: Charles Scribner's Sons, 1937.

Leighton, Clare. *Southern Harvest.* New York: Macmillan Co., 1942.

Morgan, H. T. *Chinese Symbols and Superstitions.* South Pasadena: Perkins, 1942.

Salomon, Julian H. *Book of Indian Crafts and Indian Lore.* New York: Harper & Brothers, 1928.

Sumner, William Graham. *Folkways.* Boston: Ginn and Company, 1907.

Thompson, Harold W. *Body, Boots, and Britches.* Philadelphia: J. B. Lippincott Co., 1940.

Weygandt, Cornelius. *Dutch Country; Folks and Treasures in the Red Hills of Pennsylvania.* New York: D. Appleton-Century Co., 1939.

————. *The Red Hills.* Philadelphia: University of Pennsylvania Press, 1929.

Works in *American Folkways Series.* New York: Duell, Sloan & Pearce.

Works in *River Series.* New York: Farrar & Rinehart.

Immigration, Immigrants, and Culture Groups

GENERAL

Adamic, Louis. *From Many Lands.* New York: Harper & Brothers, 1940.

————, (ed.). *Peoples of America Series.* Philadelphia: J. B. Lippincott Co. In preparation.

Alland, Alexander. *American Counterpoint.* New York: John Day Co., 1943. (A series of photographs.)

Blankenship, Russell. *American Literature as an Expression of the National Mind.* New York: Henry Holt & Co., 1931. "Introduction."

Bogardus, Emory. *Immigration and Race Attitudes.* New York: D. C. Heath & Co., 1929.

Brown, Francis J., and Roucek, Joseph (eds.). *One America: Our Racial and National Minorities* (rev. ed.). New York: Prentice-Hall, Inc., 1945.

Brown, Lawrence Guy. *Immigration; Culture Conflicts and Social Adjustments.* New York: Longmans, Green & Co., 1933.

Corsi, Edward. *In the Shadow of Liberty.* New York: Macmillan Co., 1935.

Davie, Maurice R. *World Immigration.* New York: Macmillan Co., 1936.

Duncan, H. G. *Immigration and Assimilation.* New York: D. C. Heath & Co., 1933.

Feldman, H. *Racial Factors in American Industry.* New York: Harper & Brothers, 1931.

Fields, Harold. *The Refugee in the United States.* New York: Oxford University Press, 1938.

Hansen, M. L. *The Immigrant in American History.* Cambridge: Harvard University Press, 1940.

Leiserson, William M. *Adjusting Immigrant and Industry.* New York: Harper & Brothers, 1924.

McWilliams, Carey. *Brothers Under the Skin.* New York: Little, Brown & Co., 1942.

Miller, Kenneth. *We Who Are America.* New York: Friendship Press, 1943.

Myers, Gustavus. *History of Bigotry in the United States.* New York: Random House, 1943.

Sænger, Gerhart. *Today's Refugees.* New York: Harper & Brothers, 1941.

Schrieke, B. J. O. *Alien Americans: A Study of Race Relations.* New York: Viking Press, 1936.

Scotford, John R. *Together We Build America.* New York: Friendship Press, 1943.

Seabrook, William. *These Foreigners.* New York: Harcourt, Brace & Co., 1938.

Simon, Emily P. *Strong as the People.* New York: Friendship Press, 1943.

Smith, William C. *Americans in the Making.* New York: D. Appleton-Century Co., 1939.

Stephenson, George M. *A History of American Immigration, 1820-1934.* New York: Ginn & Co., 1936.

Survey Graphic. "Color: Unfinished Business of Democracy." November, 1942.

Wittke, Carl. *We Who Built America.* New York: Prentice-Hall, Inc., 1939.

Woofter, T. J. *Races and Ethnic Groups in American Life.* New York: McGraw-Hill Book Co., 1933.

SPECIFIC

Associates in Negro Folk Education. *Bronze Booklet Series.* Box 636, Ben Franklin Station, Washington, D. C.

Balch, Emily Green. *Our Slavic Fellow Citizens.* New York: Charities Publication Committee, 1910.   —

Benson, Adolph B., and Hedin, Naboth (eds.). *Swedes in America.* New Haven: Yale University Press, 1938.

Bogardus, Emory S. *The Mexican in the United States.* Los Angeles: University of Southern California Press, 1934.

Browne, Lewis. *Stranger Than Fiction.* New York: Macmillan Co., 1933.

Chenault, Lawrence R. *The Puerto Rican Migrant.* New York: Columbia University Press, 1938.

Child, Irwin L. *Italian or American?* New Haven: Yale University Press, 1943.

Christy, Arthur E. *The Asian Legacy and American Life.* New York: John Day Company, 1944.

Clarke, T. Wood. *Emigrés in the Wilderness.* New York: Macmillan Co., 1941.

Coffin, Robert P. T. *Kennebec: Cradle of Americans.* New York: Farrar & Rinehart, 1936. (French Canadians and old-stock Americans.)

Deloria, Ella C. *Speaking of Indians.* New York: Friendship Press, 1944.

Dobie, Charles C. *San Francisco's Chinatown.* New York: D. Appleton-Century Co., 1936.

DuBois, Rachel, and Schweppe, Emma (eds.). *The Germans in American Life.* New York: Thomas Nelson & Sons, 1935.

———. *The Jews in American Life.* New York: Thomas Nelson & Sons, 1935.

DuBois, W. E. B. *Black Reconstruction.* New York: Harcourt, Brace & Co., 1934.

———. *The Gift of Black Folk.* Boston: Stratford Publishing Co., 1924.

———. *The Souls of Black Folk.* Chicago: McClurg & Co., 1904.

Ducharme, Jacques. *In the Shadows of the Trees.* New York: Harper & Brothers, 1943. (French Canadians in New England).

Embree, Edwin R. *American Negroes: A Handbook*. New York: John Day Co., 1940.

———. *Indians of the Americas*. New York: Houghton Mifflin Co., 1939.

———. *The Story of a Tenth of the Nation*. New York: Viking Press, 1943.

Faust, A. B. *The German Element in the United States*. New York: The Steuben Society of America, 1927.

Federal Writers Project. *The Italians in New York*. New York: Random House, 1938.

Ford, Henry J. *The Scotch-Irish in America*. Princeton: Princeton University Press, 1915.

Frazier, E. Franklin. *The Negro Family in Chicago*. Chicago: University of Chicago Press, 1932.

———. *The Negro Family in the United States*. Chicago: University of Chicago Press, 1939.

Gamio, Manuel. *Mexican Immigration to the United States*. Chicago: University of Chicago Press, 1930.

Glick, Carl. *Shake Hands with the Dragon*. New York: McGraw-Hill Book Co., 1941.

———. *Three Times I Bow*. New York: Whittlesey House, 1943.

Hansen, Marcus Lee. *The Mingling of the Canadian and American Peoples*. New Haven: Yale University Press, 1940.

Hark, Ann. *Hex Marks the Spot*. Philadelphia: J. B. Lippincott Co., 1938.

Havighurst, Walter. *Upper Mississippi*. New York: Farrar and Rinehart, 1937.

Hitti, P. K. *The Syrians in America*. New York: Doubleday, Doran & Co., 1924.

Hunter, Allan A. *Out of the Far East*. New York: Friendship Press, 1934.

Janowsky, Oscar I. (ed.). *The American Jew*. New York: Harper & Brothers, 1942.

Johnson, Charles S. *The Negro in American Civilization*. New York: Henry Holt & Co., 1930.

———. *Patterns of Negro Segregation*. New York: Harper & Brothers, 1943.

———. *Shadow of the Plantation*. Chicago: University of Chicago Press, 1934.

Jones, Robert Mumford. *America and French Culture*. Chapel Hill: University of North Carolina Press, 1927.

Kaplan, M. M. *Judaism, A Civilization.* New York: Macmillan Co., 1934.

LaFarge, Oliver (ed.). *The Changing Indian.* Norman: University of Oklahoma Press, 1942.

Lasker, Bruno. *Jewish Experiences in America.* New York: Inquiry, 1930. (Vocational.)

———. *Filipino Immigration to Continental United States and to Hawaii.* Chicago: University of Chicago Press, 1931.

Lin Yutang. *The Importance of Living.* New York: John Day Co., 1937.

———. *My Country and My People.* New York: John Day Co., 1936.

Locke, Alain. *The New Negro.* New York: Boni & Liveright, 1928.

Malcomb, M. Vartan. *The Armenians in America.* Boston: Pilgrim Press, 1919.

Margolis, M. L., and Marx, A. *A History of the Jewish People.* Philadelphia: Philadelphia Publications Society, 1941.

Miller, K. D. *Peasant Pioneers.* New York: Council of Women for Home Missions, 1925. (The Slavs.)

Moton, Robert R. *What the Negro Thinks.* New York: Doubleday, Doran & Co., 1929.

Myrdal, Gunnar. *An American Dilemma: The Negro Problem and Modern Democracy.* New York: Harper & Brothers, 1944.

Northey, Sue. *The American Indian.* Springfield, Mass.: Milton Bradley & Co., 1939.

Ottley, Roi. *New World A-Coming.* Boston: Houghton Mifflin Co., 1943.

Palmer, Albert W. *Orientals in American Life.* New York: Friendship Press, 1934.

Quintanilla, Luis. *A Latin-American Speaks.* New York: Macmillan Co., 1943.

Raper, Arthur F. *The Tragedy of Lynching.* Chapel Hill: University of North Carolina Press, 1933.

Roberts, Edward F. *Ireland in America.* New York: G. P. Putnam's Sons, 1931.

Romulo, Carlos P. *I Saw the Philippines Fall.* New York: Doubleday, Doran & Co., 1943.

———. *Mother America.* New York: Doubleday, Doran & Co., 1944.

Roth, Cecil. *Jewish Contributions to Civilization.* New York: Harper & Brothers, 1940.

Schiavo, G. *Italians in America before the Civil War.* New York: Vigo Press, 1934.

Smith, William C. *The Second-Generation Oriental in America.* Honolulu: Institute of Pacific Relations, 1927.

Sorokin, Pitirim A. *Russia and the United States.* New York: E. P. Dutton & Co., 1944.

Steinberg, Milton. *The Making of the Modern Jew.* Indianapolis: Bobbs-Merrill Co., 1934.

Strong, Edward K. *The Second-Generation Japanese Problem.* Palo Alto: Stanford University Press, 1934.

White, Trumbull. *Puerto Rico and Its People.* New York: F. A. Stokes, 1938.

Williams, P. H. *South Italian Folkways in Europe and America.* New Haven: Yale University Press, 1938.

Wise, James W., and Levinger, Lee J. *Mr. Smith, Meet Mr Cohen.* New York: Reynal & Hitchcock, 1940.

Wissler, Clark. *Indians of the United States.* New York: Doubleday, Doran & Co., 1941.

Wood, Ralph (ed.). *The Pennsylvania Germans.* Princeton: Princeton University Press, 1941.

Woodson, Carter G. *The Negro in Our History.* Washington, D. C.: Associated Publishers, 1937.

Wuorinen, John H. *The Finns on the Delaware,* 1638-1653. New York: Columbia University Press, 1938.

Xenides, J. P. *The Greeks in America.* New York: Doubleday, Doran & Co., 1922.

Intercultural Education

Department of Supervisors and Directors. *Americans All: Studies in Intercultural Education.* National Education Association, Washington, D. C., 1942.

DuBois, Rachel Davis. *Adventures in Intercultural Education.* Intercultural Education Workshop, 204 E. 18th Street, New York, N. Y. Pamphlet.

———. *National Unity through Intercultural Education.* United States Office of Education, Washington, D. C. Pamphlet No. 10.

"Education for Racial Understanding," *Journal of Negro Education,* XIII, Summer, 1944.

Giles, H. H., and Cadigan, Robert J. *Playwrights Present: Problems of Everyday Life.* New York: Harper & Brothers, 1942.

Lasker, Bruno. *Race Attitudes in Children.* New York: Henry Holt & Co., 1929.

Mitchell, Lucy Sprague, and Boetz, Johanna. *The People of the U.S.A.: Their Place in the School Curriculum.* New York: Progressive Education Association, 1943. Booklet.

Vickery, William E., and Cole, Stewart G. *Intercultural Education in American Schools: Proposed Objectives and Methods.* New York: Harper & Brothers, 1943.

Magazines

American Childhood, Milton Bradley Co., Springfield, Mass.

American German Review, Fourth and Chestnut Streets, Philadelphia, Pa.

American Hebrew, The, 48 West 48th Street, New York, N. Y.

American Russian Review, 215 West 23rd Street, New York, N. Y.

American Scandinavian Review, 116 East 64th Street, New York, N. Y.

American Slav, C. P. O. Box 44, Pittsburgh, Pa.

American Swedish Monthly, 630 Fifth Avenue, New York, N. Y.

American Unity, The Council against Intolerance in America, 17 East 42nd Street, New York, N. Y. A monthly educational guide. Free.

Asia and the Americas, 40 East 49th Street, New York, N. Y.

Building America, Americana Corporation, 2 West 45th Street, New York, N. Y. A pictorial magazine.

Childhood Education, 1201 Sixteenth Street, N. W., Washington, D. C.

Classmate, The, Cincinnati, Ohio. A weekly Sunday-school paper for young people.

Common Ground, Common Council for American Unity, 222 Fourth Avenue, New York, N. Y. Quarterly.

Commonweal, The, 386 Fourth Avenue, New York, N. Y.

Contemporary Jewish Record, 386 Fourth Avenue, New York, N. Y.

Craft Horizons, American Craftsmen's Co-operative Council Office, America House, 485 Madison Avenue, New York, N. Y.

Crisis, monthly magazine, organ of National Association for the Advancement of Colored People, 69 Fifth Avenue, New York, N. Y.

East and West, East and West Association, 40 East 49th Street, New York, N. Y.

Intercultural Education News, Bureau for Intercultural Education, 221 West 57th Street, New York, N. Y. Free.

International Beacon, The, International Institute of Boston, Inc., Boston, Mass. Magazine of folklore, folkways, and folk news, issued monthly from September to June.

Interracial News Service, Department of Race Relations, Federal Council of Churches, 297 Fourth Avenue, New York, N. Y.

Interracial Review, Catholic Interracial Council, 20 Vesey Street, New York, N. Y.

248 *Build Together Americans*

Junior Arts and Activities, 4616 North Clark Street, Chicago 40, Ill.
Junior Red Cross Journal, American National Red Cross, Washington, D. C.
Menorah Journal, The, 63 Fifth Avenue, New York, N. Y. A quarterly of Jewish cultural life.
Monthly Summary of Events and Trends in Race Relations, prepared for the American Missionary Association by the Social Science Institute, Charles S. Johnson, Director, Nashville, Tenn. Free.
Negro History Bulletin, Association for the Study of Negro Life and History, 1538 Ninth Street, N. W., Washington, D. C.
New Mexico Magazine, Santa Fe, N. M.
Opportunity, 1133 Broadway, New York, N. Y. A journal of Negro life.
Pacific Citizen, 25 East Second Street, Salt Lake City, Utah.
Pacific Coast Scandinavian, 435 DuBois Street, San Francisco, Calif.
Phylon. Atlanta University, Atlanta, Ga. A quarterly on race and culture.
Pulaski Foundation Bulletin (Polish), 719 Broad Street, Newark, N. J.
Scholastic, A Magazine for High School Students, 22 E. 42nd Street, New York, N. Y.
South Today, Clayton, Ga.
World Over, 1776 Broadway, New York, N. Y. Bimonthly magazine of the Jewish Education Committee.
Young Judaean, The, 389 Fourth Avenue, New York, N. Y.

Novels and Short Stories

Attaway, William. *Blood on the Forge.* New York: Doubleday, Doran & Co., 1941.
Bell, Thomas. *Out of This Furnace.* New York: Little, Brown & Co., 1941.
Bojer, Johan. *The Emigrants.* New York: Century Co., 1925.
Bright, Robert. *Life and Death of Little Jo.* New York: Doubleday, Doran & Co., 1944.
Calverton, V. F. (ed.). *Anthology of American Negro Literature.* New York: Modern Library, 1929.
Carroll, Gladys Hasty. *As the Earth Turns.* New York: Macmillan Co., 1933.
Cather, Willa. *Death Comes for the Archbishop.* New York: Alfred A. Knopf, 1936.
———. *O Pioneers!* Boston: Houghton Mifflin Co., 1913.
De Capite, Michael. *Maria.* New York: John Day Co., 1943.
Di Donato, Pietro. *Christ in Concrete.* New York: Bobbs-Merrill Co., 1939.
Dogherty, Marian. *'Scusa Me, Teacher.* Boston: Marshal Jones, 1943.

Fagin, N. B. *America Through the Short Story*. Boston: Little, Brown & Co., 1936.

Fast, Howard. *Freedom Road*. New York: Duell, Sloan & Pearce, 1944.

Fauset, Jessie R. *The Chinaberry Tree*. New York: Frederick A. Stokes Co., 1932.

————. *Plum Bun*. New York: Frederick A. Stokes Co., 1929.

Feld, Rose C. *Sophie Halenczik, American*. New York: Little, Brown & Co., 1943.

Ferber, Edna. *American Beauty*. New York: Doubleday, Doran & Co., 1931.

————. *Fanny Herself*. New York: Grosset & Dunlap, 1917.

Kerr, Annie B. *Candles in the Heart*. New York: Womans Press, 1936. Also other books by this author.

Levin, Meyer. *The Old Bunch*. New York: Viking Press, 1938.

Lucas, Harriet M., and Ansorge, Elizabeth F. *Regional America: Prose and Poetry of Today*. Syracuse, N. Y.: L. W. Singer Co., 1941.

McClellan, Mary, and De Bonis, Albert (eds.). *Within Our Gates*. New York: Harper & Brothers, 1940.

McMickle, D'Arcy. *The Surrounded*. New York: Dodd, Mead & Co., 1936.

Moon, Bucklin. *The Darker Brother*. New York: Doubleday, Doran & Co., 1943.

Rölvaag, Ole Edvart. *Giants in the Earth*. New York: Harper & Brothers, 1927. Also other books by this author.

Schwarz, Leo W. *The Jewish Caravan*. New York: Farrar and Rinehart, 1935.

Sinclair, Upton. *The Jungle*. New York: Doubleday, Doran & Co., 1906.

Singmaster, Elsie. *Katy Gaumer*. Boston: Houghton Mifflin Co., 1915.

Suckow, Ruth. *Country People*. New York: Alfred A. Knopf, 1924.

Swift, Hildegarde H. *The Railroad to Freedom*. New York: Harcourt, Brace & Co., 1932.

Underhill, Ruth M. *Hawk Over Whirlpools*. New York: J. J. Augustin, 1940.

White, Walter. *The Fire in the Flint*. New York: Alfred A. Knopf, 1924.

Pamphlets

Adamic, Louis. *America and the Refugees*. New York: Public Affairs Committee, Inc., 1940.

Allen, William D., and Shen, S. T. *Let's Try Chinese*. New York: Institute of Pacific Relations.

American Friends Service Committee. *Refugee Facts*. Philadelphia: 1939. Single copy free.

America's Tenth Man, A Brief Survey of the Negro's Part in American History. Also *Singers in the Dawn, A Brief Anthology of American Negro Poetry*. Atlanta, Georgia: Commission on Interracial Co-operation, Inc.

An American Answer to Intolerance: Teacher's Manual No. 1., Senior and Junior High Schools. New York: Council Against Intolerance in America.

Aptneher, Herbert. *The Negro in the American Revolution*. New York: International Publishers. 45 pp.

Associates in Negro Folk Education. *Bronze Booklet Series*. Box 636, Ben Franklin Station, Washington, D. C.
Booklets on the Negro in art, drama, literature, music, America, etc.

Bell, J. O., and Wilkins, H. J. *Interracial Practices in Community Y. W. C. A's*. New York: Womans Press, 1944.

Brown, Muriel W. *The Schools and Community Organization*. Education and National Defense Series, Pamphlet No. 5, U. S. Office of Education, Washington, D. C.

C.I.O. and the Negro Worker, The. Washington 6, D. C.: Congress of Industrial Organizations, 718 Jackson Place, N.W. 12 pp.

Cole, S. G., and Trager, H. G. *How Can Majority and Minority Groups Contribute to Democracy?* Trenton 8, New Jersey: Democratic Discussions, The New Jersey Education Association. Outline No. 10.

Democracy in Trade Unions. New York: American Civil Liberties Union, 170 Fifth Ave. 85 pp.

Foote, Caleb. *Outcasts! The Story of America's Treatment of her Japanese-American Minority*. New York: Fellowship of Reconciliation, 2929 Broadway. 24 pp.

A Guide to Community Co-ordination. Los Angeles, Calif.: Co-ordinating Councils, Inc., 145 W. 12th St.

Hill, Frank. *The Museum and Popular Culture*. New York: Adult Education Association.

Lambert, Clara. *An Adventure in Teacher Training*. New York: Summer Play Schools Association. (A good study in home backgrounds.)

McGavran, Grace W. *Creating Friendly Attitudes through the Home*. New York: Friendship Press.

Miller, Clyde R. *How to Detect and Analyze Propaganda*. New York: Town Hall, Inc., 1939.

Performance of Negro Workers in 300 War Plants. New York: National Urban League, 1133 Broadway. 10 pp. Free.

Racial Inequalities in Education. New York: National Association for the Advancement of Colored People. 21 pp. Free.

Singer, Caroline. *Race—What the Scientists Say.* New York: National Conference of Christians and Jews, 1939.

Smith, Lillian. *There Are Things to Do.* Reprint from *South Today,* Clayton, Ga., 1943. (A good list of things to do about the race problem.)

Understanding Our Neighbors: A Factual Study of America's Major Race Problem. Atlanta, Ga.: Commission on Interracial Co-operation.

Vickery, W., and Trager, H. *One Nation Divisible.* New York: Committee on Discrimination in Employment, 80 Centre St. A study manual on employment practices.

Wiese, M. J. *Helping the Foreign-Born Achieve Active Citizenship—A Teachers Guide.* Washington, D. C.: U. S. Office of Education, Education and National Defense Series, No. 21.

Personality Development and Intercultural Education

Allport, Gordon. *Personality: A Psychological Interpretation.* New York: Henry Holt & Co., 1937.

Baxter, B., and Cassidy, R. *Group Experience—The Democratic Way.* New York: Harper & Brothers, 1943.

Berg, L. *The Human Personality.* New York: Prentice-Hall, Inc., 1933.

Blos, Peter. *The Adolescent Personality.* New York: D. Appleton-Century Co., 1941.

Cassidy, Florence. *Second-Generation Youth.* New York: Womans Press, 1930.

Cunningham, Bess V. *Family Behavior.* Philadelphia: W. B. Saunders Co., 1936.

Davis, Allison, and Dollard, John. *Children of Bondage.* Washington, D. C.: American Council on Education, 1940.

Fenton, Norman. *Mental Hygiene in School Practice.* Palo Alto: Stanford University Press, 1943.

Frazier, E. Franklin. *Negro Youth at the Crossways: Their Personality Development in the Middle States.* Washington, D. C.: The American Council on Education, 1940.

Gesell, Arnold, and Ilg, Frances. *Infant and Child in the Culture of Today.* New York: Harper & Brothers, 1943.

Horney, Karen. *The Neurotic Personality of Our Times.* New York: W. W. Norton & Co., 1937.

Jacobi, Jolan. *The Psychology of Jung.* New Haven: Yale University Press, 1942.

Jennings, Helen Hall. *Leadership and Isolation, A Study of Personality in Inter-Personal Relations.* New York: Longmans, Green & Co., 1943.

Jung, C. G. *Modern Man in Search of a Soul.* London: Kegan Paul, 1933.

————. *The Integration of the Personality.* London: Kegan Paul, 1940.

Koopman, G. R., Miel, Alice, and Misner, P. J. *Democracy in School Administration.* New York: D. Appleton-Century Co., 1943.

Kunkel, Fritz. *In Search of Maturity.* New York: Charles Scribner's Sons, 1943.

————, and Dickerson, Roy. *How Character Develops.* New York: Charles Scribner's Sons, 1940.

Moreno, J. L. *Who Shall Survive? A New Approach to the Problem of Human Interrelations.* Washington, D. C.: Nervous and Mental Disease Publishing Co., 1934.

Newcomb, Theodore. *Personality and Social Change.* New York: Dryden Press, 1943.

Plant, James S. *Personality and the Cultural Pattern.* New York: The Commonwealth Fund, 1937.

Prescott, Daniel A. *Emotion and the Educative Process.* Washington, D. C.: The American Council on Education, 1938.

Stonequist, Everett V. *The Marginal Man.* New York: Charles Scribner's Sons, 1937.

Sullenger, T. Earl. *Social Determinants in Juvenile Delinquency.* New York: John Wiley & Sons, 1936.

Thrasher, Frederic. *The Gang.* University of Chicago Press, 1936.

Warner, W. Lloyd, *et al. Color and Human Nature: Negro Personality Development in a Northern City.* Washington, D. C.: The American Council on Education, 1940.

Plays and Related Activities

Americans All—Immigrants All, Radio Scripts. Office of Education, Washington, D. C.

Block, Etta (translator). *One-Act Plays from the Yiddish.* New York: Bloch Publishing Co., 1929.

Cannon, Fanny V. *Playing Fair: A Book of Tolerance Plays.* New York: E. P. Dutton & Co., 1940.

Childs, Jessica. *Building Character Through Dramatization.* New York: Row, Peterson & Co., 1934.

Freedom's People, Radio Scripts. Office of Education, Washington, D. C.

Gardner, Horace J. *Let's Celebrate Christmas.* New York: A. S. Barnes & C., 1940.

Giles, H. H., and Cadigan, Robert J. (eds.). *Playwrights Present Problems of Everyday Life.* New York: Harper & Brothers, 1942.

Gullan, Marjorie. *The Speech Choir.* New York: Harper & Brothers, 1937.

Koch, Frederick H. *American Folk Plays:* New York: D. Appleton-Century Co., 1939.

Niebuhr, Hilda. *Ventures in Dramatics with Boys and Girls of the Church School.* New York: Charles Scribner's Sons, 1935.

Niggli, Josephina. *Mexican Folk Plays.* Chapel Hill: University of North Carolina Press, 1938.

Plays and Pageants: A Bibliography. New York: Womans Press.

Powell, Lydia. *The Art Museum Comes to the School.* New York: Harper & Brothers, 1944.

Richardson, Willis. *Plays and Pageants from the Life of the Negro.* Washington, D. C.: Associated Publishers, 1930.

Soifer, Margaret K. *With Puppets, Mimes, and Shadows.* New York: Furrow Press, 1936.

Poetry

Barnes, Ruth A. (ed.). *I Hear America Singing.* New York: Winston Publishing Co., 1937.

Benet, Stephen Vincent. *Western Star.* New York: Farrar & Rinehart, 1943. See also *John Brown's Body.*

Brown, Sterling. *The Negro Caravan.* New York: Dryden Press, 1941.

Coffin, Robert P. Tristram. *American Primer.* New York: Macmillan Co., 1943.

Cullen, Countee. *Caroling Dusk.* New York: Harper & Brothers, 1927.

Johnson, James W. *Book of American Negro Poetry.* New York: Harcourt, Brace & Co., 1931.

———. *God's Trombones.* New York: Viking Press, 1927.

Lomax, Alan. *American Ballads and Folk Songs.* New York: Macmillan Co., 1924.

Maus, Cynthia Pear. *Puerto Rico in Pictures and Poetry.* Caldwell, Ohio: Caxton Printers, Ltd., 1941.

Sandburg, Carl. *The People, Yes.* New York: Harcourt, Brace & Co., 1936.

Van Doren, Mark, and Lapolla, Garibaldi M. *The World's Best Poems.* New York: Albert and Charles Boni, 1932.

Walker, Margaret. *For My People*. New Haven: Yale University Press, 1943.

Religion

Adam, Karl. *Spirit of Catholicism*. New York: Macmillan Co., 1935.

Asch, Sholem. *The Nazarene*. New York: G. B. Putnams' Sons, 1939.

———. *The Apostle*. New York: G. P. Putnam's Sons, 1944.

Baron, J. L. (ed.). *Candles in the Night*. New York: Farrar & Rinehart, 1940. (Jewish stories by non-Jewish writers.)

Bower, William Clayton. *Church and State in Education*. Chicago: The University of Chicago Press, 1944.

Brown, W. A., Ross, J. E., and Finkelstein, L. *Religions of Democracy*. New York: Devin-Adair Co., 1940.

Brown, William Adams. *The Church, Catholic and Protestant*. New York: Charles Scribner's Sons, 1935.

Clinchy, Everett R. *All in the Name of God*. New York: John Day Co., 1941.

Dewey, John. *Freedom and Culture*. New York: G. P. Putnam's Sons, 1939.

Edidin, Ben M. *Jewish Customs and Ceremonies*. New York: Hebrew Publishing Co., 1941.

Eliot, T. S. *The Idea of A Christian Society*. New York: Harcourt, Brace & Co., 1940.

Hall, Thomas C. *Religious Background of American Culture*. Boston: Little, Brown & Co., 1930.

Harkness, Georgia. *Religious Living*. New York: Association Press, 1938.

High, S., Kingdon, *et al. Faith for Today*. New York: Doubleday, Doran & Co., 1941.

Jung, Leo (ed.). *Judaism in a Changing World*. New York: Oxford University Press, 1939.

Kaplan, Mordecai. *The Meaning of God in Modern Jewish Religion*. New York; Behrman, 1937.

Mackey, John A. *Heritage and Destiny*. New York: Macmillan Co., 1943.

Moehlman, Conrad Henry. *School and Church*. New York: Harper & Brothers, 1944.

Page, Kirby. *Living Creatively*. New York: Farrar & Rinehart, 1932.

Sargent, Daniel. *Catholicism in Our History*. New York: Longmans, Green & Co., 1939.

———. *Our Land and Our Lady*. New York: Longmans, Green & Co., 1939.

Smith, Ruth (ed.) *The Tree of Life: Selections from the Literature of the World's Religions.* New York: Viking Press, 1943.

Valentin, Hugo. *Anti-Semitism.* New York: Viking Press, 1936.

Wieman, Henry N. *American Philosophies of Religion.* Chicago: Willett Clark, 1936.

Social Psychology

Alexander, Franz. *Our Age of Unreason: A Study of the Irrational Forces in Social Life.* Philadelphia: J. B. Lippincott Co., 1942.

Allers, Rudolph. *Psychology of Character.* New York: Sheed and Ward, 1943.

Bowers, David F. (ed.). *Foreign Influences in American Life.* Princeton: Princeton University Press, 1944.

Briggs, L. H., *et al. The Emotionalized Attitudes.* New York: Bureau of Publications, Teachers College, Columbia University, 1940.

Cook, Lloyd Allen. *Community Backgrounds of Education.* New York: McGraw-Hill Book Co., 1938.

Dollard, John, *et al. Frustration and Aggression.* New Haven: Yale University Press, 1939.

Hart, Hornell. *The Science of Social Relations.* New York: Henry Holt & Co., 1927.

Huxley, Aldous. *Ends and Means.* New York: Harper & Brothers, 1937.

Johnson, Charles S. *Patterns of Negro Segregation.* New York: Harper & Bothers, 1943.

Klineberg, Otto. *Social Psychology.* New York: Henry Holt & Co., 1940.

Kulp, Daniel H. *Educational Sociology.* New York: Longmans, Green & Co., 1932.

Lasker, Bruno. *Race Attitudes in Children.* New York: Henry Holt & Co., 1929.

Lee, A. McC., and Humphrey, N. *Race Riot.* New York: Dryden Press, 1943.

———, and Bryant, Elizabeth. *The Fine Art of Propaganda.* New York: Harcourt, Brace & Co., 1939.

Lindeman, E. C. *Social Discovery.* New York: New Republic, Inc., 1924.

———. *Social Education.* New York: New Republic, Inc., 1933.

Locke, A. L., and Stern, B. J. *When Peoples Meet.* New York: Progressive Education Association, 1942.

Lynd, Robert S. and Helen M. *Middletown in Transition.* New York: Harcourt, Brace & Co., 1937.

MacIver, R. M. *A Textbook of Sociology.* New York: Farrar & Rinehart, 1937.

McWilliams, Carey. *Prejudice: Japanese-Americans.* Boston: Little, Brown & Co., 1944.

Mead, George Herbert. *Mind, Self, and Society.* Chicago: University of Chicago Press, 1934.

Menninger, Karl. *Love against Hate.* New York: Harcourt, Brace & Co., 1942.

Murphy, E., *et al. Experimental Social Psychology.* New York: Harper & Brothers, 1937.

Park, Robert E., and Burgess, Ernest W. *Introduction to the Science of Sociology.* Chicago: University of Chicago Press, 1926.

Ries, Helen E. *A Psychology of Artistic Creation.* New York: Bureau of Publications, Teachers College, Columbia University, 1942.

Thomas, W. I., and Thomas, D. S. *The Child in America.* New York: Alfred A. Knopf, 1929.

Waller, W. W. *Sociology of Teaching.* New York: John Wiley & Sons, 1932.

Songs, Games, Music

Altman, Shalom. *The Judaean Songster.* New York: Young Judaea, Inc., 1934.

Bancroft, Jessie H. *Games for the Playground, Home, School, and Gymnasium.* New York: Macmillan Co., 1923.

Binder, Abraham Wolk. *The Jewish Year in Song.* New York: G. Schirmer, 1928.

Botsford, Florence H. *Botsford Collection of Folk Songs* (3 vols.). New York: G. Schirmer, 1930.

————. *The Universal Folk Songster.* New York: G. Schirmer, 1937.

Chen, Shih-hsiang, *Collection of Chinese Folk Songs.* New York: John Day Co., 1943.

Coopersmith, Harry. *Songs of My People.* New York: Anshe Emet Synagogue, 1937.

————. *Songs of Zion, Part II.* New York: Behrman, 1942.

Dann, Hollis. *Christmas Carols and Hymns.* New York: American Book Co., 1912.

Densmore, Frances. *American Indians and Their Music.* New York: Womans Press, 1926.

Downes, Olin, and Siegmeister, Elie. *A Treasury of American Song.* New York: Alfred A. Knopf, 1943.

Dulles, Foster Rhea. *America Learns to Play.* New York: D. Appleton-Century Co., 1940.

Eisenstein, Judith Kaplan. *The Gateway to Jewish Song*. New York: Behrman, 1939.

Fletcher, Alice Cunningham. *Indian Games and Dances*. Boston: C. C. Birchard Co., 1917.

Games with Music. Boston: C. C. Birchard Co., 1924.

Goldfarb, Israel. *The Jewish Songster*. New York: Bloch Publishing Co.

Gordon, Dorothy. *Treasure Bag of Game Songs*. New York: E. P. Dutton & Co., 1939.

Hampton Book of Spirituals. Hampton, Va.: Hampton Institute.

Handy, W. C. *Unsung Americans—Sung*. New York: Handy Music Co.

Henius, Frank. *Songs and Games of the Americas*. New York: Charles Scribner's Sons, 1943.

Hunt, Sarah E., and Cain, Ethel. *Games the World Around*. New York: A. S. Barnes Co., 1941.

Jacobs, A. Gertrude. *The Chinese-American Song and Game Book*. New York: A. S. Barnes & Co., 1944.

Johnson, J. R. *Rolling Along in Song*. New York: Viking Press, 1937.

Lieurance, Thurlow. *Songs of the North American Indian*. Philadelphia: Theodore Presser Co., 1921.

Linscott, Eloise Hubbard. *Folk Songs of Old New England*. New York: Macmillan Co., 1939.

Locke, Alain. *The Negro and His Music*. Washington, D. C.: The Associates in Negro Folk Education, 1936.

Lomax, John and Alan. *American Ballads and Folksongs*. New York: Macmillan Co., 1934.

———. *Our Singing Country*. New York: Macmillan Co., 1941.

Luther, Frank. *Americans and Their Songs*. New York: Harper & Brothers, 1942.

National Service Bureau of the Federal Theater Project. *American Folk Song Publications*.

New Brown Book, Twice 55 Songs. Boston: C. C. Birchard Co., 1929.

Odum, Howard. *The Negro and His Song*. Chapel Hill: University of North Carolina Press, 1925.

Oxford Book of Carols, The. New York: Oxford University Press, 1928.

Parrish, Lydia. *Slave Songs of the Georgia Sea Islands*. New York: Creative Age Press, Inc., 1942.

Pocket Songster. New York: Fellowship of Reconciliation.

Rohrbough, Lynn. *Joyful Singing*. Delaware, Ohio: Co-operative Recreation Service, 1943. Also *Kits P, O,* and *R*.

Ryan, Helen Chandler. *Spanish-American Folk Songs of New Mexico*. Albuquerque: Federal Music Project, 1940.

Sandburg, Carl. *The American Songbag.* New York: Harcourt, Brace & Co., 1936.

Schack, Sarah P. *Yiddish Folk Songs.* New York: Bloch Publishing Co., Inc., 1924.

Spaeth, Sigmund. *Read 'Em and Weep; Songs You Forgot to Remember.* New York: Doubleday, Doran & Co., 1926.

———. *Weep Some More, My Lady.* New York: Doubleday, Doran & Co., 1927.

Weaver, Robert B. *Amusements and Sports in American Life.* Chicago: University of Chicago Press, 1939.

Wesley, John. *Negro Work Songs.* New York: Howell Soskin & Co., 1940.

Zanzig, Augustus D. *Singing America.* New York: C. C. Birchard Co.

Sources of Information and Material

American Association for Adult Education, 60 West 42 Street, New York, N. Y.

American Association of University Women, 1634 I Street, N. W., Washington, D. C.

American Jewish Committee, 386 Fourth Avenue, New York, N. Y.

American Junior Red Cross, 17th Street between D & E Streets, N. W., Washington, D. C.

American Library Association, 520 North Michigan Avenue, Chicago, Ill.

American Museum of Natural History, Central Park West at 79th Street, New York, N. Y.

Association for Childhood Education, 1201 16th Street, N. W., Washington, D. C.

Bureau for Intercultural Education, 119 West 57th Street, New York, N. Y.

Carnegie Endowment for International Peace, 700 Jackson Place, N. W., Washington, D. C.

Catholic Interracial Council, 20 Vesey Street, New York, N. Y.

China Institute of America, 119 W. 57th Street, New York, N. Y.

Columbia Broadcasting System, Department of Education, 485 Madison Avenue, New York, N. Y.

Committee on Cultural Relations with Latin America, 156 Fifth Avenue, New York, N. Y.

Committee on Resettlement of Japanese-Americans, 297 Fourth Avenue, New York, N. Y.

Common Council for American Unity, 222 Fourth Avenue, New York, N. Y.

Consumer's Book Co-operative, 27 Coenties Slip, New York 4, N. Y.

Co-operative Recreation Service, Delaware, Ohio.

Co-ordinator of Inter-American Affairs, Department of Commerce, Washington, D. C.

Council Against Intolerance in America, 17 East 42nd Street, New York, N. Y.

Council for Democracy, Inc., 11 West 42nd Street, New York, N. Y.

Council on African Affairs, Inc., 23 W. 26th Street, New York, N. Y.

Country Dance Society, Inc., 15 East 40th Street, New York, N. Y.

Division of Cultural Relations, U. S. Department of State, Washington, D. C.

East and West Association, 40 East 49th Street, New York, N. Y.

Federal Council of Churches, Industrial Division and Department of Race Relations, 297 Fourth Avenue, New York, N. Y.

Fellowship of Reconciliation, 2929 Broadway, New York, N. Y.

Film and Sound Library, Bell and Howell Co., 30 Rockefeller Plaza, New York, N. Y.

Folk Arts Center, 670 Fifth Avenue, New York, N. Y.

Friendship Press, 156 Fifth Avenue, New York, N. Y.

Harmon Foundation, 140 Nassau Street, New York, N. Y. (Films and visual aids.)

Institute of Pacific Relations, 129 East 52nd Street, New York, N. Y.

Intercultural Education Workshop, 204 East 18th Street, New York, N. Y.

Julius Rosenwald Fund, 4901 Ellis Avenue, Chicago, Ill.

Junior Red Cross, National Headquarters, Washington, D. C.

Linguaphone Institute, 30 Rockefeller Plaza, New York, N. Y.

National Association for the Advancement of Colored People, 69 Fifth Avenue, New York, N. Y.

National Broadcasting System, Department of Education, 30 Rockefeller Plaza, New York, N. Y.

National Catholic Welfare Conference, Social Action and Education Department, Washington, D. C.

National Conference of Christians and Jews, 381 Fourth Avenue, New York, N. Y.

National Education Association, 1201 16th Street, Washington, D. C.

National Folk Festival Association, Evening Bulletin, Philadelphia, Pa.

National Institute of Immigrant Welfare, 2 West 45th Street, New York, N. Y.

National Memorial Book Store, 2107 Seventh Avenue, New York, N. Y. (Books by and about Negroes; also a full line of pictures. Will fill mail orders.)

National Recreation Association, 316 Fourth Avenue, New York, N. Y.

Near East Foundation, 17 West 46th Street, New York, N. Y.

New Tools for Learning, 7 West 16th Street, New York, N. Y.

Progressive Education Association, 221 West 57th Street, New York, N. Y.[2]

Southern Regional Council, 710 Standard Building, Atlanta, Ga.

United China Relief, Inc., 1790 Broadway, New York 19, N. Y. (Films, records, books on songs, games, and recipes. Will fill mail orders.)

United States Office of Education, Washington, D. C.

Women's International League for Peace and Freedom, 1734 F Street, N. W., Washington, D. C.

Y.M.C.A., National, 347 Madison Avenue, New York, N. Y.

Y.W.C.A., National, 600 Lexington Avenue, New York, N. Y.

Teachers' Special Aids

AUDIO-VISUAL AIDS

(Many organizations listed under "Sources of Information and Material" supply such aids, as maps, photographs, etc.)

Americans All—Immigrants All, Radio Recordings. U. S. Office of Education, Washington, D. C., and Linguaphone Institute, 30 Rockefeller Plaza, New York, N. Y.

Almanac of Films for Special Occasions. Harmon Foundation, 140 Nassau Street, New York, N. Y. (Motion pictures for schools, churches, clubs.)

Building America: A Photographic Magazine of Modern Problems. Published for The Society for Curriculum Study and distributed by Americana Corporation, 2 West 45th Street, New York, N. Y.

Catalogues listing phonograph records of various countries:
Decca Album Sets, 50 West 57th Street, New York, N. Y.
General, 1600 Broadway, New York, N. Y.
Keynote Recordings, Inc., 522 Fifth Avenue, New York, N. Y.
Musicraft Records, Inc., 480 Lexington Avenue, New York, N. Y.

---

[2] Now the American Education Fellowship, 289 Fourth Avenue, New York 10, N. Y.

Freedom's People, Radio Recordings. U. S. Office of Education, Washington, D. C.

House, Wallace. *Folk Songs of the United Nations,* 1943. Asch Records, 117 West 46th Street, New York, N. Y.

Mayo, Margot. *The Running Set,* Square Dances with Calls. Decca Album A274, Decca Records, Inc., 50 West 57th Street, New York, N. Y.

Metropolitan Museum of Art, Department of Education and Extension, Fifth Avenue and 82nd Street, New York, N. Y. Offers a service to schools for a small registration fee and cost of transporting lantern slides, photographs, color prints, paintings, etc.

New Tools for Learning about War and Postwar Problems. New Tools for Learning, 280 Madison Avenue, New York, N. Y. 1943. (A guide to films, pamphlets, and recordings for teachers, speakers, and discussion leaders.)

New York University Film Library, 71 Washington Square South, New York 12, N. Y.

Seigmeister, Elie. *The Songs of Early America,* ES1, and *Latin-American Typical and Folk Songs,* ES3, both from Bost Records Co., 29 West 57th Street, New York, N. Y.

Victor Records 20395 and 20986, *Cradle Songs of Many Lands,* English, French, Dutch, and Spanish.

Visual Aid Department of the Presbyterian Church Board of National Missions, 156 Fifth Avenue, New York, N. Y. (Films on the church and the refugee, the war relocation camps, and the American Indian.)

White, Josh, and Cuney, Waring. *Southern Exposure.* Keynote Recordings, Inc.

"Wizard of Science," a story of Dr. Carver, *True Comics,* No. 28, October, 1943. Parents Magazine Press, 52 Vanderbilt Avenue, New York, N. Y. See also *True Comics,* "Who Got the Blame?"

TEACHERS' UNITS

Arnold, J. I. *Challenges to American Youth.* Evanston, Ill.: Row Peterson, 1940. See especially "Social Inheritance: The Third Challenge"; "The Church: The Sixth Challenge"; and "Racial Cooperation: The Twenty-Second Challenge." For senior high schools.

Beach, W. G., and Walker, E. E. *Social Problems and Social Welfare.* New York: Charles Scribner's Sons, 1937. See especially Unit I: "Population Change and Social Reorganizations." For senior high schools.

Benedict, Ruth, and Ellis, Mildred P. "Race and Cultural Relations: America's Answer to the Myth of a Master Race," Unit 5 in *Problems in American Life Series*. Washington, D. C.: National Association of Secondary School Principals and National Council for the Social Studies, National Education Association, 1942. For junior and senior high schools.

Diener, Thelma D. *United We Grow*. New York: Friendship Press, 1943.

Gould, Kenneth M. *They Got the Blame: The Story of Scapegoats in History*. New York: Association Press, 1942. 25c. A comic book of this story is distributed *free* from Council for Equal Job Opportunity, 923 City Centre Building, 121 North Broad Street, Philadelphia, Pa.

Landis, Benson Y. *Adventure in Understanding: A Handbook of Discussion and Source Materials for Protestants, Catholics, and Jews*. New York: National Conference of Christians and Jews, 1941. For senior high schools and colleges.

Lincoln School Research Studies. *Catalogue, Units of Work Activities, Projects, etc., to* 1932. New York: Bureau of Publications, Teachers College, Columbia University.

McCall, William A. (ed.). *Teachers Lesson Unit Series*. New York: Bureau of Publications, Teachers College, Columbia. (More than a hundred pamphlets for teachers of all grades from kindergarten through high school. A few relate to intercultural education. Send for descriptive folder.)

McLellan, M. B., and DeBonis, A. V. *Within Our Gates: Selections on Tolerance and the Foreign Born of Today*. New York: Harper & Brothers, 1940.

Michener, James A., and Long, Harold. *A Source Unit on Immigration*. Cambridge: Harvard Graduate School of Education.

National Society for the Study of Education. *The Thirty-Sixth Yearbook, Part II*, "International Understanding through the Public School Curriculum." Bloomington, Ill.: Public School Publishing Co., 1937.

Sweeney, F. G., Barry, E. F., and Schollkopf, A. E. *Western Youth Meets Eastern Culture*. New York: Lincoln School, Bureau of Publications, Teachers College, Columbia University, 1932.

Yiser, Idabelle. *The Curriculum as an Integrating Force for Ethnic Variations*. Cambridge: Harvard Graduate School of Education.

Vocational Guidance

Council for Equal Job Opportunity, 923 City Centre Building, 121 North Broad Street, Philadelphia 7, Pa.

National Urban League, 1133 Broadway, New York, N. Y.

Science Research Associates. *Vocational Trends*. Chicago: Monthly, September to June.

INDEX